IMPOSSIBLE MAN

MICHAEL
MUHAMMAD
KNIGHT

Soft Skull Press
Brooklyn

Library of Congress Cataloging-in-Publication Data is available.

ISBN (10): 1-59376-226-7
ISBN (13): 978-1-59376-226-1
3992 4187 5/09
Cover design by Brett Yasko
Cover image by Michael Muhammad Knight
Interior design by Beth Kessler, Neuwirth & Associates, Inc.
Printed in the United States of America

Soft Skull Press
An Imprint of Counterpoint LLC
2117 Fourth Street
Suite D
Berkeley, CA 94710

www.softskull.com
www.counterpointpress.com

Distributed by Publishers Group West

10 9 8 7 6 5 4 3 2 1

CONTENTS

0 holy ghost and fire   1

1 heroes and hero-worship 15

2 the battle of swamp road 27

3 creep, jr.   35

4 helter skelter   49

5 el-hajj malik el-shabazz 59

6 prostrations and ejaculations 73

7 malik al-kafi khan   87

8 if we're lucky, his brain is
shot to shit   101

9 the one percenters   115

10 witness   131

11 actual facts   143

12 full power   151

13 a new hope   161

14 traveling through hyperspace
ain't like dusting crops, boy 169

15 mein amriken musalman hoon 179

16 the strongest man   189

17 goat head soup   199

18 drops of hellfire   211

19	going home	229
20	out of step	241
21	slayers of husayn	249
22	in the name of vince mcmahon	267
23	history of the egyptian wrestling federation	281
24	the furious cock	295
25	manchild in the north country	303
26	manned missiles	319
27	dutch sailors	327

for mothers

holy ghost and fire

0

My father's father, Calvin Sherrard Unger, was born on Christmas Day, 1895, in Berkeley Springs, West Virginia. Calvin's brother, John Wesley Unger, was a blind musician who wrote a well-known folk song, "The Miner's Doom," about an explosion in a nearby mine. The Ungers had a lot of history in Morgan County; there was an unincorporated "town" called Unger's Store (just an intersection of country roads, a post office and general store, population eighty), later shortened to Unger, where my great-great-great-great-uncle Washington Unger gave shelter to Stonewall Jackson's troops before they invaded Romney. Another Unger, also named John Wesley, served as a captain in the Confederate army.

Calvin married a local girl named Maude and left her pregnant to fight in the First World War. According to legend, Calvin's mother-in-law had disapproved of her daughter marrying a low-class Unger, and after delivering the baby in her home promptly smashed its head against a chair. Maude died in the summer of 1920. Five months later, Calvin married sixteen-year-old Martha Irene Bishop.

When he wasn't working in the coal mines, Calvin preached the Gospel on street corners and in time became a Pentecostal minister. He gave immersion baptisms in the Cacapon River and sometimes received the Baptism of the Holy Ghost and Fire, which caused him to speak in tongues. Following the Lord's orders against birth control, between 1921 and 1947 Martha would give birth to twenty children, twelve girls and eight boys. Calvin's primary instrument of discipline in that crowded house was the Devil: *If you don't eat your vegetables, the Devil's gonna get you. Do your chores, or the Devil's gonna get you.* He even let them believe that the charcoal furnace in the basement led directly to Hell, and that he kept the Devil's fire burning.

With so much work and so many kids, Calvin and Martha delegated their older children to watch over the younger ones; as one of the younger ones, Wesley Calvin Unger was mostly raised by his sisters, one of whom would claim that Calvin had molested her. Wesley's surrogate mothers all left him in turn; at least half of the Unger daughters were married by seventeen, but that's how they did things in that time and place.

The twentieth child was Calvin and Martha's eighth boy; but because one of the boys had lived only six months, they thought of this one as the seventh son—which Calvin saw as full of religious meaning. They named him David Pine Unger; David after the Bible's King David, who was also a seventh son, and Pine after the hospital in which they delivered him (he was the first Unger born in a hospital).

One morning as the Unger kids crossed the road to get on

the school bus, a Harris Express Company tractor-trailer came speeding from behind the hill. Wesley was fourteen years old and right there in the road. He saw it coming full of violence but no personality—like the violence of nature—upon six-year-old David. And he saw up close as the eighteen wheels and however many tons absorbed the blonde child into itself. In less than a second there was no more of David Pine Unger, nothing that could have been recognizable as a boy or parts of a boy. Wesley watched men with shovels come to scrape his brother off the road. And he watched his mother lose her mind and attack the trucker with a butcher knife, screaming as the men dropped their shovels and rushed to hold her back.

Martha told her remaining children that the trucker was the Devil coming to get them. She died of grief in two years and Calvin married another woman with her own kids. Calvin's new wife tried to convince him that the Devil had possessed Wesley, that after Wesley left a room, books would start jumping off the shelves and flying around her. When she became too much, Wesley would live in his car in the church parking lot. He looked to the army for a way out of Berkeley Springs, but at seventeen he needed parental permission; his stepmother happily signed the papers, and he was soon shipped to Korea. Something bad happened there. Nobody knew what, and Wesley wouldn't talk about it, but his sisters all had their own stories. One claimed that he had witnessed the North Koreans massacre a truckload of refugee children, giving him twenty simultaneous flashbacks of David's death. Another said that his brain had been fried by chemical warfare. It might have been a jeep accident (and not in Korea, but off base in Niagara Falls) resulting in neurological problems; but for whatever reason, Wesley was honorably discharged and received benefits as a disabled veteran.

After coming home, he started to get weird. During the national headlines of Richard Speck raping and stabbing eight nurses to death, Wesley drove to the FBI headquarters in Washington, handed in his gun, and confessed. The FBI let him go but kept the gun. He did do some time, for what, nobody knew, but Mom thought it was drugs. He married two or three times. One of the women was Puerto Rican, for which the Ungers briefly disowned him, but she left Wesley after he slept with her mother. Another wife, remembered in Unger history only as "Cookie," gave Wesley two kids, a boy and a girl. After Cookie left him, Wesley showed up on her front lawn with an army-surplus bazooka. None of Wesley's sisters know how the kids ended up; according to Wesley, they were killed by the Kennedys.

Living off his monthly $211 as a disabled veteran, Wesley never had to work and could drift as he liked. He wandered down to Titusville, Florida, and moved into a little bubble camper at the end of a trailer park. Driving his illegal yellow 1963 T-Bird one afternoon, he passed a tiny, dark-haired girl carrying two bags of groceries. He slammed on the brakes, then floored it back to her in reverse.

"GET IN THE CAR!" he barked at her. She was nineteen or twenty and he had a decade and a half on her. He was handsome and intense, his eyes burning through hers while he stretched his body across the passenger seat and kept his left hand on the wheel. She noticed that all of the stuffing had been torn out of his backseat. He opened the door for her, she got in, and that's how my parents met.

COMING TO FLORIDA from upstate New York, Mom had first lived with her aunt Trudy before moving into the trailer park.

After the wedding, Wesley developed a theory that Trudy was working for the Mafia, so they packed up and moved to Hagerstown, Maryland; but there he uncovered a new plot against him. At a local antique store he found a painting of a foxhunt and became convinced that his brother Jim had stolen it from them years ago. Lacking the money to buy it back, Wesley started hanging out at the store, examining the painting with a magnifying glass or chatting up the store owner, trying to trick him into admitting that he knew Jim. Once he even sent Mom in there with a camera to take pictures while he waited outside around the corner, crouching behind parked cars and mailboxes like a cat burglar in a Saturday morning cartoon. "He was trying to be James Bond about it," said Mom, "but he just looked ridiculous."

The next step was to go to Jim and confront him.

"That painting was a gift!" he shouted across Jim's kitchen table, my mother at his side. Jim listened quietly, neither calling Wesley crazy nor playing along, only causing Wesley to grow frustrated and his accusations to get more far-fetched until he finally realized that Jim was the Devil himself. Wesley stormed out of Jim's house, Mom running after him. "Jim's gonna kill me because I'm onto him," he told her. "He's a big shot down in Berkeley Springs and he knows that I'll ruin his reputation. He'll lose his family and his construction company and everything." At the time my parents lived in a retreat cabin that Wesley had been hired to build for a wealthy couple. Outside they kept a small mountain of slab wood for the fireplace, which Wesley spent an entire day rearranging into a bunker to hide my mom. "Stay in here," he ordered. "Jim would kill you too if he found you, because you know all about it." Then he covered her with wood and kept her there with a sleeping bag and flashlight, curled into a ball through the night and the next day while he waited for Jim with his gun.

Jim never showed up, so Wesley did what he could to alert politicians on the state and federal level that his brother had stolen the painting. Soon he found the Devil in his other forms. My mother's mother was the Devil, so Wesley made threatening phone calls to Nan in the middle of the night. And the Devil was head of the Mafia, which wanted to kill Wesley, so he and Mom avoided staying in one place for any length of time. When Mom became pregnant, they were hiding from the Devil in a tent in the forest, hunting deer and rabbit for food. They'd go on long hikes in search of firewood, my mother loading heavy branches onto Wesley's back to carry to their tent.

"MORE!" he'd scream at her, even when it was too much for him.

"That's enough, Wesley," she'd say softly.

"MORE, BITCH!" One of those times she decided that he wasn't going to call her a bitch anymore, so she picked up their hunting rifle and pointed it at his face. The two of them stood motionless, Wesley hunched over with the heavy load on his back and Mom ready to leave him dead right there, miles away from the civilized world and its authority. She finally lowered the gun and they walked back to the tent without saying anything. The stress of life with Wesley, combined with the physical strain of life in the woods, caused her to lose the baby.

They were back in the rich couple's retreat cabin when she got pregnant again, but by then Wesley was receiving messages from his dead brother David and seeing the Devil fly out of the ground. David told Wesley to fulfill the duties of the lost seventh son; he must have seven sons of his own, and his seventh son must in turn have seven sons, because the seventh son of a seventh son would possess special spiritual powers. But then David's story changed; the baby was not Wesley's at all but belonged to the Devil, who had seduced my mother as part of a plan to kill him. The Devil can trick you into raising his seed as your own, David told Wesley, and when the boy's old enough he'll turn on you. Wesley looked at Mom's belly, sensed the Devil growing inside it and knew that he'd have to send it back to Hell. So he wouldn't allow Mom to eat. She miscarried while he was waiting for his monthly $211, so he had no money to take her to the hospital. It was around midnight that he found her lying on the bathroom floor in a pool of her own blood.

"Jodie!" he shouted at her. Mom's name was Sue, but for some reason he called her Jodie. "Jodie, get up!" He dragged her to their bed, the blood still spilling and leaving a trail behind her. She regained consciousness and seemed okay, so Wesley sat her up, causing the blood to rush out of her head, and she blacked out. Wesley put her down and she recovered, so he brought her back up and she blacked out again. They went back and forth like that for some time, Wesley sure that she was faking, until he finally panicked and ran down the road to call an ambulance from the fish store. In the emergency room her blood pressure was measured at fifty over twenty, and she momentarily went blind.

Less than a year later she became pregnant again and turned into a basket case, refusing to get dressed or leave the bed, hallucinating blood, and waiting for the inevitable miscarriage. Turning off his disease like a switch, Wesley feared that he might end up doing wrong again and wanted her as far from him as she could get. He bought her a bus ticket back to Geneva, drove her to the station, and left her there, a scared young girl with a big belly surrounded by drug dealers and assorted shifty monsters giving her their evil eyes. A police officer, recognizing my mom as a walking target, pulled a chair over to a corner far from everyone, put her in it, and wouldn't even let her get up to go to the bathroom. "You stay here," he ordered. "I'll watch you."

MOM NEVER HAD a chance to tell Nan and Gramps that she was coming, or even that she was far along in another pregnancy; Nan was so shocked and overjoyed to see her walk in that she dropped my baby cousin Chrissy to the floor. Nan thought that my mother had freed herself of Wesley, but he'd show up a few weeks later.

It made for an uneasy house. Wesley maintained a hatred of upstate New York from his time stationed in Niagara Falls, but more important, my Nan and Gramps were Catholics, and Wesley hated Catholics. He managed to get along with Gramps, at least until losing respect for him for letting the women run the house. Wesley took charge, telling Nan what to do in her own house. He wouldn't even let Mom help her with the housework.

"Is this how you treat your own mother, Wesley?" Nan cried.

"My mother left me," he told her.

Wesley was confident that he knew how to work women, that he could tweak their minds in the right places to put himself in charge and have them accept it. He claimed that he could take a high school girl and tie her up in his house, and keep her tied up for so long that when he finally untied her, she'd stay because she loved him.

He had my mother tied up in her own head, and she was nine months with me when he decided to untie her. They were sitting together in Nan and Gramps's living room when, without saying a word, he stood up and headed for the door. Mom asked what he was doing, but he only picked up his manual typewriter in its carrying case, pushed open the screen door, and walked out. He knew what it would do. Mom cried for him from the porch and then chased after him, her screams bringing out the neighbors. Wesley picked up the pace until she was sprinting. Mom followed him around the block, her womb bouncing hard with her steps, until she couldn't run anymore and fell to her knees. Wesley helped her up, walked her back to the house, and then went to the kitchen for a beer. Mom sat at his feet and waited for the stillbirth.

IT WASN'T ENOUGH to kill me, but did complicate the labor. I came out arm-first and required the help of forceps, leaving a scar on the top of my head and another by my right eye. Wesley had wanted to name me Frederick after Frederick the Great of the Prussian Empire, but he was nowhere near the hospital; when things were looking bad, he ran out of there and booked down the street to drink all of Gramps's whiskey. My mother named me Michael. I was healthy, but she wasn't. Her bladder had completely shut down, keeping her in the hospital for eight days after I was released.

For those eight days Wesley used me as a tool to antagonize Nan. After everything that she had done for my mother during her pregnancy, including waiting on Wesley hand and foot, Wesley would not allow Nan to touch me. "The sun is shining from his eyes," he'd tell Nan, dangling me in front of her. "You see it? That's his light. You'd like to take it away, wouldn't you?" A week after Mom came home, Wesley and Nan got in a fight over her alleged involvement in the Mafia, so he put Mom and me in the truck and went south. On the road Mom caught botulism from bad truck-stop food. We settled into a nasty trailer in Bedford, Pennsylvania, where she would constantly vomit and have diarrhea at the same time. One afternoon that Wesley was gone, she had to pull herself out of the bathroom to answer the door for an older gentleman from the FBI, who expressed concern over letters that Wesley had written to senator Robert Byrd.

MOM WAS SO afraid of Wesley and what he might do that for the first two years of my life, she never let me out of her sight. In those two years, because of Wesley's growing paranoia, we lived in over twenty places. We had a gutted-out house in Morgantown, West Virginia, that was only one big room with no windows or furniture, just a mattress on the floor; and a motel room in Cumberland, Maryland, with windows that my mother had to crank open; and for a time we squatted in the servants' quarters of an old plantation house. The only meat we could afford to buy was chicken neck, so Wesley would hunt. Sometimes he'd come home and throw a fresh deer on the floor, chop off its head, and nail it to the wall for skinning. When he didn't catch anything, Mom made pancakes with just flour and water, adding ketchup or mayonnaise, or we ate off Salvation Army meal tickets. Wesley tried to supplement his monthly $211 with odd jobs like painting, landscaping, or bean picking, but they never lasted long. When he decided that it was time to move, usually without warning, we took only what fit in the car. Sometimes I had things like a crib and a stroller and toys, but they were often left behind.

Wesley was drinking hard, whipping Mom with belts and calling Nan from payphones to tell her that he was about to kill us both and bury us in the mountains. He started to shave his head to look like Charles Manson, and spent hours practicing what he called "Manson eyes" in the mirror. His stories went through revision; usually I wasn't his son, but other times I was the start of his seventh-son-of-a-seventh-son plan to take over the world. Mom just took it as he gave it until November 1978, when she heard the news coming from South America and saw piles of dead bodies on the cover of *Time*.

The bodies had once been followers of the Reverend Jim Jones at his Jonestown commune in Guyana. They used to call him "Dad." When he gave the order, they lined up to drink poisoned Kool-Aid and kill themselves in turn: first the children, then the elderly followers, then everyone else. Some of the cult members had argued for life, and Jones only told them that living, "raising up every morning and not knowing what's going to be the night's bringing," was much harder than lying down and submitting to death. Seated at his throne when it was all over, surrounded by his adoring corpses, Jones emptied a pistol into his own head.

The sign above him read THOSE WHO DO NOT REMEMBER THE PAST ARE CONDEMNED TO REPEAT IT.

My mother looked at the bodies, considering what they might have been running from or looking for at Jonestown, and why they stayed even when they knew that Jones was wrong. Mom knew all the tricks; we were living in a Jonestown of three.

She began to steal money from Wesley and hide it in a sock, never so much that he would notice. After some months, one morning she asked him to leave the door unlocked so that she could take me for a walk. Wesley agreed. As soon as he headed off to wherever he went during the day, Mom took me and scooped up what else she could—diapers and one change of clothes for me, my bottle, and my baby book—and ran to the neighbors to use their phone.

For the whole ride to the bus station, she scrunched down in the backseat of the taxi, peeking out the windows and constantly checking behind us, certain that Wesley knew. He had told her for so long that he always knew when she lied, that he could read her thoughts and knew her better than she knew herself. Wesley had powers; he could close a door behind him, sit in the dark alone, and travel through space in his mind. He could have been right there in that taxi with us. Mom asked the driver to stop at the bank so she could get some money, knowing that there was no money and she'd have to write a bad check. Still sure that Wesley was coming, she rushed in for the money, then raced back to the cab like the bank was on fire.

She got on the bus to Hagerstown, from there taking a short flight to Washington, D.C., the whole time terrified that he was driving to the airport and could catch her if there was any delay in the flight. At an airport payphone she called Gramps. Having gone the better part of two years without her calling once, he knew what was happening.

"You on the run?" he asked.

Mom held onto me and waited for the plane. Just by looking at Mom and me—me with bruises and Mom with her face gaunt from not eating, her long hair unwashed and nervous eyes surveying the place for Wesley—a random college student felt sorry for us and bought me a teddy bear. At the Syracuse airport, Nan and Gramps walked right past without even recognizing us. Mom was that far gone, the soul drawn out of her sunken face.

They took us home fed and washed us. Three days went by without word from Wesley, which scared Mom more than if he had actually shown up. When he finally called, all he said was, "When are you coming home?" "I'm not," she told him. He hung up. After that he would call constantly to tell her that he was waiting behind a tree to come snatch me away. Gramps's brother Shamo was a detective with the Geneva police and sent officers to the house to wait for his calls.

Wesley eventually came to the house and demanded to see me. Gramps stood watch over the situation, loaded shotgun in hand, but I hid behind Mom and wouldn't go near him. After a few minutes he gave up and went back to Maryland.

"It's harassment," Shamo told my mother. "You can get a warrant on him." So she did, and a week later Wesley called again.

"I'm in Geneva," he said. "I'm at the bus station, and I'm gonna go to the police and have you arrested."

"Okay," said Mom. "I'll tell them you're coming." She called Shamo, and as soon as Wesley walked through the police station doors he was cuffed. During a brief questioning, he stood up and casually walked towards the door, so Shamo handcuffed him and dragged him back to the table. A judge informally told Wesley to never step foot in Geneva again. Shamo drove him to the edge of town and left him by the road with 79¢ in his pocket. That was the last we ever heard of him.

heroes and hero-worship

1

First it was Luke Skywalker, who in 1983 had me deciding that I would train in the ways of the Jedi and restore freedom and justice throughout my own galaxy. I even had a certificate naming me an honorary Jedi knight, bearing Luke's picture and signed by Yoda himself; Mom cut it out of a package of *Star Wars* Underoos, wrote my name on the blank in calligraphy pen, and framed it for my wall. My *Star Wars* alarm clock woke me up each morning with R2-D2 beeping and whistling and C3-PO saying, "You're right, R2. This little Jedi's going to be late."

Ever since *The Empire Strikes Back*, kids talked about Darth Vader being Luke's father as though it were hot gossip about real people in our town. *Return of the Jedi* came out in May, a few months before my sixth birthday. Mom took me to see it in the theaters. By winter I had seen it a dozen times and was wearing only one black glove, no matter how cold my other hand got, so that I could look like Luke. Mom used to nag every morning that I would catch my death going out like that.

"I have to wear this glove," I would say. "Darth Vader chopped my hand off."

When Mom drove me to school she seemed nervous, like a little animal always on alert, as though moms had natural predators in the wild.

One morning I looked at my one black glove and then the question jumped out of me, catching us both by surprise. "Mom, where's my dad?"

"He ran away," she blurted immediately. "He got sick and ran away."

So I wondered what made him sick, or why being sick would make him run. Maybe a sick dog bit him, I thought, and he got lost while running from the dog, and he was still trying to get home but now the bite made him sick too. Then I felt it, my first sense of that secret history, floating in the air around my mother. It reached my side of the car and hovered over me, starting to push down with all of its weight. Mom must have felt it too, now offering assurances that she would always be there and never let anything happen to me. When we got to school, she unlocked my door and kissed me. She waited until I was in the building before driving away.

Without any knowledge or conscious memory to justify them, I began having nightmares about him, my own Darth Vader. It was always the same: Mom's driving me somewhere; the car behind us pulls up close. The driver honks his horn in a rhythmic code. Mom's entire body tightens as she tries to restrain her panic. "It's your father," she says. I wonder what the honks mean, but she knows.

ONE AFTERNOON, WHILE I performed a funeral for some *Star Wars* action figures in the dirt by our front porch, a man on a motorcycle pulled into the driveway. I sprinted inside and alerted Mom, who promised that it was okay. I looked out the window. He had taken off his helmet. He was stocky and bald with a horseshoe of black hair and a beard.

"Michael," she said, "this is Bill."

"Hey," he said.

We didn't hang out too long. They dropped me off at Nan and Gramps's house and then went somewhere together.

The first Saturday morning that I walked into her bedroom and found him sleeping there, with only shorts on and no shirt and hairy all over, I wanted to throw up. I didn't know what sex was. When a black kid at school told me that he was going to get some girls and "hump" them, I had no idea what he meant, but figured that humping wasn't something that white people did. I at least knew that Bill had corrupted the natural balance of things. As an honorary Jedi knight, I could sense a disturbance in the Force. Later I was sitting on the living room floor, watching cartoons in my Darth Vader pajamas, when he came out and sat on the couch. He was still only in his shorts. I kept my eyes on the TV, scared to turn around and look at him.

He did better the next week.

"You want to ride my motorcycle?"

My head whipped away from the cartoons. At least this time Bill had a T-shirt on.

"He's not riding that motorcycle," yelled Mom from the kitchen, playing the bad cop to help him out.

"He's nine years old," said Bill. "He's up for it."

"Yeah, Mom!"

She let us go up and down the empty street at two miles per hour, but in my head we were chasing TIE fighters in the trenches of the Death Star.

⊘

"HOW WOULD YOU feel about Bill being your father?" Mom asked. "When we get married, I'm going to take his name. You can too."

"Okay," I said. Up to that point Mom and I still had Unger, my father's name. Now our name was going to be Schutt (pronounced with a *K*, like *school*). If I wanted, she said, I could also trade in my old middle name, Roland, and make William my middle name.

I was more excited about the name than the man. Even before the wedding I took to signing homework and quizzes as "Michael W. Schutt," which led to a minor battle of wills with my third-grade teacher, Mrs. Abraham.

"That's not your name yet," she snapped at me.

"Yes, it is."

"You can use it when it's legal."

"Why are you changing your name?" asked a girl named Jackie.

"I'm getting adopted." She gasped as though I had revealed something awful. I kind of appreciated that.

Mom suggested that after the wedding, when she and Bill ran out of the church and people threw rice at them, I should go up to Bill and call him Dad. So I waited outside with everyone, and when they came out I just walked up to him and said, "Hi, Dad."

Mom and Bill bought some land from his parents out in Hopewell, a nearby farm town. It seemed like a foreign country.

The first time I saw our land it was only a field of weeds. Next door Bill showed me his father's giant tractor, with tires taller than me, and took us for a slow ride across our three acres. On another trip they showed me where the land had been dug up for our house. Sometime later we made a third pilgrimage to witness our brand new double-wide, delivered in separate halves and encased in plastic like wrapped presents. Mom showed me where my room would be—my new room in my new house, coming with a new school where I'd show up with my new name, completely reinvented at nine years old.

After we moved in, Bill went through a phase of avoiding both of us. Mom and I would be watching TV in the living room, and he'd go into their bedroom to watch the same show. He went about six months like that, but I didn't mind; before Bill came along, it had been just Mom and me, so it seemed more natural without him.

It was another Saturday morning that he broke the ice, rejoining me for cartoons and then turning the channel to wrestling. All I knew of wrestling were the posters of Hulk Hogan and Mr. T in the ring together, and kids screaming "Superfly Snuka!" whenever they jumped off something high on the playground. Bill had me watching wrestling every week. I learned the essential characters and storylines just in time for WrestleMania III, the single greatest night in wrestling history—taking place before a record-setting crowd of ninety-three thousand fans at the Pontiac Silverdome, with the historic main event of Hulk Hogan defending his championship against Andre the Giant.

The day offered its first glimpse of Hulk Hogan in a prefight interview. Standing backstage, his bronze (nearly orange) skin stretched over comic-book muscles—"the largest arms in the world," he boasted—he made it more than a matter of choreographed violence; he was our new Christ on steroids and the center of his own belief system. "ANDRE," he bellowed into Mean Gene's microphone, "YOU GOTTA FACE THE TRUTH, BROTHER, IN ITS PUREST FORM, MAN—THE PUREST TRUTH THERE IS, MAN! THE TRAINING, THE SAYING THE PRAYERS, THE EATIN' THE VITAMINS . . . AND TO BEAT ME, MAN, YOU GOTTA BEAT EVERY HULKAMANIAC— EVERY LITTLE HULKSTER IN THE WORLD, EVERYONE THAT PLAYS IT STRAIGHT, ALL THE ONES THAT DON'T TAKE ANY SHORTCUTS . . ."

I counted myself among the faithful but still wondered whether he could do it, and watched with genuine fear as Hulk Hogan entered the ring for his stare-down with the Giant. "Look at the size of Andre," exclaimed announcer Jesse Ventura. "I mean, Hogan is six foot eight!" Gorilla Monsoon then added, "Andre is seven foot five."

After roughly eight minutes of battle, our champion, his body surging with the power of Hulkamania and all of our prayers, finally hoisted five-hundred-pound Andre over his head and sent him crashing to the mat. My jaw dropped as the referee counted the pin, ending Andre's fifteen-year unde-feated streak. The Immovable Object—the mountains, the deserts, the oceans, the sun—had fallen at the feet of the Irresistible Force, man himself. It was my first religious con-version experience; I now bore witness to the truth of Hulk Hogan.

Wrestling became my life. During class I zoned out on Hulkster dreams, conjuring up fictitious Andre-sized oppres-sors and scenarios in which I would send them crashing into the earth, after which of course I'd treat the fans to a twenty-minute posedown, my theme music blaring through the speakers, the announcers hailing my triumph over evil. My older cousin Shawn had been into wrestling but outgrew it for heavy metal, so he gave me his huge box of old *Pro Wrestling Illustrated*s. I draped my walls in Hulk Hogan clippings. There were wrestlers on my T-shirts and wrestlers on my birthday cakes. When we had our moving-in yard sale, I sold all of my *Star Wars* figures and used the money to buy Remco dolls of wrestlers like Ric Flair, the Road Warriors, and the Fabulous Freebirds. Nan and Gramps would let me have parties for all the pay-per-view matches at their house.

Bill even helped me make my own championship belt. I drew designs for the plates on white poster board and colored them with gold markers, and he cut out a belt of black fabric and stapled the plates on. "WORLD HEAVYWEIGHT CHAMPION," read the center plate, with a globe colored blue and surrounded by the flags of various nations that I copied out of *The World Almanac*. I wore the belt to school, imagining each crowded hall as my aisle to the ring.

Though Bill had introduced me to wrestling, the degree of my obsession started to annoy him, and he felt obligated to kill it. "Did you see that?" he remarked as Hulk Hogan put his big boot in an opponent's face. "Did you see that kick? He didn't even touch him." I failed to catch what Bill was getting at, so he just came out with it.

"You know that wrestling's fake, right?" I turned away from the TV to face the hairy, half-naked man.

"What do you mean?"

"Remember when Willie Andrews punched you at recess and you had a black eye? And he was just some kid. But Hulk Hogan, with all of his muscles, when he punches a guy, there's no black eye or anything."

"So? Wrestlers are in peak physical condition, they don't bruise as easily."

"Look at how he punches. He's not really making contact, he just stomps the mat to make that sound." For the rest of the show, every time a wrestling hold defied common sense, Bill made sure to point it out.

The truth about wrestling never hit me in some dramatic revelatory moment, but eased its way in slowly, without making much impact. I could care less about wrestling being real or not real; *Star Wars* wasn't real. If anything, learning that wrestling was fiction only gave me a new way to enjoy it. Rather than Hulk Hogan, I would now imagine myself as Vince McMahon, the half–Walt Disney, half–P. T. Barnum creative genius who masterminded the show. My sixth-grade teacher, Mr. Plyter, encouraged me as I penned epic wrestling sagas and performed them for the class. One story, detailing every blow in a hundred-man battle royal, was too long to read at a normal pace, so Mr. Plyter and I took turns zipping through my blue-inked loose-leaf pages. He'd race his way through a section, then slap my hand like we were partners in a tag-team match. I'd read as fast as I could until running out of breath, then tag him back in. At the end of the story, the class cheered as though I had won the battle royal myself.

Mom bought me a wrestling dice game from an ad in *Pro Wrestling Illustrated* that put me in charge of an imaginary league of sixty wrestlers. I made blank character cards so that I could create my own wrestlers, and the league soon took on its own life. I brought the cards, dice, and record book everywhere, holding matches at the dinner table, on the bus ride to school, and even during class, discreetly rolling the dice inside my desk. My friends made wrestlers of themselves, and we formed a Dungeons & Dragons–styled role-playing group in which I dictated the story with original narratives of matches and feuds. It became serious and real, at least for me; I reserved afternoons for us at a meeting room in the local public library, appointed kids as secretaries and treasurers and even announced a plan to recruit members in Australia through a pen-pal service at school. That marked the end; to my friends I had lost my mind.

I did have a brief involvement with "real" wrestling in seventh grade when I joined the Junior Academy wrestling team. Compared to Hulk Hogan matches, it lacked personality; but I did feel proud in my red and gray singlet, like a uniformed soldier on his way to fight and die for Canandaigua's honor. My first practice match was against a gangly red-haired kid, taller and skinnier than me, with freckles over every inch of his body. The whole team was watching. We walked onto the red mat and entered the gray circle, both of us in our matching singlets, and shook hands. Then he dove at me and drove his shoulder into my stomach, at the same time grabbing my legs and spearing me to the mat. I heard our teammates laugh. Once we landed he didn't know what to do, so I squirmed out from under him, got behind him and locked on a half nelson. I rode him like that for the whole match, making the most of my body weight, my hand on the back of his neck, shoving his face into the mat. He tried a few escapes but couldn't get out. Kids were shouting advice to him. The coach told him not to give up. Our match had taken on a traditional pro-wrestling psychology, in which this freckled kid was the underdog, and I was the ruthless villain asshole. Someone yelled for me to try going for the pin to end the match, but I wouldn't risk losing my advantage. It was enough for me to just hold this kid down, feeling the tension inside him as he grew pissed, his body becoming slack as he grew tired, the occasional bursts of power getting smaller and weaker until I finally sensed that his spirit had broken in my hands. It was like school-sanctioned domestic abuse.

I STILL WROTE wrestling stories, but only for personal gratification or English class. In one story, "Dream Match," I was a wrestling promoter, owner of the International Wrestling Association. My character meets Vince McMahon at a party in Atlantic City and we trade business cards. "It was the most helpful and influential exchange in wrestling history," I wrote, as it would lead to a match between Vince's champion, Hulk Hogan, and mine, "Flyin'" Brian Pillman.

The story was dated January 17, 1990, as the real-life World Wrestling Federation began to build towards a match between Hulk Hogan and the Ultimate Warrior, its rising young star. Everything about him was louder than old, balding Hogan—he had a wild head of hair that he styled after glam-rock bands like Poison and Warrant, and a more ripped body that he'd accentuate by wearing tight bands around his arms, making his biceps and veins pop out. He sprinted down the aisle, ran back and forth across the ring, shook the ropes like a maniac, and pumped his fist towards the sky. He masked his face in neon war paint and screamed his interviews. He also had his own championship belt, the Intercontinental title, which he first won by destroying a man in thirty seconds.

Hulk Hogan faced his sunset. The Ultimate Warrior was the future, or so it looked in 1990.

Promotional spots for their confrontation, billed as "Champion vs. Champion, Title for Title" portrayed them as constellations in the night sky, the greatest forces in the universe colliding live on pay-per-view. Maintaining the gospel of Hulkamania, Hogan insisted, "THIS IS WHERE THE

POWER LIES," while pointing into his open palm. He then foretold that he would bring his opponent to his knees and ask him if he wanted to live forever.

"I CAN SAVE YA," he promised the Ultimate Warrior, "THE HULKAMANIACS CAN SAVE YA! WE CAN TURN THE DARKNESS THAT YOU LIVE IN INTO THE LIGHT—"

The Warrior, snarling as he paced like a caged animal in his dressing room, gave a monologue in which he promised that he had come not to destroy Hulkamania but to save it, taking the true faith to places it had never been.

Hulk Hogan was now on the other side of the equation, the Immovable Object that must succumb to the Irresistible Force. They battled evenly for more than twenty minutes, when finally the Ultimate Warrior threw himself onto Hogan's exhausted body and covered him for the win. As Warrior celebrated with his Intercontinental belt, Hogan climbed out of the ring and grabbed his own—the World Wrestling Federation championship, his crown denoting sovereignty over all of creation. He went back into the ring while Jesse Ventura noted the hush falling over the crowd. "They don't know what the Hulkster's going to do," said Gorilla Monsoon, "and neither do I." Hulk Hogan then handed over the belt and embraced his conqueror. While the old god left the ring with tears in his eyes, the new god held up both belts amidst explosions of fireworks.

The defeat of Hulk Hogan reminded me of the Norse mythology book at the school library, in which I read of Ragnarök, the final battle in which the gods and monsters kill each other and the world freezes. All that remained from the old world was hope, hope that someday a new hero would break out of the ice; I needed that much, but I wasn't sure that he'd be the Ultimate Warrior.

2 the battle of swamp road

The next hero emerged after Bill refused to let me go see MC Hammer.

"How would you feel about going to a concert where everyone was black?" he asked. "You're not really used to being around black people."

"There were black people in Geneva." Geneva was where Mom and I lived before Bill took us away to Hopewell's cows and cornfields.

"But you were a little kid then."

"So?"

"It's different."

"How is it different?"

"When I was in the army there were some black guys and they didn't like us. They'd try to play their music louder than ours, but we had better radios." Bill failed to grasp that most of the black people at an MC Hammer concert would actually be on the stage; but unfortunately for him, Hammer's safe pop-rap served as my gateway to more threatening material. If hip-hop and black people made Bill uncomfortable, I'd graduate from Hammer to Public Enemy, a group with its own paramilitary entourage, the S1W, costumed in berets and black fatigues like the Black Panther Party, and frontman Chuck D who bragged that his Uzi weighed a ton. The cover of their album *It Takes a Nation of Millions to Hold Us Back* showed Chuck D and Flavor Flav standing behind prison bars, looking badass beyond belief, while inside I found lyrics calling Farrakhan a prophet, quoting the Honorable Elijah Muhammad, and calling the government a bunch of "grafted devils." I didn't know who Farrakhan or the Honorable Elijah Muhammad were, but they at least sounded like people who scared the shit out of Bill. I convinced Mom to buy me a baseball cap with the Public Enemy logo (a silhouette of an S1W standing in a sniper's crosshairs) and a red, black, and green medallion of Africa to wear to square dances at the Hopewell town grange.

Mom worked at the local battery factory, which provided my Walkman with free batteries to kill just rewinding and playing back my favorite Public Enemy song, "Black Steel in the Hour of Chaos." I'd march through the kitchen with the headphones on, waving my hands around like a tough guy as I recited the lyrics:

> *I got a letter from the government, the other day*
> *I opened and read it, it said they were suckers*
> *they wanted me for their army or whatever*
> *picture me giving a damn*
> *I said never*

The song depicts Chuck D in prison for draft evasion and plotting his escape. He steals the gun from a sleeping guard, instigates a prison riot, and breaks out with the help of the S1W, who descend in a helicopter and blow up the prison water tower. The best part comes when Chuck D declares, "They could not understand that I'm a BLACK MAN! And I could never be a veteran!" For Bill, it must have seemed like I was siding with the black guys from his army days. At least that's what I hoped.

AFTER WATCHING SPIKE Lee's *Do the Right Thing,* I decided to imitate the Radio Raheem character, who always appeared with a boom box blasting Public Enemy's protest anthem, "Fight the Power." Radio Raheem carried himself like a wrestler challenging the entire world. If he was in the army with Bill, he would have defeated all of the white boys' transistors and maybe punched Bill out with his big four-fingered rings. My "boom box" was the little radio that Mom would take to the beach, but I still thought of myself as pretty hardcore marching around Hopewell with it, wearing my Public Enemy hat and Africa medallion swinging over a red and yellow "Hulk Rules" T-shirt. Strutting down County Road 47, there was never anyone but the cows to see me, and Mom's radio wasn't loud enough for truckers to hear. My only chance to make a scene was at the Little Store (the only store within five miles), where they sold beef jerky and rented Nintendo games. Before going in, I'd stop the tape and rewind it to the beginning of "Fight the Power"; then press play and push through the door. No one ever reacted, which made me think that I was the most intimidating twelve-year-old alive.

"Elvis was a hero to most," raps Chuck D in the song, "but he never meant *shit* to me! A straight-out racist, that sucker was simple and plain." Then Flavor Flav interjects,

"Mother*fuck* him and John Wayne!" The obscenities on my cassette were bleeped out, but I knew what they said.

To keep me from embarrassing him, Bill locked the radio in the truck when we went to the flea market and tractor store.

"Country music is stupid," I told him. "It's not about anything."

"Johnny Cash sang about prison."

"Yeah, but I'd bet he didn't break out."

Bill said I could get some summer work on his uncle Harold's farm down the road. I had already worked for my uncle Doug pulling weeds out of a bean field, but chose to spend the summer at Nan and Gramps's house where they had cable and I could watch *Yo! MTV Raps.*

"Luke's just not a farmer," says Aunt Beru in *Star Wars.* "He has too much of his father in him." Uncle Owen replies gravely, "That's what I'm afraid of." I remained sure that I wasn't a farmer either, maybe for the same reason.

AROUND THE TIME that Hulk Hogan lost his championship, Mom and Bill's marriage began to fall apart. They tried to hide it, locking me out of their bedroom during fights. The walls were thick enough to muffle the words; but whatever they said, I could tell that they screamed it. When the shouting became too much I'd go out and walk for hours down Hopewell's long, dead roads. I always started with a violent burst out the door, leaving fast and hard and almost hurting myself with my steps, then turned off County Road 47 to go down the slope of Swamp Road, which offered only scant woods of ugly, bare trees and a few ugly houses with unmowed lawns. At the bottom of the hill I passed my friend Ronnie's house, which had been patched together with mismatched sheets of whatever materials they

could find. Ronnie was a tough kid with long blonde hair that
he had vowed never to cut. He smoked cigarettes and got in
trouble at school for stuff like lighting trash cans on fire. Then
I passed Randy's trailer. Randy was a skinny kid who lived in
constant fear of his fat mom. Their trailer looked like it could
fall apart any minute.

I'd walk a long ways after the hill flattened and it seemed
as though I could trudge a hundred miles in that direction
and never see anything. My anger wore off and then I only
felt sad, and then even the sadness wore off and I just felt
glad to be alone. When it got boring I'd push on, knowing that
I couldn't turn around until Mom and Bill noticed that I
was gone, however long that would take—I'd keep walking
beyond all rational limits, suffering to make them suffer. It
proved something, I thought. They needed to see how mad I
was and how badly they'd messed up with their dumb fights.
One time Bill came in his truck to get me and I told him to
keep on driving.

Mom started to go out at night, leaving me alone to deal
with Bill. Neither of us knew where she went, but no sooner
did she walk out the door than Bill sat on the floor and bawled
about her in front of me. He had no support in that house.
Mom clearly wanted little to do with him, and I'd wave it in
his face that he wasn't my real father.

"Why do you treat me like this?" he shrieked.

"Maybe I know something you don't." That made him back
off, paranoid that Mom was planning to leave him and had
told me. I didn't actually know anything. I was a jerk to Bill,
but I was also a kid in a house with no adults.

Sometimes I took refuge in a weekend with Nan and
Gramps or my friend Jim. Jim lived on a farm, and it was
always funny to watch turds fall out of his cows. We invented

an indoor football game with his two younger brothers, in which the guy with the ball ran towards Jim's bed and tried to leap across it while everyone else tried to kill him. If you made it to the pillows at the far end of the bed, it equaled a touchdown. During the chaos I made the mistake of jumping while actually standing on the bed, smashing my head into Jim's low ceiling. It earned me a huge bump, but I stayed in the game and then did it again on the exact same spot. As I took my hand off my head and saw red, a warm stream came trickling down my face.

"Shit!" screamed Jim, his voice cracking. He ran through the house with his brothers in search of their mom while I rolled around by myself on the floor, writhing and grimacing like a wrestler, imagining what the astonished play-by-play announcers would say. OH MAH GAWD, HE'S BLEEDING PROFUSELY! HIS FACE HAS BECOME A CRIMSON MASK! I became Randy "Macho Man" Savage; he was wiry like me and small compared to the other wrestlers, so it made sense to model my movements after him. The blood kept pouring out at a steady pace, filling my eyes and nose and mouth, making puddles on the hardwood floor. Jim's mom arrived just as I reacted to Andre the Giant stomping on my back. It must have looked like I was having a seizure, but seeing her I calmly stood up and let her bring me to the bathroom. "Mike's dying," gasped one of Jim's brothers while his mom sat me in front of the mirror, applied pressure to the top of my head and scrubbed hard on my face. A pile of reddened wet washcloths lay clumped and ruined on the edge of the sink. The dried blood around my eyes was dark, looking almost like I was wearing eyeliner.

MOM AND BILL conducted experiments in separation, taking turns moving out of the house. I always stayed with Mom. For a time we had our own apartment in Canandaigua, and I'd spend weekends with Bill, during which he'd cry, yell, or probe me for information. I just sat and took it, sometimes wondering what Mom did while I babysat her husband. I never told Bill that I had walked in on her kissing her friend from work, but I asked Mom about it. "Sometimes friends kiss each other that way," she told me.

Sick of Bill and distrusting Mom, I began to think about my third parent, my father who got sick and ran away. When I finally asked the question, Mom took me over to the couch and put her arm around me. It had to be something big.

"Remember when you were little and Gramps had those strokes?"

"No."

"Well, Gramps had strokes because his heart wasn't working."

"Okay."

"And Nanny, you know she's sick because her lungs are bad, because she smokes so much."

"Yeah."

"The brain's a part of the body like anything else, and sometimes it doesn't work right. Wesley—your father—had a sickness in his brain."

"Like how?"

"You know what an alchemist is?"

"No."

"An alchemist is like a magician who turns things into gold. Wesley thought he could do that. We used to run all over junkyards on full-moon nights to find the right ingredients." That actually sounded kind of cool. "And he saw things," she added, though she didn't seem sure that she should say it. "He saw things that weren't there."

"What kinds of things?" I asked. She paused, then looked straight at me.

"The Devil. Do you want to know the story?"

creep, jr.

3

Mom gave me some photos of Wesley as a young man. In one he's standing proudly by his new car painted like a giant American flag with red and white stripes down the side, the blue hood covered with stars. In another he's wearing a suit, standing slack with hands in pockets. His chin's up and he's smirking. He looks like he has all kinds of cool things going on, but around him there's nothing but a grassy field and some trees. Mom also had a photo of Wesley and Calvin standing together on the front porch. Wesley's affection for his dad looks condescending, as though he loves Calvin but still knows that he's worlds above him and can't wait to prove it.

"Why didn't you tell me before?" I demanded.

"The last time you asked, you were six years old. What was I going to say?"

"You lied, Mom."

"Bud, I didn't know what to do."

"You said he got sick and ran away."

"In a way, that was true."

"In *a way?*"

"I was scared to death of the day that you'd ask about Wesley. I should have prepared for it; I knew it was coming, but I couldn't even begin to think of what I'd tell you. I was so afraid of how you'd feel about yourself . . ."

"How come he never wanted to see me?"

"Bud, he's sick. He's not in his right mind."

"I want to see him."

"Nobody knows where he is," she said. "When I was with him, we used to move around so much. If I knew where he was today, it wouldn't mean anything two weeks from now. Once I had lawyers looking for him. For a while he was in Montana, but that was some time ago."

"He gets money from being disabled, right? The VA knows where to send the check."

"Until you were six years old," she answered, "they sent me part of his benefits every month. But they can't say where he is; there's a rule about confidentiality."

"I'm going to find him."

I went to Canandaigua's Veterans Administration, which happened to be within walking distance of the Junior Academy. "I'm searching for a disabled veteran," I told the man at the office. "He's mentally ill and he lives in Maryland, I think. But I don't know."

"We don't have those kinds of records," he said, "and we couldn't give them out if we did. You might want to check with the VA in Maryland."

MOM KEPT INSISTING that there was no way to track down Wesley, but found herself remembering bits and pieces of their life together that she hadn't thought about in ten years.

"There was one time," she said, "when he told Nan and Gramps that he was going to let me go. So your uncles Dan and Don went all the way down to Maryland to get me, but when they showed up, Wesley changed his mind. He wouldn't even let them in the house or let me out to talk to them—I had to talk to my brother and brother-in-law through the window while Wesley waved my plane ticket at them."

That was the first time that I thought of other people in our family as participants in the Wesley stories. It was one thing to hear about Nan and Gramps dealing with him, but now I felt embarrassed in front of everyone, as though they saw Wesley when they looked at me.

DURING THE TIMES that Mom and Bill lived together, Mom would stay out late and Bill cried himself to sleep while hugging a pillow. I took to doing my country walks at all hours, ruining my sleep routine. Sometimes I'd be awake in the living room at three in the morning and Mom would show up to try to talk me into going to sleep.

"At least try."

"I can't sleep, Mom."

"Bud, do you ever pray?"

"I don't believe in God."

"You have to believe in God," she said.

"Does sex hurt?"

"What?"

"I'm sorry," I said, "I don't know why, it just—"

"No, no, it's okay. You can ask me anything. It's not supposed to hurt, but it can if it's something like rape."

"Am I a rape child?"

"What? No, no—"

"If you were afraid of Wesley, then I was a rape child."

"No. He did do that, Michael. But he wasn't like that until after you were born." Mom gave a bad answer under pressure; for Wesley to only be crazy or abusive after my birth contradicted all of the stories that she had already told me. The idea of being a rape child became fact, as far as I could know.

After Mom went to work I'd call her office with the feeling of open scissors jumbled up in my stomach, cutting my insides when I moved.

"Mom," I moaned, trying to sound like I could drop dead right there on the phone, "I can't go to school today."

"Yes, you can, bud. You can do it."

"No, Mom, I can't. You don't understand."

"Michael, you need to pull yourself up and go, and you'll feel better."

"I can't!"

"It's so easy to give up; I know. It's a lot easier to just hide in the house and give up and keep telling yourself that you're too weak until it's true. Do you want to be like Nanny and never leave the house? You're not weak, you can—"

"NO, I CAN'T!"

"Okay, bud. Stay home. But we need to do something about this." Hiding behind the living room curtains, I watched out the window as the school bus paused in front of my house, then continued on its way.

Sometimes she convinced me to go to school. I hated riding that bus; it was at least an hour and we seemed to pass the same cornfields over and over again, like the repeating backgrounds in old cartoons. The ride home was even worse because most of my friends got off before me. One of my friends on the bus was Elwin Gayheart, two years older and three times my size. He had greasy hair and always wore long-sleeved flannel shirts, even in the summer. Kids made fun of him by asking,

"Elwin, do you have a *gay heart?*" He never had any come-backs better than "No, but you do." The bus picked him up and dropped him off in front of a huge junkyard way out in the middle of nowhere. I think his dad owned it. Most of the yard's contents were hidden behind an old metal fence, but I could see the tops of dead yellow buses and piled-up cars peek-ing over. I thought it'd be cool to run away and live in one of the buses.

Feeling carsick during a ride home, I finally threw up on myself just minutes before the bus reached my house. Someone took initiative to alert the driver: "MIKE SCHUTT PUKED!" Then came the expected reactions. A few kids chanted, "CHUNK, CHUNK, CHUNKY SOUP!" They kept it up as I walked down the aisle, wearing my pink vomit like an extra layer of clothing, and stumbled off the bus.

There were times when I decided to miss the bus home, walk around Canandaigua for a few hours, and then call Mom after she got out of work; what was she going to do, not come get me? I cut across the local dairy's property, where outside they always had cartons of milk that had just passed their sell-by dates. I'd grab as many pints of chocolate milk as I could carry, run down to the chain-link fence on the far end, and hurl them all over to the other side. Then I hopped the fence and sat on the railroad tracks that ran between the dairy and my former school, Canandaigua Elementary, enjoying my plunder. The fences on either side of me gave the tracks an illusion of being a *place,* a long narrow territory distinct from the rest of the town; and I could be its king, lording over it alone and chugging my stolen expired chocolate milk.

The Junior Academy's class day ended a full forty min-utes before elementary got out; if I was willing to hop another fence, I could go see my sixth-grade teacher, Mr. Plyter. His door opened to the back of the classroom, so I walked in without being noticed by most of the kids. One turned around and saw me. I took a seat and waited for the last bell of the day.

"How's junior high?" asked Mr. Plyter as the kids grabbed their book bags and filed out.

"I don't know," I said, looking at the floor.

"Are you still writing those wrestling stories?"

"No."

"I want to show you a story that I wrote." He then opened his desk and fished around inside, pulling out a legal-sized notepad with "The Ugly Word" written at the top in red ink and classic teacher's cursive.

"The Ugly Word" was about a boy who had been locked in a closet as punishment for swearing. The opening paragraphs rolled by without my full attention, but halfway through it clicked and I knew that I was reading a terrible secret. The sounds of his evil bitch sisters laughing outside became real, and the thoughts of the boy in the dark became my own. "Sometimes you can work things out with stories," he said after I finished. "You'll find things that you never knew were there."

I told Mom about it and she bought me a journal. I started a few stories but most of them never went anywhere. The only finished one involved an alien coming from outer space to see what war was like on earth and basing his research on fights between a husband and wife. Besides that, I wrote letters to Mom's two miscarriages, just telling them how I was doing and that someday the three of us would have our revenge.

MISSING NEARLY THE entire last quarter of eighth grade, I didn't have much to give to tests or quizzes on days that I showed up, so I'd fill the margins of papers with cryptic messages to my teachers. *I have to find him . . . I must find him to save myself.* I either wanted to freak them out or get some help, maybe both, but they never reacted. Skipping school in Hopewell was boring, so I'd spend afternoons staring in the mirror and pretending to hold a gun, concocting elaborate scenarios in which I killed my father.

Wesley Unger? I ask, the two of us standing in a field. He doesn't know who I am. *I'M YOUR SON!* And then *blam-blam-blam*, he falls. In another version I come into his house, catch him sleeping, and wake him up before pulling the trigger, just so he knows who I am. There was one fantasy in which I'd come up behind him while he stood over my mother, ready to hurt her, maybe with a weapon in his hand. Before he even knows that I am there, I pick up the nearest sharp object and plunge it into his eyeball. He goes down but I keep on him, destroying his face.

I also pictured myself walking into his house when he wasn't there and finding a naked young woman chained to the wall. I break the chains, carry her to my car (not sure how old I am in the fantasy), and take her to the hospital. While she's recovering, I visit her and explain that I am the man's son. Even though I come from that same horrible place, she falls in love with me.

WRESTLEMANIA VII CAME and went without my noticing. The main storyline of the time revolved around Sgt. Slaughter, wrestling hero/G.I. Joe action figure, turning his back on America and siding with Saddam Hussein. Having lost interest in Vince McMahon's make-believe combat, I took to starting real fights in the gym during recess. My first opponent was Tony Mitch, one of the kids from our defunct dice-wrestling league. I spit on him and walked away, so he ran after me, grabbed my shirt, and swung me around. I hit him with a backhanded right to his temple, brought it back on the other side, then backhanded him again. After the three rights he fell down. Another kid picked me up and shouted, "MIKE SCHUTT BEAT UP TONY MITCH!" while I waved my arms like Ali.

Another time we were playing tag and I just punched a kid on the back of his neck in front of our teacher. For that I was sent to the "hot box," a behavior-management technique that I'm pretty sure is frowned upon by today's educators. It was just a little cell adjacent to the vice principal's office where students would sit for predetermined periods of solitary confinement. We had a whole mystique surrounding the hot box; to go there meant you were a legit bad kid. Contrary to legend, I found that the hot box wasn't literally hot, but I still bought into the gravity that teachers tried to give it. I was certain that I had gotten myself into real trouble with the permanent-record kind of consequences, and for nothing had just thrown away the rest of my life.

The hot box was located between the vice principal's office and his secretary and had no door. I could see when people walked by, but they never turned to look at me.

"Mr. Darnell," I cried, "I have problems!" Then I burst into tears. He brought me into his office. "My dad went to Vietnam," I told him (I thought that Vietnam and Korea were the same place), "and he went crazy. He saw grafted devils fly out of the ground." I didn't know what it meant to be a *grafted* devil, having only heard the phrase in Public Enemy lyrics. "And he raped my mom and that's how I was born."

"Michael," said Mr. Darnell, "let me tell you something. Vietnam was hell." He said it like he really respected the words, as though he might have known something about it. "A lot of people went to Vietnam and weren't the same when they came back." He let me go to class and wrote a late pass to give to the teacher. On the way I unfolded it to read, "Mike is a good guy."

As good a guy as I might have been, I still landed detention at least once a week, usually for things like accumulated tardiness. During the stints that Mom and I lived in town and I could walk to school, I never worried about getting there on time.

After one detention, a girl just up and asked me, "Will you go out with her?" I turned and saw her pointing at her friend, a plain brown-haired girl with a bowl cut. I had never said a word to her before. Her name was Patience. Kids teased her by singing the Guns N' Roses song of the same name, or calling for her in their best Axl Rose impressions. I immediately turned away and walked off without saying a word or looking back.

On the way home I tried to make sense of it. Why had I even done that? I must have looked insane, but I *was* insane; at least I wanted to think so. Being insane was at least more interesting than just being a loser who's afraid of girls.

Exploring the basement in that apartment house, I came across a cardboard box full of old *Playboy* magazines. Before even looking at them I moved the box into a small doorless closet in the basement that I had claimed for my fort and blocked off with a giant sheet of plywood. As dark as it was in the rest of the basement, in the fort it was pitch-black. I'd just sit there, satisfied that I now owned a box of *Playboys* even if I couldn't see the pictures. In the dark with my pointless magazines I thought about Patience. There might have been a chance that instead of being either a loser or a psycho, I could actually go out with her and be her boyfriend. For the next couple days, I tried to figure out what door she took out of the school so that I could walk her home. Observing her step out of the Main Street exit and cut behind the school, instead of taking immediate action I decided to go home and think out a plan for the next day.

Twenty-four hours later I was ready. I raced out of school to wait for her by the Main Street door.

"Hi," I said when she came out.

"FUCK YOU!" she shouted. I stood in place as she ran away.

I waited for her again the next afternoon.

"Hi, I just wanted to say that I'm sorry for not going out with you when you asked . . ."

"That's okay," she said. "I'm sorry for swearing at you, that's what I do when I'm nervous." I walked her home and asked her if she still wanted to go out with me. She said yes and gave me her phone number. After watching her go into her house, I continued on my way and sang the Guns N' Roses song with utmost seriousness: *sad woman, take it slow, it'll work itself out fine . . . all we need is just a little patience . . .* I even tried to do Axl's long whistling part.

In the parlance of Canandaigua Junior Academy circa 1991, "going out" didn't really mean that you went anywhere. For me it didn't even mean that I spoke to her in person. I made a concerted effort to avoid any interaction with Patience during the school day, but then called her at night. It occurred to me that we might at some point be expected to spend time together, perhaps even make out. But then Mom moved us back to Bill and the house in Hopewell, which for two thirteen-year-olds constituted a long-distance relationship.

Desperate to express my love but unable to tell Mom that I had a girlfriend, I reached out to Bill.

"Can you drive me into town and drop me off and then pick me up in an hour?"

"For what?"

"Can I tell you later? I promise I'll tell you later."

"Sure." So I had him drop me off in front of the florist on Gibson Street. After his truck disappeared, I went inside and bought a bouquet. I didn't know anything about flowers, and the ones I chose did not seem particularly romantic—they could have been sorry-for-your-loss flowers for all that I knew—but they were flowers anyway, supplemented with a folded note full of overblown adolescent tragedy, and also my Saint Anthony necklace ("Guide and Protect," it said). I walked with the flowers, note, and necklace to her house, trying to hide the flowers in case Bill drove by, dropped it all in front of her door, and sprinted away. Bill came by at the appointed time and took me home.

"It's kind of a girl," I said, staring at the dashboard.

"She's your friend?"

"She's like my girlfriend, I think."

"So you got to see her?"

"No, I just got her flowers."

"That sounds nice," he said. "I'd bet she likes that."

She did, but nothing came out of it. I lived a million miles away, skipped school constantly, and hid from her when I did go. When I no-showed a school dance, she told me that she had danced with another boy but that it didn't mean anything; she was only being nice to him. Our break was logical and painless. We had a conversation full of boyfriend-girlfriend sweetness, during which I promised that I'd give her the best summer of her life, and then we just never called each other again. I don't know what became of Patience, but the boy she danced with ended up as a minor-circuit NASCAR driver.

I spent another summer with Nan and Gramps in Geneva. Gramps made me pancakes and chocolate milk every morning, and Nan made chocolate cookies with chocolate frosting. Nan lived in her pajamas and bathrobe, and a permanent depression marked her place on the couch; she'd even make her cookies there, having Gramps bring them to the oven. Every day she woke up just in time to watch her afternoon soap operas (while taping her game shows to watch at night). She kept a wastebasket nearby for when she coughed up thick wads of phlegm—"hunking the gunk," she called it. Her calves were bone thin and dark purple.

When hunking the gunk became too much I put on my headphones and Public Enemy hat and sought refuge in a nearby creek that went underground. Exploring without a flashlight, I wandered knee-deep until reaching its conclusion at Seneca Lake, past the edge of downtown. Back on the surface, I looked across the road, spotted our local Greyhound station, and walked over in my soaked shoes. The outside of the station looked rough and tired, with cracks in the cement and rust on the metal and weeds growing unchecked in random places. Everything inside wore a slight film of dirt that permanently dulled the colors, as though the place had the same furniture, vending machines, floor tiles, and signs for thirty years. Sitting in a corner to stay out of the way, I watched the sketchy characters file in and out and wondered what kind of rottenness in Geneva had attracted them.

The Greyhound station became my hangout, and I started to identify the sketchy ones as my own culture. They often looked worn-out and mentally frazzled, sometimes unaware of where they were, seeming ready to slit their own throats just for a chance to rest. Unwashed, unshaven, and wearing the same clothes for hundreds of days, their natural smells blended with sour beer smell. One day a greasy creep with sores on his arms had scared me so bad that I walked out, but I knew that these were my countrymen; I came from one of their own. This was the station where Wesley hopped off a bus and called my mother to say that he was having her arrested; and years before that, she had arrived here pregnant with me. It was like a sacred place in my own history.

I started to think up a story in which the bus station hosted an afterlife purgatory for the mentally ill. The story's hero, a schizophrenic named Bill—with a wife who fears him and son who has become the center of his bizarre personal mythology—hijacks a bus and crashes it into Seneca Lake, only to drive it out on the other side after crossing into a parallel dimension. The dripping bus pulls up in front of the alternate-reality Geneva station and Bill is greeted by all the unwell people who ever lived. He strolls in and there's a guy plunging his left hand into scalding hot coffee because he's afraid of his own hand killing him, and of course a guy who thinks he's Jesus, and miscellaneous goons who just don't have any tools for competing in the world. None of my fictional psychotics ever had a chance, I decided; they were fucked at the start, twenty steps behind everyone else for whatever reasons, and with every new step they only fucked themselves more. With lives like that, it seemed that all you could do was just check out and decide to go insane. From what I knew of Wesley's life, it was clear that he never had a chance either.

And he started me off in a bad way: Mom told me that when I was two years old, the stress of our condition caused me to bite myself and bang my head against the wall, resulting in black-and-blue tooth marks on my arms and bruises on my head. That all stopped once we got away from Wesley, but at Nan and Gramps's house I would run around a tree for hours. I did not speak until I was nearly four, instead repeating one syllable (*jah!*) over and over. One of my aunts thought that I was autistic, but it turned out to be post-traumatic stress disorder.

I did all of my writing for "Bus Station" at the actual bus station, hunched over my work in a plastic seat, scribbling in aggressive fits and starts, and sometimes looking up to dart my best Manson eyes at people. It was all performance, like I was living a movie just for myself. Hoping for a maniac-genius aesthetic to the physical story, I became deliberately careless with the papers—sloppy in my handwriting, filling the margins with unnecessary notes, putting creases and Pepsi stains in strategic places, violently crossing out mistakes until my pen ripped through the page. I rewrote "Bus Station" a few times and kept all of my drafts in the same haphazard pile, which I'd hold close to my body while walking downtown, eyes aimed at the sidewalk, trying to look disturbed and scary to match my own conception of Wesley.

IN THE PROCESS of divorce from Bill, Mom asked me if I'd want to switch schools for a new start at her alma mater of DeSales.

"It's a Catholic school," she warned. "You'd have to wear a tie every day."

After spending the summer at Geneva's Greyhound station, the idea of clean uniforms seemed like a step in the right direction.

helter skelter

4

Unlike Geneva's public schools, DeSales Catholic High School was entirely white. Kids would joke that the one mulatto boy and his sister added up to DeSales having a single black student. We also had a half-Filipino brother and sister that together equaled one Asian.

Mom got us an apartment on Pulteney, the same street as the school and a mile or so from Nan and Gramps's house, where I'd spend most afternoons and weekends. For the first month of freshman year I wouldn't talk to anyone. Every morning I participated in the Pledge of Allegiance as led by our principal, Mr. Tracey (the kids called him "Fat Ed") on the PA. After the "liberty and justice for all," Fat Ed added his own line, "born and unborn." Then we prayed the Our Father and Hail Mary. Having never been in Catholic school before, I treated it with respect, standing solemnly with my hands folded and making the sign of the cross when appropriate. The other kids had already gone through eight years of it and felt free to talk and goof off. Still an atheist, I thought of myself as at least being mature for having manners about it.

While other kids socialized in homeroom I'd examine the liner notes of the new Public Enemy album *Apocalypse '91: The Enemy Strikes Black*. One morning the half-Filipino boy saw it, sat at an empty desk by mine, leaned over, and asked, "So, you like Public Enemy? You a Public Enemy fan?" The way that he said it came off as though he imagined me a guest on his late-night talk show.

"Yeah," I said without looking up from the album. There was something intimidating about that kid. First off, he dressed way too sharp for a DeSales freshman. All the boys had to wear shirts and ties but most of them tried to act like they were too cool for it, requiring prompts from teachers to tuck in their shirts and tighten their ties. This guy dressed with the crispness and precision of military school. His shirts seemed to fit him better, with none of that clumsiness of gangly teenagers trying to wear grown-man clothes, and he had better ties than the teachers— nice Italian silk ties that you couldn't get anywhere in Geneva. On top of that, he read the *New York Times* before class. He was geek-smart but didn't use his brain as a withdrawal from the world. He walked briskly through the halls and with perfect posture, eyes straight ahead, carrying himself as though he was headed somewhere important. I was sure that he could throw jocks to the floor just with mental power.

WHEN OUR EARTH science teacher told us to make groups for a lab project, I had no friends to partner with. He lumped me with the two nearest kids, Tom and Kyle. They soon became embroiled in a pen fight while I stared out the window.

"Look," said Tom, showing me the line of ink on his arm. "I'm really black, and he scratched the paint off." I half smiled. Before class was over I had joined in and received black and blue lines all over my face and hands. Tom and I walked home together, on the way stopping at the corner store. Tom bought a soda and I got a jar of green olives. Heading up William Street, we were stopped by two black kids from Geneva Middle School.

"Did you just call me a nigger?" one of them asked me.

"No."

"Yeah he did," his friend chimed in. "He called you a nigger, I heard him."

"I've never seen you in my life," I said.

"You got any money?" he asked.

"No."

"Give me an olive, then."

"No."

"Give me an olive!"

"I'm not giving you an olive," I said. Then he punched me in the face. The kid was smaller than me and couldn't hit, so I just stood there, not sure of the appropriate response. His friend landed another weak hook on my jaw. After that they walked off so Tom and I continued on our way, the jar of olives undisturbed in my hand. A moment later I was ashamed to find that the whole incident had been witnessed by a bunch of white guys installing windows on someone's house.

"I'd have kicked that nigger's ass," said one of them.

A week later Tom invited me to go with him to a basketball game, DeSales playing at his old school of South Seneca. His dad drove us.

The junior varsity teams played first. Most of the kids were freshmen so I knew them. Afterwards they put on their mandatory post-game shirts and ties and joined us in the bleachers for the varsity game. On our way back from the bathroom, I remarked to Tom that South Seneca was a dumb name for a school. "It's not like there's any North Seneca," I told him. The kids in front of us turned around with dirty looks. Mike and I walked back to where the junior varsity kids sat and we told them what had happened.

"There they are," said Tom, pointing directly across the court to the home team's section. "There they are; they just sat down." I thrust my finger in their direction like Hulk Hogan challenging Macho Man or somebody. A DeSales JV player dared me to go over there and sit on their side. I looked at Tom.

"My dad's here and we know people," he said. "Nobody's kicking your ass tonight." I stood up, left the bleachers and walked alongside the court to sit behind South Seneca's varsity bench. Whenever DeSales scored I jumped up and danced like Flavor Flav. On the far side of the gym, I could see the DeSales kids cracking up and their reactions inspired me to top myself every time, getting more intense and ridiculous with every basket. At one point Tom gave a subtle wave for me to come back to the visitors' side of the court. "They're getting pissed over there," he said.

"Man," said Dan, the half-Filipino kid, "you're a comic genius. You should have your own show."

The next day, when our English teacher stepped out for a moment, Tom and Dan had me stand on my desk and show the Flavor Flav dance to all the kids who weren't at the game. The basketball players laughed hardest but everyone loved it.

"Very nice," said Ms. DeSain as she came through the door. "Would you like to come up front and do that for the rest of the period?" I quickly sat down, assured by the surrounding whispers and giggles that I had finally secured a place for myself in DeSales society. I went to the rest of the season's games as an unofficial mascot. When Fat Ed mispronounced my name as Mike *Scoot* in the morning announcements, my mascot name became "Scooter" and my Flavor Flav impersonation was dubbed the "Scooter Dance." I developed the ability to fall on cue as my trademark move. I could be standing, walking, or doing the Scooter Dance when out of nowhere my feet would fly up and I'd land on the gym floor so hard that people thought I had split my head open.

I even took that act to the regular school day. In the hall on my way to class, some kid would just say, "Scooter, fall" and I hit the floor. There were some tricks to it: If falling on my side, I'd tuck in my arms to protect my ribs, and if going on my back I'd spread my arms and tuck in my chin. My legs and arms were covered in bruises and sometimes I knocked the wind out of myself. When Mom spotted my massive purple bruises after a school dance, I told her that I was "moshing," aggressively slam-dancing to heavy metal songs. She never knew that it was only me slamming myself against the gym floor while kids stood around and laughed.

Nor was she aware that I carried photos of Wesley in a manila folder and spent entire class periods shuffling through them, wishing I could hop on a bus with Gramps's shotgun to kill him. I did it most during math, where I had to sit behind Dan and watch him do his Letterman routine with everyone around him. One time he turned around to say something to me and ended up seeing my Wesley file.

"Who's that?" he asked.

"It's someone I'm looking for. It's someone I'm going to kill."

"Don't be a dick."

"I'm serious. It's my dad." Dan's smirk disappeared. I then poured out the whole story for him, which he interrupted with counselor-type questions ("How does that make you feel? That must be really difficult, how do you handle it?") while turning away sometimes to stay up on the banter with other kids. After school we talked more. He said that he had always wondered why I fell on the ground for people and danced like an idiot at basketball games.

"They're degrading you," he said.

"They think it's funny."

"That doesn't mean you have their respect. You're getting a reputation for being seriously crazy." I secretly wanted to smile; I was my father's son after all. Mom had told me that Wesley's only career goal was to convince the VA that he was crazy enough to warrant a 100 percent disability rating, which would result in better payments; and whenever his benefits went under review, he tried to freak out his interviewers with the wildest shit he could come up with.

"I don't really care what they think," I told Dan.

"You can be more than a mascot," he said. "Have you ever read *The Autobiography of Malcolm X*?"

"What's it about?"

"Dignity."

FOR SOPHOMORE YEAR Dan moved up to calculus while Tom and I were placed in the math class for average or below-average sophomores and smart freshmen. One of the smart freshmen was a blonde girl named Bridget, whose lawyer dad owned the house that Mom and I lived in. Bridget was a cheerleader and had a cheerleader friend named Shannon, who dated a basketball player named Mike Sweeney. In math class Mike showed me her notebook, on which she had written "I love Mike S." at least a hundred times.

"She loves you!" he exclaimed. I looked up and saw Shannon blushing a few seats ahead.

"It's not you," she said. "It's Mike Sweeney."

"No way!" said Mike Sweeney, a huge smile on his face. "It's Mike Schutt." I looked at Shannon growing terrified and Mike trying hard not to laugh.

"Mike, it's not you," said Shannon. "I think you're awesome and so funny, but me and Mike are going out—"

"She's lying," said Mike. "We're not going out; I don't even like her."

"YOU'RE SUCH A JERK!" she snapped at him.

"Hey, just because you love Mike Schutt and can't admit it . . ."

I decided to give the people what they wanted. My face lit up; my eyes opened wide and locked on Shannon. Her jaw dropped and Mike Sweeney turned to hide his laughter while his friends roared. It was that easy to convince them all that I had become obsessed with her; having already done so much to cement my image as legitimately crazy, I could do anything and they'd think I was serious. I started applauding whenever Shannon got an answer right in class. I would forego eating to buy her boxes of doughnuts with my lunch money, and the seniors would quiet down the entire lunchroom so that I could serenade her. The kids all laughed, and most eventually recognized that I was joking, but no one told Shannon. She usually tried to be cool and shrug it off, but sometimes looked genuinely uncomfortable.

Her actual boyfriend helped to keep it going; Mike Sweeney even switched seats so that I could sit next to her in biology, turning to stare at her for the whole forty-five minute class without moving. "Look at his eyes," I heard another girl whisper. "He could stare a hole through the wall." It reminded me of Mom's stories about Wesley practicing his Manson eyes in the mirror.

I knew about Manson as a little kid, even before I knew about Wesley. I wasn't sure how I had ever heard of him; maybe Wes would talk about Manson to Mom while she was pregnant and somehow I retained it. In fourth grade I invented a game for our labyrinthine wooden playground at Canandaigua Elementary and named it Helter Skelter after Manson's apocalypse. One of the nooks in the playground became our bottomless pit, where we'd wait until Armageddon had finished. The girls were supposed to pretend to shave their heads. After a while the game evolved, and *Helter Skelter* became the name of our spaceship.

Around the start of my fake obsession with Shannon, I began reading *Helter Skelter*, the story of the Manson murders as told by Manson's prosecutor. At the Geneva public library, a man saw me with the book and asked what I thought of it. Suspicious of someone who wanted to make small talk about Manson with strangers, I told him that it was okay. "They say that if Manson lived somewhere like Iran," he remarked, "he could have taken over like an ayatollah, but I don't think so. They don't take any nonsense over there; they would have chopped his head off."

Manson struck me as a superstar version of Wesley. I even wrote him a fan letter:

Mr. Manson:

This is the first letter I have ever written to a celebrity. I was wondering if you could explain to me your views on American culture and the impact you had on the twentieth century.

Enclosed is a self-addressed stamped envelope. I am anxiously awaiting your reply.

Sincerely,
Michael Unger

I signed it with Wesley's last name, just in case Manson still had followers on the outside who would come and get me. Charlie wrote his reply on my letter and sent it back; above my words "views on American culture," he had scribbled "upside down." Where I wrote "twentieth century," he wrote "backwards." At the bottom of the page he wrote in large cursive "upside down and backwards, wheels and rolling" and signed his name. After staring at it for hours, I discovered that he put an "A. C." between his first and last names (for "Antichrist," I guessed). On the "Charles" he had drawn an infinity symbol, and he crossed his last name with a large curvy swastika.

I was sitting with *Helter Skelter* on a stairwell after school as Shannon passed me on her way to cheerleading practice.

"Oh my god!" she shrieked.

"What?"

"Why are you reading that?"

"This?"

"Yeah, why are you reading that? Oh my god, you're crazy." I looked at her and knew what the moment called for.

"It's okay, Sharon."

"SHARON? DID YOU JUST CALL ME SHARON?" She took off running in her pleated blue-and-gold cheerleader skirt. I hung around the school until they finished practice and then followed Shannon, Bridget, and Fat Ed's daughter Colleen to a pizza place downtown. I didn't have money to buy anything but sat at a booth ten feet away from them and watched them eat.

"Don't look at him," Bridget whispered. They switched sides so that Shannon had her back to me. I whipped out a pen and scribbled *I love Sharon* all over the table before leaving. Shannon went home and told her mom, who in turn called Fat Ed, who accepted my assurance that it was only a prank with all of the popular kids and basketball players in on it. I promised to stop my stalker act, and even Shannon nervously laughed it off and we became friends, or at least friendly, though part of me still wondered if she really knew that it was a joke.

5 el-hajj malik el-shabazz

Besides the underground creek and bus station, Geneva had a brand-new Wegmans supermarket to keep me busy when I wasn't scaring cheerleaders. The store preferred to hire DeSales kids, so I'd go through the checkouts and say bizarre things to the ones that I knew, just to make them laugh and talk about me. The best thing about Wegmans was that it stayed open twenty-four hours, providing a quiet refuge when I really needed it.

Late one night I walked past Wegmans' paperbacks and spotted *The Autobiography of Malcolm X*. In 1992 Malcolm was everywhere, the hype around Spike Lee's upcoming biopic having spawned a fad of X baseball caps and T-shirts of Malcolm's face. Dan was always referring to Malcolm but I knew nothing of the man, beyond Public Enemy's assertion that both Malcolm and Martin Luther King, Jr., had been killed by the FBI. I did not know the years in which he lived or anything meaningful that he had said; I did not recognize his voice when Public Enemy sampled him. His name was absurd and dangerous and cool. He was a symbol without form.

The cover painting showed Malcolm with his gleaming glasses and stoic glare, the clouds behind him growing darker, and two angry Malcolm faces cascading down as though depicting his fall. Above the painting it had a quote by Spike Lee saying that this was the most important book he would ever read.

I picked up the book and held it with both hands. It was small but thick, nearly five hundred pages, its thickness only telling me how clueless I was about him. Five dollars was not a light investment for an unemployed fourteen-year-old, but I took Malcolm home.

Dan called that night and I told him that I had bought the autobiography.

"That's a good step," he said. A good step towards what, I didn't know.

In the first few pages of the first chapter, "Nightmare," I learned that when Malcolm's mother was pregnant with him, a gang of Ku Klux Klansmen circled the house on their horses. They wanted Malcolm's father, who was preaching the Black Nationalist Gospel of Marcus Garvey. I read of how they killed him when Malcolm was young. When Malcolm said that he could notice white people looking at him differently for who his father was, somehow I thought that I could relate, forgetting that while his father was a martyr, I hadn't lost mine to any kind of struggle against injustice; mine was just a crazy asshole.

Still in the first ten pages, Malcolm described how he'd sit in church "goggle-eyed," failing to make sense of Jesus as a divine being. I couldn't believe what I was reading; it somehow felt illegal and dangerous—what would happen if I brought this to DeSales tomorrow? But I also sat goggle-eyed at our mandatory masses and homeroom prayers, and when Gramps had read his book of prayers for all of us every morning, I had no idea who he was reading them *to*. At seven years old I was baptized in the Catholic Church, which might have been more for Gramps's benefit, or possibly Mom's final gesture of divorce from Wesley, but I never really knew what it meant. Around that time I even decided to read the entire Bible, but couldn't get through Genesis with all of its long lines of who-begat-whom.

DeSales had been my first real brush with Catholic life, and I couldn't find anything there to respect, just Fat Ed talking bullshit on the PA every morning, and the kids pretending to believe it. I couldn't actually say that they believed or disbelieved; even worse, they didn't seem to ask themselves the question, just standing up and doing signs of the cross and eating the wafers when they were supposed to. Reading Malcolm as he spoke of black Christians as "brainwashed," I thought of white DeSales kids. At first, my reaction to Malcolm was like the way we react to songs. He drew out emotions that I was already feeling, even if only for my own unrelated reasons, and showed them to me.

Malcolm described how he "conked," painfully burning his scalp to straighten his hair, and called it his first act of degradation. I missed its significance as a commentary on black self-hatred, instead reflecting on the bruises I'd earned trying to entertain these DeSales kids. I remembered myself dancing like an idiot at their basketball games (and Malcolm had a chapter titled "Mascot"), even working hard to convince them that I was crazy.

I brought the book to school and held it in my lap to read

under the desk during class. I read about Malcolm's hustling days and the life lessons that he learned from pimps and prostitutes—that women were inherently weak and attracted to strong men. Then came the part where Malcolm's in prison and he learns of the Honorable Elijah Muhammad, who had been chosen by Allah Himself to teach the so-called Negro in America the truth about himself. Black people were once kings and queens and rulers of glorious civilizations, taught Elijah, back when the white man lived like an animal in the caves of Europe. When the white man finally emerged from his cave—only after the black man taught him civilization— he rose up to enslave black people, bringing them in chains to the wilderness of North America.

In the Honorable Elijah Muhammad's theology, the black man was God, which logically assigned the role of Devil to the white man. The Devil's enslavement of black people was not only physical, but depended on their *mental* bondage as well; so the Devil taught his slaves that, instead of recognizing themselves as true and living gods on the earth, they should worship a god that they couldn't see. Even worse, these Christian slave masters taught their slaves that God was a white man with blonde hair and blue eyes. God now looked like the slave master, while the slave—who had been removed from his true religion, culture, and language—was taught that black people had never done anything but swing from trees in the jungle.

As part of Malcolm's entry into the Honorable Elijah Muhammad's Nation of Islam, he gave up his "slave name" of Little to become Malcolm X—the X representing his true name that had been lost in slavery. He gave up cigarettes and pork, forced himself down to his knees in prayer, improved his vocabulary by hand-copying the entire dictionary, and lost himself in the prison library. Checking out stacks of books, he'd lie awake in his cell long after lights-out, reading by the faint glow of a corridor light. He learned of the nonwhite origins of European civilization, as well as the evil and bloodshed brought by the white devil wherever he went on the earth. Whether it was Africa, India, China, or the Americas, whenever devils arrived somewhere they did nothing but rob, rape, and enslave, and then use Christianity to brainwash the people into accepting their oppression.

Having read the earlier chapters devoted to Malcolm's life in Harlem and Boston underworlds—drugs, hustling, pimping, robbing, the inevitable bust—and state prison, where he earned the nickname "Satan," I saw he had fallen as far as anyone could, only to be transformed by knowledge. Deciding that I'd turn my life around too, I went to the musty used bookstore on Exchange Street and scooped up an armful of books from the shelf marked BLACK, including writings of the Black Panthers and a volume on Christ's true skin color. When I finished them I went back and got more. Next I hit the shelf marked PHILOSOPHY, grabbing Penguin's *The Portable Nietzsche*, Plato's *Republic*, some Schopenhauer and Camus. Malcolm mentioned reading Nietzsche in prison, and Huey Newton had dabbled in him at fifteen. I read Nietzsche in biology class and failed all of my tests. Besides praising Islam as more life-affirming and full of masculine virtue than feminizing, antilife Christianity, Nietzsche had a cool factor with me for having lost his mind. There was even a legend attributing his mental breakdown to having deliberately contracted syphilis from a prostitute. The syphilis rendered him not only insane but also blind, finally killing him after a decade of suffering and writing crazy letters. There's no better suicide for a genius, I thought, than crucifying himself on his own giant brain. Naturally I saw myself as Nietzsche's Zarathustra character, standing outside the school dance to curse everyone's herd mentality while they had fun inside. *Your neighbors will always be poisonous flies; that which is great in you, just that must make them more poisonous and more like flies:* Who doesn't want to hear that?

"YOU KNOW THAT Jesus wasn't white?" I asked Nan and Gramps during *General Hospital*, feeling like Malcolm when he confronted that white Bible teacher in prison.

"Who cares what Jesus was?" Nan replied. "Why can't God be everything?"

"Because he was a historical man who lived in real life, and the Catholic Church tells us to accept a blonde-haired, blue-eyed Jesus that's not historically accurate. That's not what he looked like. He came from a part of the world where people were dark. But when black people are forced to worship this Jesus with white skin, you see . . . that's why there was slavery."

"That's not why there was slavery," said Nan.

"Slavery of the mind, Nan!" There was no hiding how proud I felt for hitting her with that. From there I started ranting about how the United States had killed hundreds of thousands of innocent Japanese with the A-bomb. Nan and Gramps didn't know what to say. When I told them that I had gotten it all from Malcolm X, Gramps warned that Hitler had started the same way, by writing a book and brainwashing teenagers. He didn't even know that Malcolm was dead.

MOM WAS THRILLED with all of my reading and even claimed some credit for it. "When you were little," she said, "I put books in your crib, and when we went to the store I wouldn't always buy you toys, but I never said no to a book." She suggested that I go to the big library at Hobart and William Smith College down the street. Compared to any other library I had seen, it was overwhelming, but once I figured my way around I felt innately superior to all the college kids—I was only fifteen years old and killing all kinds of books for my self-improvement while they were drunk idiots just half-assing their way through papers. Give me any of them in a debate, I smirked to myself. I dove into the history section and found books that Malcolm had mentioned in his autobiography, starting with Will Durant's *Story of Civilization*, which turned out to be not one but eleven huge volumes. I scanned down the titles: *Our Oriental Heritage, The Life of Greece, Caesar and Christ, The Age of Faith, The Renaissance, The Reformation, The Age of Louis XIV, The Age of Reason Begins, The Age of Voltaire, Rousseau and Revolution, The Age of Napoleon.* Ten volumes just for Europe; one for the whole rest of the world. Still I would read them all, just like Malcolm, to find the truth hidden behind the Devil's words. I grabbed the 938-page hardbound *Our Oriental Heritage*, doubting myself as I felt its weight transfer from the shelf to my hand. I also considered a series of books on ancient Egypt and the green and red Cambridge volumes on Iran but decided that Durant would keep me busy. Just carrying it under my arm to the front desk, I already felt stronger, like I could walk as Dan did at school.

I consumed *Our Oriental Heritage* at a rate of at least two hundred pages a day, easy. Even if it had nothing to do with what we were learning in class, I could raise my hand and drop knowledge: "The earliest statues of Greek gods had the facial features of Asiatic peoples," I told my English teacher as we read Sophocles. The next week I went back to the library for the second volume, *The Life of Greece*, which, along with *Caesar and Christ*, helped me to understand the pagan contributions to Christian doctrine. It was hard not to skip ahead to volume four, *The Age of Faith*, which covered the development of Christianity, the birth of Islam, and the Crusades.

Finally stumbling into the library's religion section, I started with the Qur'an. The library had a green-covered Yusuf Ali translation with the same intimidating weight as the Durant when I pulled it off the shelf. I sat by a window and delicately turned the thin pages, briefly confused until learning that the book actually started in the back.

The original Arabic text accompanied the English translation. The Arabic script and elaborate ornamentation in the margins washed in the natural light of the windows gave me a sense of having discovered a treasure that no white Catholic boy had ever seen before, at least not in Geneva, New York. I felt like Indiana Jones. The first sura, al-Fatiha, read quickly at only eight verses. *There*, I thought, turning the page; *I've just done something*. Then came al-Baqara at almost three hundred.

The Qur'an is a collection of prayers and commands. When non-Muslims try reading the Qur'an as a straight narrative like the Bible, they usually find it boring and give up—especially in English, with much of the power and beauty sapped out of the words. I didn't know any better so I sat there and trudged through al-Baqara for what felt like forever; but to wimp out, I was sure, would mean that I didn't deserve to undergo a dramatic Malcolm-level transformation. I trudged through, and after completing al-Baqara, respectfully placed the Qur'an where I had found it. Leaving the library with the next Durant volume, I felt a buzzing sensation, which I took as verification that something had changed.

On another visit I picked up a copy of Hammudah al-Ati's *Islam in Focus*, which outlined Islam's basic tenets and practices for the non-Muslim reader. The library's copy had been autographed by the author, which had me wondering when and why he had been to the campus. It had me respecting the college, as well as the *idea* of college, while resenting DeSales. My grades remained horrible, but I justified it with the notion that I was learning things on my own that went over the teachers' heads.

I spent every lunch period in the cafeteria with Dan and a few cast-offs from our class while Tom and the cool kids rode around town with upperclassmen. Dan always had the kids at our table talking about some news item or international conflict and he dominated every conversation.

"We've got to do something for Gary Graham," he told us.

"Who's Gary Graham?" I asked, since no one else did.

"Didn't you read the *Times* this morning?" In Geneva, when most people besides Dan said "the *Times*," they meant the *Finger Lakes Times*, which carried no mention of Gary Graham.

"No," I said.

"Gary Graham's a black prisoner in Texas, and they're going to kill him."

"For what?"

"For being a black man in Texas, what else? They say he killed someone in a parking lot, but there was no case against him. Four witnesses say that he was miles from the scene when the murder happened, and they've all passed lie detector tests. The firearm examiner said that Graham's .22 could not have been the one that was used. There are no fingerprints or ballistics, but his court-appointed attorney just assumed that he was guilty and never bothered to build a defense for him, and now he's on death row."

The other kids could never really follow Dan. He was growing visibly frustrated with them, as though our lunch table could have been the vanguard of a new revolution if only they'd listen.

"The problem isn't that they're white," I told him after school. "It's that they have white *minds*."

"Oh my god," he exclaimed. "That's the most brilliant thing I've ever heard."

That evening I had Mom drive me to K-Mart to buy a big sheet of white fabric and fistfuls of black permanent markers. SAVE GARY GRAHAM, I wrote on the sheet in giant block letters. Mom sat with me on the living room floor and helped to fill them in. The next day I brought it to school. "We should take that to the college," said Dan. "There's all sorts of radical thought on college campuses." During lunch we carried the banner between us and walked up Pulteney Street towards the college, still in our white shirts and ties. Nothing happened; we just walked to the edge of the campus, a two-man silent march, and returned to DeSales. On the way Dan explained that he was given the middle name Nicholas after his grandfather, who had gone his whole life in the Philippines without wearing shoes. Dan was getting heavy into Filipino nationalist Jose Rizal and wanted to learn Tagalog, the islands' indigenous language. Someday, he promised, he'd go back to the Philippines and build it into an economic power and model for developing nations all over the world.

"That's awesome," I replied.

"If you look at the word *black* as Malcolm understood it," he said, "then socially and politically I'm black."

"I've been reading a lot about Islam. It's like the solution to everything wrong around us. You know, because Muslims don't drink, they don't have to deal with all of the alcoholism afflicting the West; and because Islam allows polygamy, Muslim societies don't have the rampant divorce and lesbianism that are destroying America." I had gotten all of that from *Islam in Focus*, which also informed me that a woman does not have the right of consent when it comes to sex with her husband—but I could see the good in that too, since it prevented adultery and prostitution.

"I was going to suggest that you consider Islam," said Dan. "It would be a good choice for you, there's a lot of discipline to it. I almost looked into Islam myself."

"Really?"

"It would have been a cultural statement. There are Muslims in the Philippines, but the Spanish wiped out a lot of them."

"I've been thinking about Socialism too," I said. "Maybe I'll be a Muslim Socialist."

"I could see you getting into Socialism, because your family doesn't have a lot of money."

Upon our arrival at DeSales, a senior football player took our Gary Graham banner and ripped it in half.

BY THE TIME Spike Lee's *Malcolm X* came out, Dan had his license and could drive us to the theater. The movie opened with the famous video of Los Angeles cops beating on Rodney King, interchanging with the image of an American flag burning into an *X* while Denzel-as-Malcolm told us that there's been no democracy on the streets of Harlem or Brooklyn or Detroit or Chicago, that instead of the American Dream it had only been an American nightmare. I would have paid the full ticket price just to see that intro a dozen times, but there was more, nearly four hours of Spike Lee extracting fantasy scenes from my head and putting them on the giant screen in front of me: Malcolm in prison as the truth hits him; Malcolm at the Nation of Islam's headquarters in Chicago; Malcolm hunched over and weeping as he meets the Honorable Elijah Muhammad; Malcolm speaking at rallies; Malcolm putting down devils; Malcolm standing tall and damning the world. When Malcolm led a disciplined Muslim march against the NYPD, I thought that the police captain who said "that's too much power for one man to have" in his New York Irish accent sounded just like Fat Ed.

Then there was Malcolm's final metamorphosis, in which he abandoned the heretical Nation of Islam and became an orthodox Muslim. An electric charge ran through me during the scenes of Malcolm's pilgrimage to Mecca, where it showed him before the Ka'ba and shaking hands with white Muslims and reemerging with a new vision as El-Hajj Malik El-Shabazz. White Muslims were better than white Americans; only white Muslims showed Malcolm the way out of racism. And when Spike showed the assassination, Malcolm/Malik cracking a half smile as his killers rushed the stage, I couldn't quite understand how it made me feel; of course I loved Malcolm and wanted to cry for him, but I also loved his death, I loved that he would do that. Part of me wanted to watch it a thousand times and swim in his blood.

"I think it was a good thing for you," said Dan as he drove

me home. He had a way of talking to me as though he was ten years older.

Dan thought that the film had done a good job of portraying Malcolm's lifelong search for a working model of manhood. Ever since the Ku Klux Klan murdered his father, Malcolm searched for men to fill that role: In Harlem he looked to his buddy Shorty, then to the underworld boss West Indian Archie. The motif was furthered during the film's depiction of Malcolm in prison by Baines, a fictional composite of Malcolm's brother and a real convict named Bimby. With Malcolm's prison conversion and redemption, the Nation of Islam offered him a father figure in the Honorable Elijah Muhammad. Each of these men in turn let Malcolm down, leaving him to seek comfort only in Allah, the Father of us all. "You can get something out of that," said Dan.

"Do you want to see it tomorrow?" I asked him.

"We've already seen it, and you've already read the book. You'd be better off putting your time and money towards new knowledge." I went and saw it again anyway but was too embarrassed to tell him. The third night I got Mom to see it with me. That time, I closed my eyes during the assassination scene and pretended that I could feel those bullets ripping through my own chest. The whole ride back I couldn't stop talking about Malcolm and Islam.

"When he said that white people were devils," I assured her, "that wasn't real Islam. That's not what Islam teaches. That was the Nation of Islam, a whole separate thing."

"Okay," said Mom while keeping her eyes on the road.

"Malcolm left the Nation of Islam, and then he went to Mecca, where he saw that there are white Muslims too. And they all prayed together."

"I saw that in the movie."

"Islam's against racism. It does what Christianity couldn't do. Christianity is racist because black people are taught to worship a white Jesus who doesn't look like them . . ." For the rest of the ride home, Mom nodded and answered most of my commentary with "yeah" or a flat-affected "interesting."

I called Dan when we got home but lied and said that I had been reading about the Hittites, an obscure Anatolian kingdom going back to the eighteenth century BC.

"You're reading a lot," he said. "Vic thinks you're brilliant."

"Really?" Vic was Mr. Harris, our history teacher who first nicknamed me "Scooter" and the only member of DeSales' faculty for whom I had any liking.

"Yeah, but you know, you don't have to carry yourself like you're always preoccupied with something. It's the way that you walk. In the halls you look almost mean."

"Really?"

"Nothing wrong with mental activity, but you could be putting people off." I was okay with that, maybe even proud. Did Malcolm ever walk like he needed a hug?

6   prostrations and ejaculations

It still hurt that my grandparents couldn't look past their white Jesus for the truth of Islam. One night I became so enraged at their ignorance that I decided to walk home. I shoved myself through our door and slammed it behind me, then pushed on Mom's bedroom door to see if she was there.

"Wait a minute," she said. I pulled the door shut and waited. She came out in a satin nightshirt. "Michael, what are you doing here?"

"I'm not spending the weekends there anymore," I told her. "They never want to learn anything new or improve themselves. I try to talk to them about important things but all they care about is TV! Here I am reading all day, studying history, studying Islam, and I want to share it and nobody wants to hear it! And they think I'm crazy just because I don't play baseball or drink beer like everyone else—"

"I think you should go back there."

"No, I'm not going back there. They don't respect me."

"You should go back."

"I'm going to stay here."

"I think you need to stay there tonight."

"I'm not going to sleep under a roof where they don't respect Islam."

"Can you stay at your friend Tom's house?"

"Why should I stay at Tom's? I'm right here."

"Michael, go back to Nan and Gramps."

We went back and forth like that for five minutes, Mom unable to give a good reason for me to walk back to Nan and Gramps's house in the middle of the night when I was ten feet away from my own bed. Then I saw it: a man's jacket hanging off a chair in the dining room. It wasn't mine. I looked at Mom in her little nightshirt.

I knew what was going on, and I knew who it was: that guy from work, the one that I saw her kissing back when she was still married to Bill. Sometimes friends kiss each other that way? I turned and went out the door to bolt down the street like I used to do in Hopewell, like I was trying to stomp holes in the road. Instead of Nan and Gramps's house, I walked to the creek behind the Big M supermarket. It was hard to reach the water in the dark, tripping over stray branches and banging my shin on a tipped-over stray shopping cart. A fluorescent light from above glimmered on the water. Squatting on a stone by the creek's edge, I looked at the mouth of the tunnel going under the Big M and thought about how long I could hide there. This was the same creek that emptied at Seneca Lake; I knew every inch of the underground parts. If I was really determined about it, I could stay for months and no one would have any idea. I could hunt crayfish for food if I had to or come out at night to hunt from the Big M's dumpsters.

This is where I'll hide after I stab him, I decided. I was sure that I'd do it. He couldn't have respected my mother; if he did, would he put himself in her bed? Would he do that to her if he respected *me?*

I hope you know what you've done, I said out loud as though I could speak to him through the creek. *Get ready for me to show up with a machete and lop off your fucking arm*. He was done; he was dead. And I'd have fun with it. I'd stab him in the face for disrespecting my mother and me. Just a couple of years ago I had been such a messed-up, crazy kid trying to sort out all of this bullshit between Wesley and Bill, and in steps this asshole at the worst time to take advantage of Mom and fuck up the whole world. Manipulate her into throwing me out of my own home? *I'll kill him*, I said. *I'll do it and be right. I'll blow up his fucking car*, I told the water. *I don't take any nonsense; I'll rip off his head*. Then I cried in the especially pathetic way that, if people heard me, they would have thought I was choking.

I SPENT NEW Year's Eve at home watching MTV's lousy annual special with a kid named Jamie, who had been coming up from Brooklyn every year to stay with my cousins as part of the Fresh Air program. By then I had known him for nearly ten years. About half an hour into 1993 we decided to go outside and play one-on-one football, which basically amounted to wrestling. Some drunk girl walked by yelling, "Happy New Year!"

"Happy New Year," we both yelled back. She stopped and turned around.

"What are you guys doing?" she asked.

"Nothing," Jamie answered.

"I'm just looking for somewhere to go," she said. "I've got nowhere to go, my mom's having a party and I'm fucking wasted." Jamie laughed. We introduced ourselves. Her name was Tracy. She had me sit with her on the back steps while Jamie lay on the hood of my mom's car. "How old are you?" she asked.

"Fifteen."

"Have you ever had sex?"

"No," I answered, trying to smile in self-defense.

"I have," she said with an ugly laugh. "I've done it all, everything that you can do. Have you ever kissed a girl?"

"Yes," I lied.

"I've kissed a lot of people. A *lot* of people." She looked right at me. "Can you smell my breath? I have this cherry mint, it's supposed to cover up the booze. Does it smell like cherries?" She leaned over and breathed on my face, but before I could offer insight on the mint, she kissed me. I kissed her back and my hands went straight for her breasts, first over the shirt, then under. I pulled her coat off and tried to take her sweater but she refused. "I'd freeze," she pleaded. I went back to mauling her under the sweater, pulling her out of her bra. While sucking on her tits I thought about the section in *Islam in Focus* that explained why Muslims did not drink. If this girl was a Muslim, she would have respected herself enough to not get drunk and let fifteen-year-olds molest her. On the other side, if I had lived in a Muslim society, I would have been protected from girls like her.

I wasn't a Muslim, but still took it seriously that Islam would have considered this to be sinful behavior. Then I remembered reading in *Islam in Focus* that when someone converts to Islam, his previous sins are erased. It's like a baptism, a born-again moment that wipes the slate clean. If someday I decided to be a Muslim, I wouldn't have to worry about anything that I did with this girl.

Up until then my erection had seemed bigger than normal and even angry somehow, but as soon as she touched me it died.

"Was it okay?" I asked, forgetting that Jamie had been right there this whole time. "I mean size-wise, was it okay?"

"It was great," she said. "Let's see if we can get it back." I kissed her again and began a second mauling of her breasts, stretching the neckhole of her sweater. She tried jerking me with just her index finger and thumb, but I was too scared to get it up. For plan B she leaned backwards, took my hand and plunged it down her pants. They were already unbuttoned. Upon first contact with her curly hair I pulled out. "You could have," she said.

"But I respect you."

"Oh yeah," she answered with a smirk. "I forgot." She stood up and walked away. Jamie and I went back inside. About half an hour later she knocked on the door. "Do you think I could stay here tonight?"

"I'm sorry," I whispered, holding her hands, our fingers interlocking. "My mom's here." Tracy asked when she could stop by. We agreed on Monday afternoon, and she kissed me goodnight. On Monday I cleaned up the apartment pretty good, took a shower and scrubbed under my balls just in case, but she never showed up.

After the winter break, I found myself much more conscious of the teen chests all around me at DeSales. During our first week back in school, I went home and jerked off for the first time. It was while flipping through Mom's stack of *Redbooks* and *Cosmopolitans* that I came across a Victoria's Secret catalog and began holding myself differently, as Tracy

had done before I went soft. Almost by instinct I grabbed a
pink towel from the bathroom and spread it out on the living
room floor. It was clumsy and I moved my body more than my
hand, humping myself in a way. After emptying out on the
towel I looked at it, studied it, contemplating my sperm for
a long time before suddenly panicking that I had ruined the
towel.

I did it every day after school and before bed. If Mom went
out for the night I did it a few more times. Towels were too
much of a hassle with clean-up so I just laid down some notebook paper and shot on that. I learned how to do it well and
imagined distinct possibilities for each of the Victoria's Secret
models. Sometimes I'd bring out last year's DeSales yearbook
and do it to girls' pictures.

Perhaps as a balance against my new entertainment, I
decided to start praying. *Islam in Focus* listed numerous benefits to a Muslim's five daily prayers, some of them having
little to do with God or religion. For one, the prayers offered
a "lesson in discipline and willpower," which I liked in the
Malcolm way. *Islam in Focus* provided detailed instructions
for each of the five prayers, even with diagrams of the various
positions and what to say at certain points. The prayers were
not only translated into English but also given in transliter-
ated Arabic, so I could read the Arabic sounds without having
to learn Arabic script. I photocopied that whole section and
vowed to learn it. At first I read only the English; there was
no point in saying the Arabic words until I knew what they
meant.

I immediately felt the discipline. *Islam in Focus* told me
that if a Muslim has had sex, he or she must perform a bath
called "ghusl" before praying. Counting my compulsive masturbation as sex, I would have to shower at least three times

a day, so I had to schedule my beat-off sessions around the prayer times. This is the brilliance of Islam, I thought, in governing our animal desires.

THAT SPRING MOM bought a house for us in a neighboring town called Phelps. The house was red brick and used to be a one-room school back in the 1800s. I noticed the initials "J. T." carved by the side door, probably by a kid who had been sent outside as a punishment.

Though I no longer lived in the Geneva school district, I could still go to DeSales. The DeSales bus came and got me in the morning, and then after school I'd go to Nan and Gramps's house until Mom picked me up after work. While most DeSales guys changed clothes after school, I chose to stay in my shirt and tie until well after dinner. Thanks to Malcolm, I associated ties with being revolutionary.

In the course of a thousand after-school masturbations, I realized how unattractive a bathroom my grandparents had. Nan had smoked so many cigarettes in that house that when I made a hot ghusl in the shower, the steam would cause liquid nicotine to drip down the walls in long brown lines.

Between orgasms I went downstairs to keep the fights going.

"You have to admit that the church is responsible for most of the bloodshed in history!" I yelled at Nan.

"You're Catholic," she said without looking away from the television.

"No, I'm not! The Catholics have opposed every effort at human progress, from the printing press to astronomy to the abolition of—"

"You were baptized."

"That doesn't mean that I'm Catholic, Nan! What religion you believe in has nothing to do with someone sprinkling water on your head when you're too young to consent to anything or even understand what it means. It's what's in your heart, and in my heart I can't believe that some old man sitting on a throne in Italy having people kiss his ring is holier than anyone else!"

"So what are you, then?"

"I'm Muslim!"

Back then I knew that Islam was widely misunderstood in America, but still had not grasped the particular ignorance of my grandmother. At the time I imagined her shock and horror, but it's more likely that she did not even know what a Muslim was. While I stood there waiting for a response, she just looked at the screen and chewed her gum. Nan's preferred gum was Bubble Tape, which came in six-foot rolls in pink plastic containers, because once she finished a roll she could keep the container. Then she'd maintain the last wad of Bubble Tape for as long as she could, storing it in the container when she wasn't chewing it.

Her chewing slowed, as though she was reflecting on whether enough flavor remained in the gum to put it in storage. Deciding on the affirmative, she took it out of her mouth, placed it in the empty Bubble Tape container and snapped the lid shut.

"You're so mad," she said, still facing the TV. "You're mad all the time. You're breaking your grandfather's heart."

"Would he rather I did speed with the baseball players? Should I get drunk and impregnate a cheerleader? Maybe he should be their grandfather."

"Maybe he will." Her eyes stayed locked on *General Hospital*. I gave her a look like I wanted to stab her, my worst

Manson eyes—the kind that could burn a hole through the wall like they said at school—waiting for her to turn and see. I stared until it hurt, at which point I could detect the processes involved with a hard stare; it's not really your eyes that do it, it's the fatty part under your eyebrows squeezing down on your eyes. My temples started to hurt too but I kept at it. She'd have to feel the psychic aggression, and anyone can sense when they're being stared at; *turn your damn head!* My jaw was clenched and I felt my head start to rattle but she kept attending to *General Hospital* like I wasn't even there. Finally I turned and left the room. "He's mad at the world," I heard her say, "just like his father." I went outside, hitting only one step as I flew off the porch. Wesley had built that porch years ago, at least the brick part of it.

Wesley was mad at the world and fucked in the head because he was too smart for them, but there were so many of them everywhere that he couldn't win. Wesley didn't watch soap operas, he read books; he probably tried to talk to Nan about books, and she wouldn't even look at him. So he went crazy and I'd go crazy, I could tell already. I didn't need to go back there. Wesley had grown up surrounded by hicks, but he knew that he was bigger than all of them and so he went out into the world to prove it. Wesley went to Korea, but his father couldn't have found Korea on a map. I was bigger than Geneva and everyone in it and knew that I'd get out of there too; I'd go conquer the world and prove to them how big I was.

Wesley was right to hate this town. People in Geneva stayed away from books, I knew, because books would only show them how small they were. I knew from the books that I read. By its original name, Kanedesaga, Geneva once stood as the capital for the Seneca Nation. Kanedesaga was brutally destroyed during the Sullivan raids against Native American tribes, and in its ashes Geneva was born. That was our history: Everything around me, all of these stupid houses and churches and schools, had been literally built on mass graves and genocide. Then, around the start of the nineteenth century, nearly all the white Genevans died from dysentery, which meant that they didn't know how to wipe their asses properly.

I arrived at the last intersection before Geneva became wilderness. At one corner was a convenience store owned by some asshole named Rusty who sold baseball cards and always ripped kids off. At the opposite corner was a gas station; behind it stood a Native American burial ground and stone memorial to the Sullivan Raids, but no one ever saw it or even seemed to know that it was there. The other two corners were home to Cornell University's Agricultural Experimental Station and an apple orchard. I wasn't really sure of what they did at the Experimental Station. In first grade we went there on a field trip, but all I could remember was their collection of dead Monarch butterflies pinned down inside glass cases. One of the smart girls at DeSales did special summer work there.

I still hated Nan and her goddamned recycled Bubble Tape, but the adrenaline had worn off and I now questioned whether I could really make it all the way home. Beyond that intersection, the streets became country roads and the houses sat farther back. For a second I imagined Gramps's cop brother leaving Wesley at the edge of town and wondered where they dropped him off, maybe just a little ways down from where I stood. I turned right at that intersection and kept walking alongside the apple orchard towards Phelps, considering hopping the little chicken wire fence to steal some apples, but then envisioned Nan laughing at me. "I thought you were

Muslim," she'd say. "I didn't know that Muslims stole apples."
I left the apples alone.

It might be time to pray, I thought. *If I had a rug to pray on,
I'd drop right here and do it.* Though I hadn't jerked off yet, I
wasn't clean for prayer. Even when a full ghusl isn't required,
Muslims perform a lesser ritual washing called wudhu, and I
had no water. There was a way to do it if water wasn't available, but I hadn't learned it yet. Of course, I didn't know how
to pray either; I knew the motions, but not the words. Finally
I said *fuck it* and decided to trust in Allah's compassion, praying while unclean and saying what I could remember, so I
undid my tie and unbuttoned my white shirt. I turned to what
might have been vaguely east and spread out the shirt in front
of me. I should have worn an undershirt, I thought.

So I stood shirtless in front of my white shirt by the road,
my sneakers off too, my tie hanging out of the front pocket of
my black Bugle Boy pants, and I tried to remember what to
do. The first and most important thing, said *Islam in Focus*,
was to make the proper intention in my heart. I didn't know
how to do it beyond just telling myself that I was about to
pray. Staring at the ground, I put my hands up by my head,
touching my ears with the tips of my thumbs, and said "Allah
is the Greatest." Then I folded my hands over my belly button
and thought hard. The next part was recited by Denzel in the
Malcolm X movie, but all I knew of the Arabic was the rhym-
ing *eeeeen* part at the end of each line. I heard a car go by and
wondered what they thought of this skinny, pale kid standing
by the road in front of his shirt.

"In the Name of Allah, the Most Merciful," I said quietly.
"Lord of all the worlds, master of the judgment. Guide me on
the straight path, not that of those who have gone astray." I
knew that I messed it up, but was at least in the ballpark. I

didn't know anything else but had the physical movements down, so I bent over, straightened up again, and then prostrated myself on the ground. Sharp little rocks underneath the shirt poked at my forehead and knees. I knew what to say while on the ground—in English, at least: "Glory to my Lord the Most High," three times. Then I stood up again and repeated the process. At the end of my second cycle I stayed in sitting position longer, extending my right index finger; that's what the book said to do, though I hadn't learned the words that accompanied it. Then I stood up and repeated the cycle.

It was during one of my prostrations that I could detect a car pulling over on the opposite side of the road. It stayed there with its engine running.

"Mike?" asked a girl's voice. I could tell that it was my cousin Chrissy, but to acknowledge her would have broken my prayer. Who comes first, Allah or my cousin? I rose from my prostration, said "Allah is the Greatest" under my breath and went back down on the ground. "Mike?" she repeated. I said my "Glory to my Lord the Most High" three times and sat back up. For about a minute I just sat there with my right index finger pointing up, trying to remember just a fragment of the words. "I bear witness there is no god but Allah," I said to myself, "and Muhammad is the messenger of Allah." Then I turned my head to the right to say the customary *as-salamu alaikum* to the angel on my shoulder—avoiding eye contact with Chrissy—and then to the left. Then I jumped up and put my dirty shirt on.

"I'm sorry," I told her. "I was praying and I can't interrupt the prayer."

"What are you doing out here?"

"I got in a fight with Nan. She doesn't understand anything."

"Do you need a ride?"

Chrissy didn't know anything about Islam either, but at least she was young enough to understand how it felt to be young in a town like Geneva with shitty, stupid people and to want to get out more than anything in the world. I got in the car and hurriedly buttoned up my shirt. Chrissy turned around and took me home.

"So you're Muslim?" she asked. "What does that teach?"

"It's mainly about there being only one God," I told her. "You know, Christianity isn't a monotheistic religion. In Christianity you have the Father, the Son, and the Holy Spirit, right? How can that be one God?"

"I always wondered about that," she said.

"And you have God coming down to earth, having a son, and then the son dies, and because of that we're all saved. Does that make sense?"

"Not really."

"But the son is not just God's son, he's also God. How does that work?"

"I have a hard time with religion in general," she said.

"In Islam it just makes more sense. God isn't running around trying to have kids. That actually comes from Greek mythology; there are lots of examples of—"

"You know what my dad told me?" she asked. "He said that if I was ever going to join a religion, the first thing I should ask is whether a woman can have the highest position in that religion. If a woman can't be the pope or whatever, then it's not the religion for me."

"That's the great thing about Islam," I answered fast. "There aren't any popes or priests or anything like that. There's no hierarchy or institution, so everyone's equal: black or white, man or woman, whatever."

"That's cool," she said.

After Chrissy dropped me off at home I performed proper wudhu in the bathroom while looking over my photocopied pages from *Islam in Focus*. About halfway through, I had to start over because the dog licked my arm. I then spread out a towel on the floor and read my prayers.

malik al-kafi khan

7

The real Man of the House stared down at me from my bedroom wall, his stern expression rendered in black Sharpie by my unsteady hand: Ayatollah Ruhollah Khomeini, with Santa Claus beard and giant black turban. I hoped for it to convey his years of struggle and suffering but also his power—his face had awesome power, like he was father enough not only for his house but a whole nation of people. It made perfect sense to blanket Iran's cities with that face on every billboard. Some people even saw his face on the moon. I drew him by using the cover of one of his books as a reference.

Next I taped photos of Muammar Qadhafi and Sheikh Omar Abdel-Rahman (the "blind shaykh" behind the 1993 World Trade Center bombing) in my locker. Mr. Harris walked by when I had it open and just shook his head.

"What the fuck are you doing?" asked Tom when he saw them.

"I'm Muslim," I told him.

"You're not Muslim," he said with full certainty. "You're Dan's little puppet, is what you are."

He walked away and I turned back to the men in my locker. For all the white DeSales kids these faces were strange and scary, and the names were scary too. Muslim names were hard to say; I wasn't even sure I said them right, but tried to sound them out in militant and *foreign-sounding* ways, going extra hard on the *k*'s and *h*'s. In Geneva Muslim names read like stop signs: go no further, you're not part of this. Muslim names were so cool that someone who had been born in American jahiliyya (ignorance) and found Islam later in life would of course forfeit his parents' name for a new one.

"Did you know," I asked Dan at the lunch table, "that I don't have the same last name as either of my parents?"

"What do you mean?"

"My mom has gone back to Knight, her maiden name. My father's last name was Unger, but my last name is still Schutt after my stepdad, who I'll never see again."

"That says something about the American family, Scooter. You don't even have a name."

"I don't."

"You're like Malcolm; Schutt's only your slave name. We should call you Scooter X."

I went upstairs to the school library and sat down with one of its *World Almanac*s to look up various Islamic nations, mixing and matching their heads of state until coming up with my new righteous name: Malik al-Kafi Khan. I had no idea what it meant or whether it even made sense cultur-ally, but it sounded tough and had me imagining a future version of myself, how I might end up with a name like that: exiled to a place hot and dusty and harsh, someplace where people hated Americans (but they'd love me, the one American who dedicated his life to their struggle). I'd wear a patterned kifeyyeh scarf traditional among Arab men, but solid green and ridiculously oversized, going all the way to my ankles—enveloping me almost like a burqa but looking dramatic and awesome in the breeze, flowing behind me like a cape attached to my head. *There goes Malik al-Kafi Khan,* they would say. For my efforts as a legit third world revolutionary, the United States government would demand my arrest and issue million-dollar rewards for information leading to my capture. Finally the gung-ho Republican president sends his troops to my bunker, forcing a standoff with my supporters. To save his adopted people from further bloodshed at the hands of AmeriKKKa, Malik al-Kafi Khan surrenders, walking out to greet the troops with his infant son in his arms . . . and then sets off a grenade blowing up himself, the baby, and hopefully some Marines. *Tie a yellow ribbon on that, assholes!*

I came up with a few scenarios. One involved my capture, after which I'd lead a new American revolution from my prison cell. Another had me crashing a 747 into the White House.

Without even knowing of my insane inner life, the DeSales guidance counselor told Mom that I needed to see a psychiatrist. They set me up with Dr. Margaret Kennedy at Geneva General Hospital. I had low expectations; back in junior high, Mom had sent me to a few therapists, and once I even spoke to her marriage counselor, but they never gave me anything that I needed.

Every Wednesday after school, I'd walk to the hospital and see Dr. Kennedy. At first we talked about Wesley; it was from Dr. Kennedy that I first heard the term "paranoid schizophrenic." Later sessions turned into my lecturing her about

Islam, and her asking if I ever wanted to do "normal high school things" like play football.

"I'm not into having fun in this world," I told her. "This world is a prison for believers." While talking to her I had my right index finger firmly pointed to my own temple, like I was pressing a button on my head that would turn me into Malcolm.

"What about girls, Mike? Do you think about girls? Are there any girls at school that you like?"

"They call DeSales a Catholic school, but that's a joke. There was one girl who let her boyfriend finger her right in the hall; how is that Catholic?" I secretly imagined that decadent DeSales hallway to be the street from *Malcolm X* in the scene where Malcolm's walking past a slew of prostitutes and they all try to tempt him. Like Malcolm, I'd ignore the girls and just look straight ahead, but after school I'd go home and furiously jerk off to their pictures in the yearbook.

"Okay, Mike," said Dr. Kennedy. "What I'd really like you to do is think about the status of women in Islam—"

"Have *you* thought about the status of women in America? Did you know that women in Muslim countries view *American* women as oppressed and degraded? Here a woman is taught to go outside with everything hanging out and show it off and get raped." I was using Malcolm's voice, or Denzel's voice when he did Malcolm, and not the angry street-preaching Malcolm but Malcolm on the college lecture circuit, Malcolm at Harvard calmly explaining his point. "When a woman dresses in a way that shows how she respects herself," I told my therapist, "then men respect her too. That's why there aren't any rapes in Muslim countries." At least that's what I read. Men are sexual creatures, said the books, and easily distracted from the path. If a woman truly cared for a man and respected him, she would avoid attracting his attention unless they were married.

If a man truly cared for and respected women, he would avoid looking at them, because to look at or talk to them would be to secretly degrade them in his thoughts—it was unavoidable, a built-in part of his nature.

That's what scared me when I was sitting in front of DeSales with *Islam in Focus* and a girl asked me about it. She was a blonde girl in the year below me, petite with big breasts that she showed off in tight shirts. I couldn't understand why she wasn't more popular.

"I don't know much about Islam," she said. I turned to look at her but couldn't lift my head.

"Islam is like the true Christianity," I told her knees.

"Really? How so?"

"To be a Christian would mean to follow the teachings of Christ, right?" It was surprisingly easy to talk to her, maybe since I had already rehearsed these kinds of dialogues with myself.

"I would think so," she said.

"Because if you look at what Jesus actually taught, it's not anything like what we call Christianity today."

"I'm sure."

"On the Day of Judgment, these so-called Christians are going to run to Jesus and call him their savior, call him God, and he's just going to turn to God and say that he never made those claims."

"So what did Jesus teach?"

"Jesus was a prophet of Islam. When we say that Muhammad was the founder of Islam, it's not historically accurate. Islam was the religion of *all* the prophets, and Muhammad only restored it to—"

"Hey, I gotta go." Her bus was waiting. She took out her notepad, scribbled something down and ripped the page from its metal spiral. "Can we talk later? I really want to know more about Islam." She gave me the paper. It had her name, Melissa, and phone number.

As she ran to the bus, I called out to her.

"If you take one step towards Allah, He will take two steps towards you!" I had stolen that from the Malcolm X movie. Melissa smiled and disappeared into the bus.

I called her that afternoon.

"It's crazy," she told me. "DeSales is supposed to be a Catholic school, right? But you're the first person I've met there who really cares about religion or God."

Melissa wasn't like other girls at DeSales, the cheerleaders who publicly exemplified our Catholic pride but still got drunk and fucked Hobart guys. She didn't have one of the traditional Geneva surnames that you see in every DeSales generation like Smaldone, Valerio, or Evangelista. She had grown up in Phelps and went to public school there until ninth grade, another reason for her outsider status among the girls who had known each other since St. Stevens Elementary. And supposedly there was a terrible secret story behind her switching schools, but I never learned it.

I called Melissa every day after school. Our conversations were more like lectures. She'd listen to me ramble about whatever book I was reading, sometimes asking questions like she was hosting me on a panel. Though we were starting to develop a connection, I couldn't picture us actually hanging out. Even in school I'd avoid contact; if we were about to pass each other in the hall, I'd immediately open one of my books and hide in it.

Once when I called, she asked if I was embarrassed of her.

"Why would I be embarrassed of you?"

"Because you'll talk to me for three hours on the phone but run away from me in person."

"That's out of respect for you. I need to protect you from myself. If a man and woman are alone together, the Devil is the third present."

"Oh."

"If I look at you once, it's allowed, because that's unavoidable; I can't control what passes in front of my face. But if I look at you a second time, it's for the Devil, and the third look is a sin."

"Okay. I'm sorry. You think it's a sin to look at me?"

"You're beautiful, Melissa, and—"

"I'm beautiful?"

"Of course. And that would bring out bad things in me."

"Why?"

"Because that's the nature of man. It's my nature to want to violate you. Do you know what the word *jihad* means?"

"Holy war, right?"

"No." Of all the misconceptions about Islam, that was my favorite to correct. "*Jihad* means *struggle*. And that can be all kinds of struggle. For a woman, giving birth is jihad. Did you know that?"

"No, I didn't."

"Islam loves and respects the mother. The Prophet Muhammad, peace be upon him, said that paradise lies at the foot of the mother. A woman who dies while in labor gets the reward of a martyr."

"Wow."

"Yeah. And Muhammad, peace be upon him, said that fighting was only the lesser jihad. The greater jihad is jihad against yourself—to struggle with your own sinful nature."

"Is it our nature to be sinful? If that's nature, then how is it a sin?"

"Look, I'm trying to be a Muslim. I'd be happy to teach you about Islam—that's an obligation incumbent upon all Muslims—but we have to stay within the bounds." It was satisfying to use words like *incumbent* that weren't normal for fifteen-year-olds.

Another time she called me to say that she was going for a jog and wanted to stop at my house for water. I said that she could, so I poured a glass of water and left it outside. Then I locked the doors and hid in my room.

She knocked a few times but I wouldn't answer. I couldn't even look out the window, though I wanted to see what she wore. Tight shorts and a little top? A sports bra? I wanted to injure that girl with my dick, really give it to her hard and make it hurt. Maybe it'd hurt her in such a way that she loved it. *She wants to have sex with me*, I was sure. *I can't hold it against her; it's her nature to want to seduce men, and American culture has taught her that this is her only purpose in life. She doesn't know better yet. I'll have to look out for both of us.*

"Thanks for the water," she yelled before leaving.

The final straw with her came at a school dance. I had no reason to go, since I never danced with anyone; but Dan didn't either, and he went, so we could at least sit on the bleachers together and complain about how stupid it was.

Tom was on the gym floor with the football players. Too small for a fully formed clique system, DeSales just had football and nonfootball.

"Hey Scooter!" called one of them. "Let's see you fall!"

Tom turned and said something to him, but I couldn't hear it. After that they left me alone.

"They call this a Catholic school?" I scoffed as football play-ers slow-danced with their girlfriends and felt them up. There was one guy who even bragged about putting his finger in girls' assholes as he danced with them, but I couldn't begin to comprehend how that worked. "Does Fat Ed know what half these songs are about?" I asked Dan. Then Melissa came up to us, jittery and not seeming right.

"Can I talk to you for a minute?" she asked. We left Dan and walked out of the gym to sit on a quiet stairwell. "I just did speed," she told me.

"Why did you do that?"

"I don't know." She brought her hand up to my face and played with the curl in my hairline. "What if I kissed you?"

"You can't kiss me, Melissa."

"Why not?"

"Because I'm Muslim."

"There's no love in Islam?"

"Of course there is. We love Allah, and we love each other for Allah's sake. I'm sorry." Then I stood up and walked out of the school.

"Hey," said the teacher at the door. "Once you go out, you can't come back in." I ignored him and went to my grandparents' house. While other DeSales guys were fingering their girl-friends' assholes, I sat in Nan's bedroom with a stack of choc-olate cookies. I wondered what Dan was doing without me, but couldn't worry about him; he always seemed in control of things.

The next day I'd go to Hobart to lose myself in books, find-ing a new addition to the Islam shelf: Penguin's translation of the Qur'an. It was disappointing to hold, just a regular book with none of the holy power that I felt in the Yusuf Ali version. The front cover spelled it "Koran," the inside had no

Arabic, and I was sure that no Muslims were involved in its translation; the only conclusion I could reach was that neither Penguin nor Hobart and William Smith Colleges had any respect for Islam. If I was going to command right and forbid wrong, as all the books told me to do, I'd have to defend Islam against its enemies and remove the Penguin Koran.

The library had an electronic alarm, so I'd have to find whatever set it off inside the book. At an isolated desk on the third floor, I flipped through the pages and couldn't spot it, so I just ripped off the covers and put them between two books on a random shelf. That should do it, I figured. After stealing the Penguin Koran, I'd dispose of it in a respectful manner, lest the evil of Penguin reach any vulnerable person and lead him or her away from Islam.

I put the book in my backpack, walked downstairs and headed for the exit, scared but knowing that it was worth whatever would come. I couldn't believe myself: I was really doing it, heading for the exit, and everything looking good, until the alarm sounded. I froze.

"Hold it," said the librarian, a middle-aged man with a moustache. He walked around the front desk. "Do you have anything that you didn't sign out?" I opened my backpack with nothing in it but the library's half-destroyed Penguin Koran. "What's this?"

"It's the Qur'an," I told him.

"The cover's ripped off."

"I'm a Muslim," I said, my voice trembling and my eyes glued to the floor. "This edition is offensive."

"What's offensive about it?"

"There's no 'K' or 'O' in the Arabic language. And if you're going to translate the Qur'an, you have to have the Arabic side-by-side with the English, because it's impossible to *really* translate the Qur'an. The English doesn't do justice to the original Arabic, and . . ." My words trailed off into nothing. The guy looked me up and down.

"Do you speak Arabic?"

"No, sir."

"Do you have a card here?"

"Yes."

"We're going to have to suspend it."

"Okay."

Maybe stealing the Penguin Koran wasn't the right course of action, but still I showed that I'd be willing to suffer whatever that librarian might have given me. And now my library card was suspended, but I had done my best to correct error and injustice in the world. I would have taken whatever they had for me; if the library put thieves before a firing squad, all the better, I'd go out a martyr.

Even so, I broke down crying as I told Mom the story. She didn't seem angry in the way that I expected, and she knew that losing my library card was punishment enough (though fortunately, the used bookstore downtown had a complete set of Will Durant books, so my quest through *The Story of Civilization* could go uninterrupted). If anything, she gave me a look of worry like she knew something about me that I didn't, like she had seen this behavior before.

WHILE CUTTING THROUGH a cemetery one night on the way to Tom's house, I stopped to look at a large stone cross and thought of how sad and pathetic it was that someone wanted a cross (a pagan symbol if you dug into its history) to stand over his bones for all time. The Qur'an said to respect Christians, but some commentators wrote that the Christians of Prophet

Muhammad's time were not the same as Christians now. I leaned my back against the cross, allowing it to support my full weight. The next logical step was to stretch out my arms and pretend to be Jesus. Then I started to fall backward—the cross was giving way! It was too heavy to even consider trying to catch. I watched it tip over and crack against the base of the tombstone with a dull thud.

The cross lay broken in half. As soon as my brain registered what had happened, I ran. Escaping the cemetery into an adjacent public park, I blasted across it to Jefferson Avenue and bypassed Tom's house until reaching 5 and 20, the main road going through Geneva. Crossing it put me on the Hobart and William Smith side of town, which felt like a different country, safe enough to slow into a jog. Hopping some fences removed me even further from the crime.

Lying on my back in the middle of their turf lacrosse field, looking up at the stars, I thought that maybe Allah had shown me something that night; perhaps I had become spiritually advanced enough to begin living in parables. Back home I still had F. E. Peters's 1,216-page *Judaism, Christianity and Islam: The Classical Texts and Their Interpretations*, which I had borrowed from the Hobart library and never returned since they took my card away. In it I had read an excerpt from Tha'alibi's *Stories of the Prophets* detailing the return of Prophet Isa (Jesus), saying that when he comes back he will break crosses . . .

I pulled myself away from those thoughts, but remained sure that I would at least become a hero for Islam in America: maybe Malik al-Kafi Khan, first Muslim president of the United States of America (Muslim Socialists Party). The lacrosse field was flanked on either side by rows of empty bleachers; standing up, I turned in a full circle with arms outstretched and pretended that I was basking in the cheers of an audience.

WE GOT OUR sophomore yearbooks the last week of school. Dan signed mine, "You have emerged from the depths of being a nonthinking imbecile to a brilliant, cutting-edge Muslim. Have a great summer, Malcolm X rules!" Tom signed it, "ASS-lom alaikum." Carlene, a sweet girl whose picture I jerked off to, wrote, "Have a great summer and keep reading the Koran." A freshman named Justin signed my book to "Mike, the Prophet of Islam." I told him to cross out "Prophet" and write "humble student."

8   if we're lucky, his brain is shot to shit

I failed two classes that year, math and biology. Mom wanted me to do better but I pleaded that I wasn't some dumb kid; I only got bad grades because I was reading my own stuff that went far beyond anything that DeSales could offer. I brought my photocopied prayers to summer school every day and looked through them during class, trying to teach myself to say the Arabic without having ever heard it. The only part I might have had remotely right was the opening sura of the Qur'an, al-Fatiha, because Denzel recited it in the movie. I'd try to say it as he did, stretching the end of each line: ar-Rahmani R*aheeeem*, al-hamdulilahi rabbil'Ala*meeeen*, maliki yawmi-*deeeen*. Soon, I knew, I'd be a real Muslim, and then things would change.

"You ever think of getting your learner's permit?" Mom asked as she drove me to Kmart.

"Kids want to drive because they think that makes them independent, but they still don't have *mental* independence."

"I have something for you." She then reached into her purse with one hand, fished around and pulled out a folded sheet of lined yellow paper.

"What's this?" Unfolding it, the first thing I saw was "18 Oct 1991" in blue ink. And then my mother's name. After that, the handwriting was too sloppy to read easily:

Sue,

For sometime now the rating on my disability benefit has been sufficient that Michael Roland will qualify for GI Bill Benefits educationally, when it is time for him to go to school. I thought it a good idea to let you know.

Wesley C. Unger

"He sent it to Nan and Gramps's house," she said.

"He wrote this like two years ago? Why didn't you tell me?"

"I wasn't sure if you were ready then. You were pretty angry, bud."

"I know, Mom."

"We had a hard time, remember?"

"Yeah."

"I don't know what you would have done if you saw him. And I don't know what he would have said to you."

"Islam has given me some perspective, I think."

"There's something else I'm going to give you. Bud, I'm doing this because I think you've really come a long way and I trust you and I'm proud of you." She reached back into her purse and gave me another folded sheet of paper.

This time the handwriting was Mom's: the name "Naomi" and a phone number.

"Who's Naomi?"

"One of his sisters. You can call her if you want."

"You think she knows where he is?"

"If anyone did, it'd be her. They were really close."

I wondered what kind of shape Wesley was in, whether he'd try to kill us if we showed up. He might have been like a guy that Mom sometimes pointed out as we drove past him on Exchange Street; she told me that back when they were in high school, the guy was heavy into drugs and got into crazy trouble, but now he was burned out and just spent his days walking up and down Geneva. His legs were incredibly powerful, she'd say, because all he ever did was walk, but he had nothing in his brain. Maybe schizophrenia was like that, and Wesley had mellowed out. Our meeting could be like the scene in *Malcolm X* when Malcolm goes to visit his old rival West Indian Archie, years after they nearly killed each other, only to discover that Archie can barely stand up and his once-brilliant mind is gone. I didn't know what Wesley looked like, but used my old pictures to imagine him, and thought of Charles Manson. They were about the same age, and I could see Wesley aging like Charlie—with the same twinkle in his crazy eyes and deep ancient lines in his face and the same kind of scraggly wild-man facial hair, charismatic and Biblical in the way that only comes with mental illness. I also imagined him with the charm of ancient violence, a monster too old to threaten anyone—a rapist who can't get it up anymore, but recalls that in his glory days he was a real devil. Perhaps he even carved the Manson swastika into his forehead, just to complete the look.

I didn't call Naomi right away, but carried her phone

number everywhere I went and wrote multiple copies in case I lost it. I didn't know what I'd say to her or how the Ungers felt about me; I wasn't even sure if I still existed in their history. Did they remember when Wesley had a scared little girl? Did they know that she gave him a baby and then took it away? Was that even worth remembering?

❃

WITHOUT ANY WARNING to the Ungers, I popped back into existence.

"Hello?" said a woman in her fifties with a slight Southern dialect.

"Hello, is Naomi there?"

"Yes, this is Naomi."

"Hi, Naomi. Aunt Naomi. My name is Michael Schutt, I'm Wesley's son, and my mom gave me your number. I was hoping that maybe—"

"Oh, hi, Michael! We were wondering about you!"

"Uh, hi."

"How have you been?"

"Uh, pretty good. I'm doing okay."

"What grade are you in now?"

"I just finished my sophomore year."

"Oh, that's great! Are you trying to find your dad?"

"Yeah."

"He doesn't live too far from me. I'm in Berkeley Springs; you know where that is? That's where we all grew up. He's doin' good; he's got a little house. You should come down sometime; he'd love to see you."

"I've been wanting to come down."

"We'd all love to see you! You know, the last time I saw you, you were just two years old!"

"Yeah, it's been a long time."

"When you're gonna come down, you just let me know."

"Okay."

"He's doin' good, Michael."

"That's good."

"How's your mom?"

"She's okay. She just bought a house, actually."

"Good for her. Tell her I said hi."

She told me that she looked forward to seeing me, and then added, "We're *all* looking forward to it." How many Ungers was that—my grandparents had what, twenty children? Naomi said that I might have been the youngest of seventy-some-odd cousins, but she wasn't sure; she'd have to ask around.

All of a sudden I was an Unger and belonged to the Ungers. I had been one once before, and then a Schutt put his name on me. For a while I had gone to Schutt family parties, with Schutt cousins and Schutt grandparents, and they all claimed me as though I had always been theirs. Now the Ungers might claim me as though I had never left.

A few days later I received a phone call.

"Michael Roland?" asked a man.

"Yes," I answered, though it was legally Michael William, and spiritually Malik al-Kafi Khan.

"My name is Chris. Is your mother in the room with you?"

"Yeah."

"Okay, don't say anything. I'm a friend of your father's."

"Hi."

"So you want to meet your dad?"

"Yeah."

"I want to ask you something, Michael. But just say yes or no, don't say anything else."

"Okay."

"Would you consider running away with your father?"

"No."

"Okay. But you're going to come see him?"

"I want to."

"Okay. I'm not your father, just so you know. I'm a friend of his."

"Sure."

MOM SAID THAT she'd drive me to see Wesley after I finished summer school. I hustled to finish Will Durant's *The Age of Faith* so that I could start his next volume, *The Reformation*, fresh on our nine-hour drive to Berkeley Springs.

We left early in the morning, early enough that I did my presunrise prayer as Mom loaded the car. She was nervous, but it appeared to have less to do with Wesley than the fact that she had never driven as far as Rochester (forty miles from our house) by herself. I fell asleep and didn't wake up until we had crossed into Pennsylvania. On the other side of the highway I saw eighteen-wheelers wearing decals on their front grills of giant mouths full of sharp teeth, like the truck was a giant metal shark in search of prey. They made me think of what it'd be like to stare one down at six years old as Uncle David had, and I can call that trucker the Devil too—if it's not the Devil who grinds up little boys under his tires, who is it?

Then I cracked open *The Reformation*. "Listen to this, Mom, the first line of the book: 'Religion is the last subject that the intellect begins to understand.' What do you think about that?"

"I don't know, bud. What is he saying?"

"He's saying that religion doesn't agree with logical thought, that it's a hard thing for the mind to grasp because it's so irrational. That's because he's coming from a Western Christian background, you know? Of course he would say that; I would say that too if I wasn't a Muslim."

"I remember when you didn't believe in God, bud. You didn't seem too happy."

"But Islam is a religion for intellectuals. You can be Muslim and not have to surrender your brain to superstitions that were borrowed from Roman pagans." It went like that for hours. If I was awake, I was talking about Islam. Mom mostly just listened.

SHE HAD MADE us sandwiches and brought sodas to avoid spending money on the road. We ate during one of our stops for gas. While Mom went inside the station to use the restroom I sat on the curb of the parking lot with my peanut butter and jelly and Will Durant. When she came out she sat next to me.

"Mom, how'd you even end up with him?"

"I don't know, bud, I was pretty young. I had to get out of Geneva; I felt abandoned by my mother . . . Nanny, you know, she used to drink a lot. We were really close when I was little, but when I got older I wouldn't even bring friends home because she was always passed out on the floor."

"How'd you leave?"

"I had a boyfriend; we saved up our money and after graduation went down to Florida. Remember the story of a lacrosse ball knocking my teeth out?"

"Yeah."

"Well, he was the ball. The lacrosse-game story was just what I told Gramps. So I broke up with him, and then I lived in a house with eight other people—one of them was this guy named Blue who grew his fingernails really long, like *really* long, at least four inches, and put glitter in his beard. Then I moved out of there, and used to ride my bike up and down the beach collecting seashells to make candles. Then I'd sell the candles . . ." Then she was somewhere else that I couldn't see, as though, like Wesley, she had the power to travel through space and time in her head.

"Muslims don't drink," I said. "Alcohol destroys the family, that's why it's forbidden. And remember in *Malcolm X*, when he's saying how the white man sends alcohol and drugs into the black neighborhoods to pacify people? That's why everyone at DeSales is dumb, all they do is drink. I'm glad that I'm a Muslim or I'd be right there with them." Mom came back to the world in front of her.

"That's good," she said.

"There's nothing in Catholicism to protect them from it, either. When Catholics go to church, the priest holds up a cup of wine, this poison that would turn them all into criminals and rapists. This wine, you know, that would ruin their lives, the priest says it's God's blood. Can you believe that? Isn't it crazy?"

"I never thought of it like that."

"You see Mom, Islam isn't only a religion. It's actually a complete way of life." I couldn't remember which book I had gotten that from. Probably *Islam in Focus*, but it was one of those sayings that would seem to have given birth to itself, true because it had always been there.

"How are you doing, bud?"

"I'm okay."

"Are you ready for this?"

"Yeah. But it's time for me to pray." I went to the car and pulled my towel out of my backpack, the same backpack I took to school. Made me think of DeSales for a second. Even

though it was summer, I imagined that all of the assholes at
DeSales were still trapped inside while I was out here, whatever *here* was, having the adventure of my life. I had no concept of where we were on a map, but it seemed like Geneva
was nine thousand miles away. And I hadn't felt so healthy in
at least five years.

Before prayer I needed to make wudhu. Certain things violated your ritual cleanliness, like defecating, farting, or sleeping (since you might fart in your sleep and not know it), and
I had already done all three, so I went into the men's room
and locked the door behind me. It was poorly lit and smelled
sour. Wudhu involved washing your hands and arms up to the
elbows, your face and head and neck, but you also had to wash
your feet—the hardest part of wudhu in a public restroom,
when you can't sit on the piss-covered toilet to take off your
shoes and you don't want your bare feet to touch the nasty
floor. With my rolled-up towel and photocopied *Islam in Focus*
pages resting behind the sink knobs, I stood on my shoes and
used the sink for balance.

I slipped my wet feet back into my shoes and walked behind
the gas station, behind the dumpster and stacks of metal
crates (couldn't pray in front of Mom; that'd be weird). I didn't
know the right direction to face, but by then I had read in the
Qur'an that Allah was Lord of East and West and you'd face
Him whichever way you turned. The towel unrolled in front of
me, I took off my shoes again, placing them neatly to the side,
with my *Islam in Focus* pages near the place where I'd put my
head down. After a breeze came and sent them skating across
the pavement, I found a stone to pin them under.

Then I stood straight and put my hands up to my head.

"Allahu Akbar." God is the Greatest.

I folded my hands over my navel and paused before

reciting. "Bismillahir Rahmanir Raheem," I said under my breath, loud enough only for me to hear. "Al-hamdulilahi Rabbil'Alameen. Ar-Rahmanir-Raheem. Maliki yawmi-deen . . ." And I never looked at the sheets once. I went through the motions and knew the words, and the world around me started to disappear.

At the end of the prayer I was in sitting position. I greeted the angels on my shoulders and then it was done. I was warm inside, like when I read the Qur'an for the first time, but this felt more mature and valid—as though I knew something now that I didn't know then, like I saw more of the picture.

"We should be coming to Maryland soon," said Mom in the car.

"Mom, I did the whole prayer in Arabic!"

"Really? And you know what it means?"

"Yeah, I have a translation of it."

"You're a quick learner," she said. "When you were in first grade, your teacher used to say that you'd just stare out the window all day, but you still knew everything that you were supposed to know."

❧

NAOMI LIVED ON a short country road called Calvin Unger Lane. She came out of her house to greet us in the driveway. I watched her hug Mom but it still came as a surprise when she hugged me too.

We all sat at her kitchen table and she asked questions like how long it took us to get down there, and what Mom did for a living.

"Did you see the sign?" She asked me. "Calvin Unger Lane?"

"Yeah," I said softly.

"That was your grandfather. We all grew up right here. The old house got torn down not too long ago. It's too bad, you could've seen it." She turned to my mother. "You've seen it, right Sue?"

"Yep, I've seen it," said Mom. Naomi turned back to me. "You ready to see your dad?"

"Yes," I told her.

"He doesn't have a phone, so I'll call your Uncle Bill to come get him. He's doing okay, your dad, but you gotta be firm with him. You know he's not right."

"I know."

"We were really close growing up. We were about the same age . . . I remember when we were little, he'd stay up all night crying about the Devil. Anytime there was a creak in the hallway outside our room, he'd say that the Devil was coming for him."

"So he was always like that?" I asked.

"And then when he was in Korea, he signed a form allowing the army to test chemicals on him, like mind-control drugs, things like that."

"Really?" I remembered how Mom had compared Wesley to Jim Jones, and the Hobart library had that book suggesting that Jonestown had been a CIA mind-control experiment.

"Oh yeah. And he talks crazy sometimes, but he knows that I won't put up with any of that. I tell him, 'Wesley, I don't want to hear any crazy talk,' and then he'll shape up. But that's what you gotta do."

"Okay."

"He used to be in the Hell's Angels, did you know that?"

"No."

"After he came back from the army, he disappeared for a while. Came back on a Harley and had a Hell's Angel girl with him, and they both stayed with us at our parents' house. Then your grandpa opened up Wes's duffle bag and found books about Satanism and Nazism, things like that, and had him committed to the veterans' hospital."

"Oh my god."

"We went up there and saw him. They had him strapped in a bed, all drugged up."

"Oh my god," I said again. Mom didn't say anything.

"After you guys left," Naomi told us, "Wesley called me and said, 'I'm gonna go up there and get Michael Roland.' He wanted me to help him kidnap you. I told him, 'Wesley, you stay right here, you let them be.'" I felt dizzy, like Naomi had taken me by the hands and swung me in circles in the air. She said something to my mother, and my mother said something back, but for two or three exchanges I couldn't understand words.

Neither of them noticed that I was mentally gone from the table, but Naomi brought me back in by addressing me: "I've got a picture of him, you can have it." She then stood, walked over to the counter and came back with a little photo. "I dug this up when you called me." It was Wesley sitting on a bench in a park—the photo taken from some distance away—and he was waving at the camera. He had something in his lap but I couldn't tell what it was. "He would take his little manual typewriter to the park and write," she said.

"He writes?"

"Sure. He might have been published somewhere, I'll have to look into that. But he writes poetry. Your dad's real smart, always was. Did you know he has a PhD in psychology?" She looked at the photo in my hands. "You know, sometimes he talks about people living inside other people's bodies. The day I took that picture, I asked him, 'Wes, you like this park?' He said, 'Sure I do.' So I told him, 'All right, Wes, I'll tell you what I'm gonna do: I'll leave this park to you in my will.'" I smiled and pushed air out of my nose as a half laugh. "So your dad," she continued, "he says, 'Naomi, you don't own this park.' And you know what I said to him?"

"What'd you say?"

"I said, 'I know, Wesley, but the person living inside me does!'" Naomi and I both laughed. Her laugh was real and effortless; mine was real but still I had to work to get it out. I don't know what Mom did; I kind of forgot that she was next to me.

Naomi called her brother Bill and told him what was going on. I remembered that Mom was there and looked at her. She smiled to imply that we were all right. "Bill's gonna go get him," Naomi told us. "He's right down the road from your dad." So then we just waited. Maybe ten minutes later, Naomi's phone rang. "Hi, Wes, they're here. Yep, she's here in my kitchen right now. You want to talk to her?"

Mom stood up and took the phone. While I sat there attempting to eavesdrop, she responded to whatever Wesley said with only *yeah, sure, uh-huh, okay,* nothing to give me a clue. I stared hard at the table, trying to figure out what I'd say when he asked Mom to put me on the phone, but he never did. Mom finally hung up, and Naomi said she'd draw us directions to his house. It was that easy.

the one percenters

9

Wesley used to keep her up all night going off on his madness, whatever madness it was each night, just pounding away at her will until she was too tired to think anymore. He'd put her in the corner and hover over her with a fistful of her unwashed hair, his knuckles pressing down on the top of her head like the point of a drill, threatening to burrow his whole arm into her skull. When he started on her, she'd be afraid and hope for someone to hear them and call the police; but she eventually stopped hoping or fearing or caring either way, finding the switch inside herself that turned it all off. Once she numbed up, that's when he had her. By sunrise, whatever he said became true. *All little boys have lights in their eyes, Jodie*—he called my mom Jodie; why, she didn't know—*and that light's the sun, but you took Michael Roland's light away, and that's why he bites himself, that's why he bangs his head on the floor.* Or Nan had stolen my light, since she worked for the Mafia and sold little boys' lights on the international black market. Or I never had any light to start with since Mom had slept with the Devil and I was really Satan spawn, born with horns on my head and a tail.

Sometimes, when Wesley wasn't getting the effect that he wanted, he'd pull the big knife from his belt and put it to my throat. When Mom said whatever she was supposed to say, he'd put me back in my crib and go to bed, lying flat on his back with the Bible placed under his T-shirt. In the morning he'd put the Bible on a chair outside, opened to a certain passage to ward off the Devil, a pair of stones keeping the page. And he'd lock us in while he went to the campus. Without having slept the night before, Mom still had to stay awake to watch me.

That's what ran through my head like a movie montage as she drove me to the man's house. If I had to, I thought, I'd defend her against him, and it was Islamically proper to do so. I had read a story in which someone came to the Prophet Muhammad and asked him, "Who should I respect?" The Prophet answered, "Your mother." The man asked two more times and the Prophet gave the same answer. He wouldn't say "Your father" until the fourth time.

We pulled in front of his little house and he was sitting there on the porch. He wore jeans and a white muscle shirt—a *wifebeater*, they call it now. He had a beer gut but still looked strong with thick arms, like he had workingman power, though I knew he hated work more than anything.

We got out of the car and he walked over to meet us. He put out his hand and I took it. His grip was firm and I felt that he could crush my hand if he wanted to. Before I could say anything to him, he looked at Mom and told her, "You did a good job." Then he turned around and we followed him to the house. In the doorway he hugged her. I joined them uninvited and he put an arm around me, the three of us standing there silently for a long time.

Mom left to go find a motel room. It was just me and him.

"How do you like the place?"

"It's nice," I said. It was cleaner and better organized than I had expected. We sat at his kitchen table. I noticed a small painting of white Jesus on the wall.

"So the gist of your agenda down here, in seeing me, is an attempt to figure me out?"

I could only nod my head and mumble. His West Virginia dialect actually made him sound erudite, like a professor. Mom had warned that his sisters' stories weren't always reliable, but perhaps he really did have a PhD in psychology. Mom did say that he had spent something like nine years bouncing in and out of various schools with the GI Bill, but she thought that his studies had been too scattered to amount to any degree. "All right," he said. "I'm going to start out by giving you a piece of advice, and you can say that this is the only piece of advice that I ever gave you. How's that?"

"Okay."

"You ready?"

"Yeah." My voice cracked.

"Here it goes: No pussy on this earth . . . you with me?" I nodded and he said it again. "No pussy on this earth is worth the woman's game." Just like an old-school prophetic parable, he repeated himself a third time, now with thoughtful pauses to help my comprehension. "No pussy . . ." So I thought about pussy, what a pussy was and what it was worth. I had never seen one in real life and couldn't bring myself to look at one in *Playboy*, though I had once come close to touching it. Even if it scared me, I understood that a pussy was something of value.

"On this earth . . ." Then I thought about the earth and all of its billions of people, slightly more than half of them having pussies. A lot of pussies on the earth, all makes and models and years; must be some good ones out there. "Is worth the woman's game," he concluded. In his autobiography, Malcolm X said that he could never trust a woman more than 25 percent. They all had games. I considered the devious white girl from his hustler days, and the girls I knew at DeSales. Shannon, Bridget, all the girls I masturbated to. I remembered Melissa trying to seduce me away from my studies and that drunken Tracy girl on New Year's putting my hand in her pants. The girls appeared as in a lightning-fast montage, like in the movie when Malcolm reflects back on all the Caucasians from his story and realizes that yes, the white man is the Devil. Wesley could see the truth sinking in. "Woman," he added with his fullest authority, "is the true nigger of the world."

"Okay," I said, paralyzed by the word.

"The black man is not the true nigger of the world, because in some places the black man is king. But the woman is a nigger wherever she goes."

"I could see that." The shock wore off and I grew ashamed that I couldn't fight him, that something kept me in the chair.

"You hear me? That's what it means to be a bitch. When you're a bitch, you're the nigger's nigger. I'm having coffee; would you like some?"

"No thanks." He got up and opened the cupboard to get a cup. The insides of his cupboard doors were covered with taped-up clippings from pornographic magazines. The women arched their backs and opened their legs, sometimes holding open their pink labia; or they bent over, again arching their backs, to show off their wide gaping anuses. They stared at me with awful looks in their eyes—I couldn't tell if they were having fun or being tortured. There was one who clearly seemed to love it. She posed in a close-up with a brutal cock in her face. It had a swollen purple helmet head that looked mean like a weapon, a genuine instrument of destruction engineered only to hurt people. A string of sperm bridged from its tip to her lips, and a thick white blob dangled from her chin.

"You like my girls?" I smiled and looked away. By then it had been five minutes since Mom left. "You want to know the story of your mother and myself?" he asked while pouring the coffee.

"Sure," I said. Then I realized that she had been in this kitchen with us while his girls were hiding in the cupboard. It seemed that this wronged her in some way.

"The story of your mother and I begins before she was born. I was seven years old and your mother appeared to me. She was there in front of me, like you are right now. She came to me and I knew that she was mine. She was mine before she was born." He drank from his cup. "By the way, how's she doing now?"

"Good. Real good."

"How are her parents? They still alive?"

"They're good."

"You know, any and every accusation they might deliver to you against me is completely unfounded."

"Okay."

"How about her brother Danny?"

"He's married and has four kids. Two boys, two girls."

"I'm going to tell you something about Danny now. Sometimes a man needs to get his ass kicked, you understand?"

"I think so."

"Your uncle Danny is someone who needs to get his ass kicked."

"Okay."

"Now where do you lean religiously?" I was hoping he wouldn't ask, because I couldn't lie about it.

"Muslim," I told him. He gave me the once-over as though he had missed some detail of my appearance that would have given it away.

"You don't like niggers, do you? Do you like niggers?"

"I guess I don't really have a problem with them," I mumbled, unable to look him in the eye.

"I am what you would call a racial separatist. I have found there to be profound psychological differences between the white man and the black man that prevent them from living together."

"Oh."

"I don't like niggers. You can call that white nationalism. You can call me a militant or whatever you want to call me."

"Okay."

"There was this woman talking about the black people this, and the black people that, and I walked into that room and I said to her: Look, nobody wants to hear about the black people! And then she shut up."

I felt so nauseous that he could read it on my face. "Dr. Pepper's what you need," he said.

"What?"

"You don't feel good?"

"My stomach hurts."

"You need Dr. Pepper; it's good for that."

"Okay."

"So what's 'Muslim' all about?"

"One God." We missed a beat as he waited for me to elaborate, but I drew a blank.

"Fair enough," he replied. "You know about the Ku Klux Klan?"

"Yeah."

"You know what the Ku Klux Klan calls its book?"

"What do they call it?"

"The Kloran."

"I didn't know that."

"Now I'm going to tell you something about the Catholic Church," he said. "Are you ready?"

"Sure."

"I'm going to ask you a question. If I'm right, you're going to be my friend. If I'm wrong, all bets are off. Okay?"

"Okay."

"Wait a minute." He looked around for a scrap of paper, took a pen from his pocket and wrote something down. Then he folded the paper and gave it to me. "Here you go," he said. "I'm going to ask you a question, and then you can find the answer right there and tell me if you're my friend."

"What's the question?" I asked, holding the answer in my hands.

"Is the Pope Catholic?"

"I don't know," I said. Wesley gestured to the paper. I unfolded it to read in bold capital letters, "NO, HE'S QUEER."

"Can you give me some skin on that?" he asked with his hand out. I slapped it and we were now friends. "All right, let's get you some Dr. Pepper."

We got in his truck and went to the gas station. "I'm going to get five dollars of gas," he said. "You go in and pay." He gave me the money and I left him standing at the pump. Bringing my Dr. Pepper to the counter, I told the girl, "My *dad's* getting five dollars' gas," as though bragging, making sure that she understood who I had out there.

"That Dr. Pepper will settle your stomach," he told me in the truck. When we got back he made a bed for me. Lying in the dark with my eyes open, I thought of all the stories I had been told as though they had taken place in that house. For a second I wondered if Wesley would kill me in my sleep, then decided that it didn't matter since I was Muslim. For a Muslim to fear another human being was almost like shirk, the worst sin in Islam, the worshipping of others than Allah. I couldn't ascribe power over my life to anyone or anything but my Creator.

My eyes closed but I stayed awake for some time. That night was the first that I could really see myself as others might have: people at DeSales, Nan and Gramps, teachers back in junior high. How would I look at someone like me throwing himself on the floor to get a laugh, pretending to idolize Charles Manson, hanging out in the creeks and bus stations, concocting new names for himself, and marching up and down the halls looking mean? Everything I had done or tried to be was a lame joke, including my attempt at being a Muslim. I didn't know what Islam was; I hadn't stepped foot inside a mosque or even met a Muslim in real life. But if somehow I could go from being this creepy little bastard, "born in the mouth of a dragon" as Dr. Kennedy put it, to being a *real* Muslim, wouldn't that be a story? People would say, "Look at that mixed-up kid and what Islam did for him. Allah saved him from his crazy neo-Nazi father—he must have been special, destined for something great." And then I could be a Malcolm X for white boys in trailer parks, Allah's Mercy shining through my life.

WESLEY DIDN'T HAVE a shower or bathtub, so I just took a washcloth and scrubbed my body with it—but not too thoroughly since he had no hot water.

He fixed me breakfast: eggs, toast, and bacon. I looked at the bacon. It smelled good and tasted good and I made sure to enjoy every bite of it as long as I could, since this was going to be the last bacon I'd ever eat in my life. When I'd finally go to a mosque and take shahadah—bearing witness that there was only one God, and Muhammad was His messenger—this particular act of eating pork, along with all of my other sins, would be erased from the record.

"Do you still live in Geneva?" asked Wesley.

"Actually we live in Phelps now, but I go to school in Geneva."

"You go to the Catholic school?"

"Yeah."

"I'm going to tell you something about Geneva," he said. "The citizens of that town hate themselves."

"I believe it."

"There's a very specific reason, and you can accept this or not. It's fine by me either way. This has to do with Nazi doctors and scientists who fled Germany at the end of World War II. They went to Geneva, you hear me? Geneva was a center of operations for these people."

"I didn't know that."

"You can accept this or not; I don't need you to accept it. Now listen: These Nazi scientists, okay, they're continuing forward with their experiments and they are performing these experiments on minority children in basements on Exchange Street."

"Oh my god," I said, performing amazement to keep him going.

"Now everyone in town knows what's happening, but they're not ready to accept it or deal with it. When they see the missing minority children's pictures on the milk cartons, they know what it is. But they're not ready for that thought, so they bury it down, and their guilty consciences spread throughout the town, completely taking over."

"Wow."

"Geneva is full of terrible personalities and terrible attitudes. That's their collective guilt rising to the surface." It did make for a good myth to explain why Geneva was so rotten, but I couldn't tell where Wesley was coming from; I thought he *liked* Nazis.

"How do you know this stuff?" I asked.

"I have the authority of my experience. I've been around, you understand? I met the president, I stood as close to him as I am to you right now." He looked down to measure the distance between us.

"Which one?"

"Eisenhower."

"How'd you meet him?"

"I was an MP; I was standing by the door. I was here, the door was right there, and he walked in through the door."

HE DROVE ME around to meet some of my aunts and uncles and cousins. One of his sisters had a lot of trees around her house. I never caught her name. We walked outside and Wesley spotted a deer. His sister's lean black dog ran after it in vain, Wesley walking ahead of us to watch. The doe skipped out of the dog's reach without really trying.

"None of us were born in a hospital," his sister told me. "David was the first."

"Was that the norm back then?"

"Sure. And when your dad was born, the labor took a whole week. Mom was just lying there in the house for days and days, no doctor or nothin.'"

"Really," I said, missing the point.

"Yeah, that might have done something." Then I understood. "He was always different. I was in school with him and he always went off on his own thing, you know what I mean?"

"I think so."

"A couple of months ago he showed up and told me, very seriously you know, 'One of your blonde-haired grandsons and blonde-haired granddaughters are gonna get together, and they're gonna form a gang.' But I don't have any blonde grandchildren! Where does he come up with that?"

Wesley took me to the gas station at the time that Mom had appointed, so that she could call me at the pay phone and see how we were doing.

"How do you identify your heritage?" he asked me that night.

"Irish, I guess. On Mom's side."

"We are Austrian; that's our heritage. We are of the Prussian Empire. You're Frederick the Great."

"What do you mean?"

"That's who you are; you are identified as him. You're of the Prussian Empire; it would pass on through to you."

"So I'm Frederick the Great . . . reincarnated?"

"I'd prefer not to use that term," he said. In bed I'd lie awake and try to figure out what it meant, why he would see Frederick the Great in me. The Prussian Empire was still a few volumes ahead in the Durant books.

In the morning Wesley gave me a copy of his story, "Harley Hill," on the same yellow legal paper that he had used to write my mom.

"My handwriting's pretty bad," he said, "so I'm going to read it to you first." He put on his glasses and pushed them to the edge of his nose. I just sat there and took it in. "Harley Hill" read like a poem and told the story of two kids on a motorcycle, a guy and a girl, riding through North Carolina in October. "One Percenters," he read, then put the pages down. "Okay, before I proceed, I need to explain to you what a One Percenter is. That's biker language. The American Motorcyclist Association said that ninety-nine percent of bikers were productive, law-abiding members of society, so I'm talking about the other one percent." These two One Percenter bikers are riding and the leaves start falling and the girl screams that she wants out, she wants to die. The guy tells her, *Okay bitch, you want out? You're gonna get out.*

"Throw off your helmet," read Wesley from the page. "Open up the gas. Lean way back, listen to them pipes blast. That curve up ahead, you know it's gonna be your last. Lay it way over now and dig that screamin' mill. You're gonna ride forever when you make that impossible turn . . . onto Harley Hill." He then folded the yellow legal paper to fit inside an envelope. I didn't say anything.

Mom came by and the three of us went in two separate cars to a diner for breakfast. The booths were made from old church pews. Mom and I sat on the same side. From across the table, Wesley explained a new story that he was writing. "It fits into the categorization of a comic book character," he said. "His name is Impossible Man."

Impossible Man's special power was self-explanatory: He could make impossible things possible. Once a disbeliever declared something to be "impossible," Impossible Man would swoop down from the sky and make it happen.

When the disbelievers proclaimed that it would not be possible for Impossible Man to find a wife, of course he shut them up by doing just that. Her name was Possible Wife. Then the disbelievers said that Impossible Man and Possible Wife could never have a son, that in fact it was *impossible*. So Possible Wife gave birth to a boy who they named Torker.

As the boy grew older, his incredible displays of strength earned him acclaim as "Torker, Strongest Man in the World." For his greatest feat, he announced his plans to lift the Empire State Building with his bare hands and rotate it three hundred and sixty degrees before setting it back down. Reporters from all over the world came to cover the challenge, with talking heads on every television channel offering their analyses of the event's importance. Torker gave sound bites and posed for pictures before powdering his hands and approaching the Empire State Building. He took his time finding a proper grip, breathed deep, and heaved with all his might.

The skyscraper wouldn't move.

He breathed again and pulled, but the Immovable Object would not submit. Then Torker tried a third time and failed, finally causing a heckler to jeer, "It's IMPOSSIBLE!" At that moment, Torker's father descended from the heavens to tell his son that anything was possible. Torker then not only lifted the Empire State Building but pushed it high over his head in a military press before successfully rotating it three hundred and sixty degrees.

When it came time to go, Wesley made the waitress take his money right there at the booth. To go up and pay after eating, he said, ruined the experience. In the parking lot, he shook my hand and said good luck. Then I got in Mom's car and he watched us leave him again.

NEITHER OF US said anything until we crossed the threshold of an interstate ramp, placing us onto the long road that would lead home.

"How was it?" she asked.

"He's a lot to deal with. I couldn't have been there any longer than we were."

"Try five years," she said with a smile.

"I can't begin to imagine."

"You know what made me leave him?"

"You told me," I said. "When Jim Jones got all of his followers to kill themselves—"

"It wasn't just that, bud. I had given up on both of us. We were starving, you were banging your head on the floor, and I just went through the motions to get us through the day, but I was gone. I was *so* gone and I thought that you were too; you were only a baby but you felt everything."

"So how'd we get out?" I asked.

"You know that he used to put a knife to your throat, right?"

"Yeah."

"One day he did that—I don't remember what he wanted me to confess to that time, but I said whatever he wanted— and then he put you back in your crib. A little while later he picked you up again, and you know what you did?"

"What?"

"You bit him. On the neck, as hard as you could, so hard that he had to put you down."

"No way," I said.

"Here's this little baby who can fight," she said. "You still had that, I don't know what to call it, that *spark* inside. So I had to fight too. And that's what got us out."

I pushed back my seat and put in a Public Enemy tape. Chuck D was angry, Flavor Flav was Flavor Flav. After some time I turned down the volume.

"Islam is the solution for all problems," I told Mom. "None of this ever would have happened in a Muslim country, because parents help their kids find suitable partners. If Nan and Gramps were Muslim, you wouldn't have been left on your own to find a husband. They would have been there for you and helped you find a good man—a man who would really protect you and provide for you and respect you. That's why Muslims have stable homes and American divorce rates are through the roof."

"That sounds reasonable," Mom said flatly. I couldn't tell whether she really meant it or was only half listening, maybe concentrating on taking the right highway exits and such, or numbing her brain to get through my rambling like she had with my father. Either way, I kept on going: "Family means nothing to Americans. An American family builds a whole life together and then throws it in the garbage. Americans don't know how to love each other because they don't love or even respect themselves! And of course they don't love or respect God, not like Muslims. Muslims are always remembering God, and that's why a Muslim man would never mistreat his wife—he honors her and protects her; he cares for her. They respect their children, and their children respect them. We should just tear everything down and start over, you know what I mean?"

witness

10

I still had a few weeks before school
started, but couldn't wait to get back
and show everyone that I wasn't a lunatic
anymore. Bumping into Mike Sweeney at Wegmans, when he
asked what I was up to I answered, "I met my dad."

"That's cool," he said. "Did it help?"

"Probably so."

WESLEY CALLED SHORTLY after our trip to discuss my health.

"Lethargic responses are a sign, a signal," he said. "While I
am not attempting to produce a diagnostician's offering here,
I am suggesting a circumstance with both the respiratory system and the epidermal neurological system." He recommended
that after bathing, I apply a special balm—he'd send me the
ingredients, he promised—and wear full-length pajamas,
as well as braces on the "points of the body that define the

form." He even claimed to know a doctor in my area who could help me out, and strongly advised that I make an appointment. "His name is Carl Jung," he said. "He'll be in the yellow pages." When Mom told me that Jung was actually a famous psychologist who had died more than thirty years ago, I just took it as Wesley trying to give me another veiled message in his spooky mystical way. Perhaps he wanted me to read Jung but didn't want to come out and say it. Or maybe he really did think that Jung had an office in upstate New York and could cure my respiratory/neurological problems, who knows. For whatever reason Wesley had in mind, Mom did buy me a collection of Jung's writings.

I liked Jung; his psychology, at least what I read of it with the symbols and archetypes and universal subconscious, seemed more religion than science. There was something revelatory about him. I could see his appeal for Wesley, who lived in a schizophrenic's world of symbolic interactions.

IN JUNIOR YEAR Fat Ed taught religion, with an ostensible focus on Church history. Religion class was a sham every year, but even worse with Fat Ed: He spent forty minutes each day rambling on about Notre Dame football and his gritty Irish upbringing in Hell's Kitchen, then had us open our books for the last five minutes while he read verbatim from the text about obscure saints and Vatican councils. The beautiful thing about Catholic schools is that the state can't come in and hold your religious instruction to any standards.

I looked ahead in our textbook and found that soon we would be approaching Islam and the Crusades. My assigned seat was in the front row, barely three feet from his podium; as soon as the word "Islam" came out of his mouth, I'd be right there to take Fat Ed down. Could he have known what was coming—that the weird kid in the front row was training for him like a prizefighter?

The day of the Crusades chapter I sat on the edge of my seat while he droned on about the film *Rudy*, terrified that the bell would ring without him even cracking open the textbook. He did know, he *had* to, and now he was killing time, dancing around until saved by the bell. When he finally brought out the book with just minutes to spare, I clenched my fists on my desk and gave him the Malcolm X stare-down.

Fat Ed read the text like he always did, without even bothering to look up from the page to at least pretend that he was teaching us. Then he closed the book and finally turned in my direction.

"Now Islam," he said straight to me, "they have a lot of idols." I raised my hand as a formality.

"No, they don't," I said.

"Well, in Mecca they have idols."

"The pagans did in pre-Islamic times but Muhammad destroyed them, peace be upon him." I was so quick with my answer you'd think we had rehearsed our lines.

"But the Muslims have the Ka'ba, which they believe is Allah."

"No, they don't."

"Yes, they do."

"The Ka'ba was a house of worship built by Abraham, peace be upon him."

"Okay," Fat Ed huffed as he adjusted his pants. "Now Muhammad had a son named Fatima—"

"Fatima was his daughter."

"He had a son too."

"Died in infancy."

"Now Fatima was in charge of everything—"

"No, she wasn't," I said. Then the bell rang. I got up without acknowledging Fat Ed and went to my next class, smiling ear to ear.

"Way to go, Mike," said a girl who otherwise never spoke to me.

"What?"

"You made a fool out of Ed."

"You whipped his ass!" exclaimed a boy.

"Thanks," I said with a warm but diplomatic laugh, the way that I thought El-Hajj Malik El-Shabazz would have handled it. If I wasn't a real Muslim yet, I had proven myself at least ready for the next step.

The nearest mosque was nearly an hour away, in Henrietta, a suburb of Rochester. I figured that because of the Malcolm X movie, it must have been getting lots of calls from poseurs trying to be Muslim without really knowing their stuff. If I was going to call the mosque, I'd need a legit reason.

"As-salamu alaikum, Islamic Center," said a frail accented voice on the other end of the phone.

"Wa-alaikum as-salam," I said, confident that I had said it right from hearing it in the movie. "I was just wondering what month it is on the Islamic calendar."

"It is Ramadan, brother."

"Thank you." Then I just blurted, "I am converting to Islam," and instantly regretted it. *Now it's all fucked and he's going to think I'm just some punk kid—*

"Al-hamdulilah, brother!" I could feel through the phone that he was smiling. "You should come to the masjid so we can talk, insha'Allah."

"Yes, I would like that very much. As-salamu alaikum."

"Wa-alaikum as-salam wa rahmatullahi wa barakatuh," the frail voice answered.

"Bye," I said and hung up. My body shook. Whoever that was, he was a real Muslim. I felt more nervous after the conversation than before it, nervous only because I hadn't ruined it and would have to keep going.

Mom took a half day off from work to drive me to the mosque. She picked me up from DeSales at lunch and we hit the road. I kept my tie on.

My first visit to a mosque, the way I envisioned it in the car, would go down like the scene from *Malcolm X* in which Malcolm meets Elijah Muhammad for the first time. A Muslim swings open the heavy wooden door for Malcolm, and behind it stands the Messenger, his back turned, his little frame filled with Islam's power. On the road to Henrietta I remembered the shame that kept Malcolm's head low as he walked into that room, the fear in his trembling steps, and the ones that I would make as I came to admit the ignorance in which I had lived—Tracy the New Year's Eve girl, Shannon the cheerleader that I had scared to death, all the nonsense, the destructive emotions that I had cultivated, the pork eating, the weirdness, any negative impressions of Islam that I had given others for being such a freak, any disrespect I had ever displayed to my mother or grandparents, and of course the masturbations. There had been a lot of masturbation.

The Islamic Center of Rochester was a concrete gray cube, nondescript compared to gorgeous mosques that I had seen in books. I saw no domes or minarets; there was something that looked like it could have been a minaret, but it wasn't functional and looked as much like a tall chimney. The parking lot was empty except for two cars.

I knocked on the wooden door, then figured that it was okay

to go in. I held the door open for Mom. In the lobby was a sign asking us to take off our shoes and cubbyholes to put them in. Straight ahead, behind glass doors, was a big open room soaked in sunlight with plain white walls and tall windows. A tiled niche in the wall, the mihrab, indicated the direction of Mecca. To our immediate right was the office.

"As-salamu alaikum," I said quietly, standing in the open doorway.

"Wa alaikum as-salam," said a smiling South Asian man, middle-aged, clean-shaven with curly hair.

"My name is Michael; I called the other day."

"Nice to meet you, Michael. My name is Iftekhar." We shook hands.

"This is my mother," I said. She offered him her hand and I wanted to shoot myself for not instructing her about Muslim manners, but Iftekhar showed no offense. They shook hands and introduced themselves. Iftekhar had us sit and then asked to hear my story.

"I started reading," I told him. "First it was the *Autobiography of Malcolm X*, and I wanted to do what he did, you know, just read everything that I could . . . and I guess it just went from there; Islam seemed to make a lot of sense."

"The most important thing in Islam is that we worship only God," he said. "There is no god but God, nothing that deserves worship but God. In the Arabic language, we call Him Allah, but this is only the same God that the Jews and Christians worship, the God of Abraham. We believe in all of the prophets—Noah, Abraham, Moses, Jesus, and the last prophet was Muhammad. Peace be upon them all."

This was pretty basic stuff; why would he tell me this? Did he think I didn't know what I was doing? He could have been doing it for Mom's sake, but it still felt good to hear. These were the simple truths of Islam, and Iftekhar took his time on them, even explaining the psychological significance of washing before prayer. It sounded even truer coming from a real-life person than from *Islam in Focus*.

He turned to my mother. "And Susan, how do you feel about your son choosing Islam?"

"I'm proud of Michael," she said. "He's always reading, always learning something new. He tells me that the day is wasted if he doesn't learn anything."

"You know what the Prophet said about seeking knowledge?" Iftekhar asked me. "He said to seek knowledge from the cradle to the grave. And he said, seek knowledge even if you have to go all the way to China to find it."

"The Catholic Church opposed the invention of the printing press," I told Mom.

"Brother Michael," said Iftekhar, "do you have wudhu?"

"I made it before coming."

"Good. Let's go pray."

He led us into the big room—the masjid, he called it, which was the proper Arabic term for a mosque—and held the glass door open for us. I made sure to enter right foot first, as I had read somewhere that it was better, and hoped that he noticed. Iftekhar picked a random spot in the room and started a silent prayer. It was a sunna prayer, not one of the required five daily prayers but a good practice anyway. I stood right next to him and made my own while Mom stayed near the back wall.

Having perfected the prayers all alone in Phelps, I still knew nothing of praying with other Muslims. The whole time I couldn't think of anything beyond doing it right. After completing my prayer, I stayed in sitting position and waited for Iftekhar to finish his, internally wrought with fear that I had prayed too fast and failed the test and now these real Muslims would have nothing to do with me.

After completing the official part of his prayer, Iftekhar seemed to be still praying, mouthing words to himself with his hands cupped in front of him. Then he put his hands up, as though washing his face, and rose to his feet. I stood with him. He called my mother over and showed us around the masjid, though there wasn't much to show: no statues, no images, nothing too fancy, just some calligraphy on hanging plates and in the mihrab tile. I wondered what it said.

Then we were joined by about a dozen children of various backgrounds coming into the mosque, none of them as pale as me, the girls with their hair covered in hijab—the real hijab of real Muslims! Behind them was a skinny, bearded South Asian man who introduced himself as Dr. Shafiq. I recognized his voice from the phone. His handshake was relaxed, almost limp. I watched him shake hands with Mom. Iftekhar informed him that I had already learned wudhu and the prayers on my own. "Mash'Allah," said Dr. Shafiq. I didn't know what that meant, but it sounded positive and did have "Allah" in it.

Dr. Shafiq sat us all down in a circle and explained my story to the kids. I sat between Dr. Shafiq and my mother.

"This is brother Michael," he said. "Brother Michael has spent a great deal of time studying all the religions, and he has decided to embrace Islam. Al-hamdulilah, brother Michael." *Al-hamdulilah* meant "all praise is due to Allah," I knew that from my prayers. "Brother Michael, please tell us how you came to Islam."

"I, uh, I became interested in Malcolm X and read his auto-biography, and then it just led me to keep on reading, I got all sorts of books about history and philosophy and religion and, uh, I came to Islam and . . ." Dr. Shafiq could see that I was nervous and just said that it was "very wonderful" how I had devoted so much time to studying at an early age and that my mother had accepted my decision. Then he had me repeat the shahadah, the declaration of faith, first in Arabic, then in English: I bear witness that there is no god but God, and Muhammad is the messenger of God. With those words I became Muslim, as real a Muslim as anyone.

Dr. Shafiq, Iftekhar, Mom, and I left the children in the masjid and went back to the office, where we were joined by another brother, a big copper-complexioned Jamaican in orange leather jacket and sturdy kufi skullcap. He exchanged greetings of *as-salamu alaikum* with each of us, *hello* with Mom, then sat with a large leather book in his lap. After gathering from our conversation that I was a new Muslim, he interjected himself: "You understand now, brother, that your shahadah is a contract. Praying five times a day for the rest of your life is no little thing, brother."

"Yes," I answered.

"Does he have a name?" the man asked Dr. Shafiq and Iftekhar.

"Not yet," said Iftekhar. I was too ashamed to say anything about Malik al-Kafi Khan.

"What's your name right now?" the Jamaican asked me.

"Michael."

"Mikail," said Dr. Shafiq.

"That's the Arabiyya," said the Jamaican, somehow pulling three syllables out of the *-ail*, like *Me-kye-ee-al*.

Then a round, balding man, who I hadn't even noticed was there, said "Muhammad."

"Mikail Muhammad," said Dr. Shafiq.

"Brother Mikail Muhammad, my name is Siddique," said the Jamaican. We shook hands. "Can you read Qur'an?"

"Uh, not in Arabic."

"We have a set of audio tapes and a booklet you can borrow," said Dr. Shafiq. "It will help you to learn the alphabets." He dug them out of his desk and handed them to me, along with a VHS copy of the great Muslim movie *The Message*, starring Anthony Quinn as the Prophet's uncle Hamza. Iftekhar went to the shelves behind Dr. Shafiq's desk and pulled out a big book called *The 100*.

"Brother," he said, turning to a page near the beginning, "I just wanted to show you this while you were here. This is by a Jewish man, Michael Hart, ranking the one hundred most influential people in history. You see he ranks Prophet Muhammad, sallallaho alayhe wa salam, number one, most influence out of anyone.

"Most historical personas are influential in just one area. They're military leaders like Hannibal, political statesmen like Caesar, religious teachers like Buddha, you know what I mean? Or literary figures like Homer and Shakespeare, or social reformers like Martin Luther King, Jr. But Muhammad, peace and blessings be upon him, Muhammad belongs in the top five of each of these categories, so he's easily the most important human being of all time."

Siddique then explained that Islam was not simply a religion but, as I had told Mom on the way back from West Virginia, a perfect way of life. It touched on everything: not just morals and family but also government, law, and economics. As a Muslim, you don't put away your religion for six days of the week and then dust it off to bring out on Sunday; a Muslim is mindfully, actively Muslim every minute of every day, in everything that he or she does.

"And we are presently in the month of Ramadan," said Dr.

Shafiq. "You know, in this month we fast from the sunrise to the sunset."

"It's a very special time for Muslims," said Iftekhar to my mother.

"Because you have just accepted Islam," continued Dr. Shafiq, "al-hamdulilah, you are not responsible for the month up to this point. Starting tomorrow, insha'Allah, you should take up the fast." I didn't know what *insha'Allah* meant, but wasn't going to ask.

"The Prophet, peace and blessings be upon him," said Siddique, "broke his fasts with dates, so it's a good practice to pick up. Everything we do reminds us of Allah and His Prophet."

They all gave me their phone numbers. I shook their hands and took the books and tapes, along with an Islamic book catalog and a schedule showing me the times for each of the five daily prayers (and the exact minute to break my fast every day). When we left I held the door for Mom again. She went first and then I followed her outside, reborn back into the world as Mikail Muhammad.

actual facts

11

Allah gave signs to those with understanding. The Arabic word for sign or proof, *ayat*, was what we called a verse of the Qur'an; but in reality, Allah filled all of creation with ayats. If you look at a fetus in the womb, its position resembles that of a Muslim bent over in prayer! And I read about how Allah's Name was popping up in all kinds of places. A little girl in England found it in her beans. A beekeeper in Turkey found it in a honeycomb. They found Allah's Name in watermelons, tomatoes, and fish. Astronomers even saw it on the moon.

The proof of Islam was everywhere. I read about how the Qur'an was a thousand years ahead of modern science, and the best minds in the western world had no choice but to recognize and submit. There was a famous American scientist, former advisor to Jimmy Carter, who discovered that most of a mountain was actually underground and shaped like a wedge, which served to help steady the earth's crust; but then someone showed him the verse of the Qur'an saying, "and He has set up on the earth mountains standing firm, lest it should shake with you." Stunned that his scientific work had been anticipated fourteen centuries ago in the Arabian desert, he immediately became Muslim. Another story had Jacques Cousteau lecturing about how the waters of the Atlantic Ocean and Mediterranean Sea did not mix, causing a Muslim in the audience to explain that this "advanced" knowledge was already in the Qur'an. As the story goes, Cousteau immediately recognized that the Qur'an could not have been written by a man, and he bore witness that Muhammad was a prophet of God.

EVEN BETTER THAN proving Islam with science was proving it with the holy books of other religions—you could use a Christian's own Bible against him to show the truth of Islam! Ahmed Deedat, a South African scholar who had memorized both the Qur'an and Bible, revealed that Muhammad was mentioned by *name* in the Song of Solomon, chapter 5, verse 16: In the English translation it said "altogether lovely," but the ancient Hebrew word for that was "Muhammadim." The truth was right there; all you had to do was show it to the world.

Whenever I read something cool I had to call Siddique and tell him about it.

"Did you hear about the mathematical code of the Qur'an?" I asked him. "This guy ran all the verses through a computer and found the number 19 running through the entire Qur'an; it's totally unexplainable—"

"Brother," he said, "there is an integrity to Islam that

makes it stand on its own. Once you really have it, you don't have to prove it." So I put away the gimmick books and wondered if I really had it or not. What was Islam's integrity? I had already grown ashamed of those early Malik al-Kafi Khan daydreams, tearing down the Qadhafi and blind sheikh from my locker and covering the giant Ayatollah in my bedroom with a *National Geographic* map of Mars. Skipping lunch at DeSales for Ramadan, I learned that fasting wasn't just deprivation; more than just *not* eating, fasting felt like a proactive thing; it was what you *did*. I stayed mindful of it. Eating dates when the sun came down and then doing my Maghrib prayer alone, I felt what hadn't been there before: a calm in my stomach that spread up to my neck and shoulders. It might have been the same grounded peace that I heard in Dr. Shafiq's voice—or at least the start of it, since Dr. Shafiq had been cultivating it all his life, and I had just started.

Juggling two jobs, sometimes three, and still with that boyfriend from the battery factory, Mom wasn't home much, leaving me alone to practice that peace on the prayer rug she bought me. The prayer rug was green and had an image of a gold-domed mosque on it.

Peace. This until the rise of morn, as the Qur'an says. Iftekhar's brother told me that the word *Islam* even came from the Arabic word for peace, *salam*. Siddique explained that this wasn't true in a linguistic sense—two words sounding alike didn't always make them related terms—but he could still see beauty in the idea. *Islam* meant submission; in submission, we find peace. In obedience, we find love.

That was Islam's integrity: The more I practiced it, the greater space in my life that I gave to Allah, the truer it became. And I could feel the difference. I was Muslim because

I *believed* in God, because my heart had arrived at the truth—but I knew that it didn't get there on its own. Mash'Allah.

I couldn't be sure when that moment really happened. They say that you're a Muslim when you make the declaration of faith in front of witnesses. For me, that might have only been the planting of the seed.

Muhammad, too, had previously been an abstract concept or collection of concepts. I had read about all the varied greatnesses of the Prophet: Muhammad the benevolent ruler dealing justly with all of his citizens; Muhammad creating a model society; Muhammad the philosopher and defender of the poor, the ideal husband, the equitable businessman; Muhammad the judge, the liberator of slaves, the antiracist, the perfect man. He was also a father. In my little book *Daughters of the Holy Prophet*, I read about Fatima watching him ridiculed by the pagans, who spread camel intestines on his head while he prayed; and I read of Zainab, who was struck with a stick and knocked off her camel while pregnant.

I could feel sorrow for the Prophet in ways that I could never have felt for Christ as a Catholic; if Jesus was God, what did it mean that he was crucified? What could anyone take away from God, and how could you really hurt Him? But the Prophet and his daughters were only human beings; their suffering was real and their losses mattered. I pictured these girls screaming and crying—Fatima was only eight or nine at the time of the intestines episode—and their father accepting whatever God gave him. The unbelievers made plans, he knew, but Allah was the best of planners.

It was coming; I could feel it. Maybe the first hint of it somewhere inside, pushing its way out. I was afraid of noticing it, as though noticing it would push it back down. I was going to cry.

Thoughts got in the way and I lost the feeling, so I went back to whatever had made me feel it in the first place, the Prophet's daughters and their suffering and their sad father enduring it all for God's sake, and I forced my brain on it as hard as I could, waiting until the twitch and tingle came under my eyelids . . .

Crying for the Prophet was like a minor physical trauma; not to disrespect him or the experience, but I could only compare it to bodily ejections like vomiting or orgasms. There was that initial tension, when my condition transformed; the escalation, the build; the paralyzing moment at which I sensed it on its way, ready to propel out of me—the point at which it becomes an involuntary function—and then the all-consuming flood, the release, the relief. The suffering of the Prophet and his family would enter into my body, take hold of my own emotional poisons—whatever hurt I had from somewhere else—overwhelm them, transform them, and pull them out with the tears. To cry for Muhammad's daughters was to cry for myself in a less selfish way. Afterwards I felt better about everything.

ONE AFTERNOON I happened to call and Iftekhar had special news. A qari from Pakistan would be coming to Rochester for the summer, and I was invited to stay with him and his associate.

"What's a qari?" I asked.

"A qari is someone trained in the recitation of Qur'an. The Qur'an, you know, it is meant to be recited with a beautiful voice. This qari is a master of reciting and is coming to teach the community." And he was a near-celebrity in Pakistan, since he served as muezzin at Faisal Mosque—the largest mosque in the world—and his performance of the adhan came on national television five times every day.

Mom wouldn't let me live with the Qari unless I passed all my classes and evaded summer school. I did the bare minimum—how could I really care about French when I was teaching myself Arabic at home?—and after finals she drove me to the Qari's apartment. It was in a suburban development of apartment houses, almost like a neighborhood unto itself and with its own public swimming pool, and a healthy mile-or-so walk from the Islamic Center.

The Qari's associate opened the door and seemed happy to see me. He wore a white button-down shirt and black pants and introduced himself as Mukhtar, then brought us to the kitchen where the Qari was making tea. The Qari was short and stocky, with graying hair and beard. He wore a shalwar kameez, baggy white pants with a matching shirt that went down to his knees.

"As-salamu alaikum, brother Mikail," he said with our handshake. There was an instant sweetness coming out of him as he smiled his greeting.

"Wa alaikum as-salam," I answered. At the time I was still more comfortable returning the salam than giving it first. Mom gave me a hug and then left me there in my new Muslim life.

"You here, you learn Qur'an?" asked the Qari. I nodded. "Very good brother, you new Muslim? You just Muslim, now? Al-hamdulilah, brother. Mash'Allah, very good." He didn't speak English as well as his associate Mukhtar, who had come to the States essentially to help him get around, but he taught me a new sura of the Qur'an: al-Kauthar, just three short verses about a fountain waiting for us in paradise. He took the time to see that I pronounced the Arabic right. Throughout the evening, as various brothers from the community came

by to practice their reading with him, the Qari would periodi-
cally drop everything and give me a surprise quiz to keep al-
Kauthar fresh in my brain.

There were several of us in the apartment when it came
time for Isha, the last prayer of the night. It was customary
for the man who knew the most Qur'an to lead the prayer;
naturally that was the Qari (everyone called him Qari Saheb,
which meant "Mr. Qari" or "Qari sir"), so we all formed a line
behind him. In the parts of the prayer where the imam would
recite a short passage from the Qur'an, the Qari chose al-
Kauthar for my benefit. After the brothers left and I went to
bed, I recited the lines to myself until falling asleep.

That Friday marked my first participation in a jum'aa,
Islam's congregational prayer. I was told not to go on the
Islamic Center's second floor, since on Friday it belonged to
the women. Downstairs the masjid was crowded with men
of all backgrounds, some dressed in shirts and ties, some in
shalwar kameezes or long robes, others in T-shirts and jeans
and varieties of hats, individually performing sunna prayers
or making supplications to Allah. The Qari got on the microphone and gave his glass-breaking adhan, and Dr. Shafiq came
in wearing a special brown mantle with gold trim over his
clothes. It seemed like a major event, something that couldn't
just happen every Friday. I told the brother on my right, a
middle-aged South Asian man who looked like he could have
been a doctor, that it was my first jum'aa and I didn't know
what to do. He smiled and congratulated me on accepting
Islam.

"Just do what everyone else does," he said. Before the
prayer, Dr. Shafiq stood and gave khutbah, the sermon. About
what, I didn't know—it was half in Arabic and I missed some
of the English because there was so much else for a first-timer

to take in, like being a Muslim in a room full of Muslims, or the hundreds of brothers' musks and oils blending into a single scent. When we stood up for prayer Dr. Shafiq told us to make sure our lines were straight and that we stood shoulder-to-shoulder, feet-to-feet. My pale bare feet touched almost bluish-black African feet on one side and that doctor's golden-brown feet on the other. After Dr. Shafiq recited al-Fatiha, the group's collective "AAAAAAAAAAM-MEEEEEEEEEN" was so loud and strong that my knees almost buckled.

full power

12

When you're a new Muslim who doesn't know anything, every Muslim you meet becomes your teacher and inspires a kind of awe. I couldn't dream of what it was like to be born and raised in Islam. The blinding truth, which arrived out of nowhere and changed my whole life forever, had been with them since they came into the world. The first word ever said to a newborn Muslim is *Allah*, whispered into his ear by his father. Comparing my almost-a-year of study to their whole lives, I felt like a baby who needed adults to watch out for him, to teach him how to walk and talk and count, and to keep him away from the stove.

The feeling wasn't helped at Islamic Summer Camp, since my Arabic reading abilities placed me in the little kids' class. I sat in a circle with the eight-year-olds and read for Mukhtar from my little alphabet book, making the sound for each letter and then learning to put the sounds together, while from the other side of the masjid I heard the teenagers flowing smoothly through their suras with Qari Saheb. There was even an eight-year-old girl over there, too advanced for our group. She kept her hair in a long black ponytail and always wore sparkly shalwar kameezes, and later I'd learn that she was Iftekhar's niece. Sometimes she'd listen to me read after class and correct my mistakes. "Needs work," she'd say, "but you're doing good."

I still practiced with the book and tapes that the mosque had given me, and Qari Saheb would listen to me read at the apartment. Before the second week was over, I had graduated from star reader of the little kids' class to the slowest reader among the teenagers, where instead of alphabet books we used Qur'ans with not a word of English inside. Those green-and-gold-covered Qur'ans had been given to the Islamic Center by the Saudi embassy. They had smooth pages and beautiful margins around the ayats. The words themselves were pretty and it felt good to be able to read them, though I didn't know what they said.

Some mornings Siddique would come to the apartment, and after making Fajr prayer we all took turns reading from Qur'ans with side-by-side English and Arabic. Qari Saheb corrected each of us in Arabic recitation (my turns always took the longest, since it was like trudging through a tar pit just to finish one verse), and then Siddique offered the English interpretation. A voracious reader who also lifted weights and studied martial arts, Siddique had everything that I thought a man needed. Plus he was a convert like me, and I got the sense that his pre-Islamic life had given him some kind of practical authority on the bad things in the world. Compared to the detached academic way in which born-raised Muslims like Dr. Shafiq lectured about drugs or sex, Siddique spoke like he really knew things.

As important as anything, Siddique was fearless. It's an inherent quality of the Muslim, he told us, to long for your Creator and hope for a quick exit from that which keeps you separated.

❦

SIDDIQUE TOOK US for morning runs up by the water tower, doing laps until making a mile. Only Siddique and Qari Saheb did any real running. Siddique's son Little Siddique, who was my age, Mukhtar, and I just walked most of it.

"Come on, Mikail, girly man!" the Qari joked. "Why brother, you girl?"

"We should get Dr. Shafiq running," said Siddique as they lapped us. "Qari Saheb, Dr. Shafiq needs to exercise with us, maybe put on some weight and get strong. Then he can be *full power*, Qari Saheb."

"Full power, like Cherbuzi?" asked Qari Saheb with a laugh.

"Ha-ha, yes brother. Full power, brother! Like Cherbuzi!" After the run, Siddique asked Qari Saheb if he wanted yahoodi food.

"What is?" asked the Qari.

"I'll show you yahoodi food, brother. Let's go see about some yahoodi food, it's healthy." Yahoodi food turned out to be a bagel shop. We got a big bag and took it back to Siddique's house.

"What's Cherbuzi?" I asked on the way.

"Cherbuzi!" said Siddique in the driver's seat. "That's an inside joke from Pakistan, brother. There was this king Cherbuzi, and he had four wives, so that's *full power*, brother—"

"You've been to Pakistan?"

"That's where I met the Qari. Right, brother?"

"Yes, brother!" said the Qari. Siddique then told me about the Daw'ah Academy in Islamabad, which ran a program every year for new converts from around the world. The academy was located in Faisal Mosque, a gift from King Faisal of Saudi Arabia to the people of Pakistan.

"It's beautiful," he said. "That's where Qari Saheb is muezzin."

"Yes, brother," the Qari repeated.

"Faisal has a unique design for a masjid," said Siddique. "It looks like a spaceship."

Pakistan was good for his din, he said. What's better than surrounding yourself with Islam? Going to a restaurant, you never have to ask what kind of meat you're eating; there's no pork for thousands of miles. You never have to worry about girls trying to tempt you away from Islam, and Siddique even claimed that in Pakistan he had no sexual desire at all: "After your first couple weeks in the country, you just kind of forget about it." Then I wished that I hadn't been stuck in a country where I was surrounded by kafrs, pressured towards alcohol and sex by my peers, and where my religion was disrespected at every turn.

At Siddique's house we had our yahoodi food and then took naps. Siddique and Little Siddique went to their rooms. Qari Saheb stretched out on the living room floor, while I slumped into a couch maybe five feet from him. Looking at the Qari, I remembered Iftekhar teaching me the proper etiquette for handling a Qur'an. Before reading the Qur'an, it is good practice to make wudhu. Never put anything on top of the Qur'an. In a stack of books, the Qur'an always goes on top, and always occupies the highest bookshelf. The Qari had memorized the entire Qur'an by heart; he was, in a way, a walking Qur'an, or his brain carried a Qur'an that I had to respect. So I quietly slid off the couch and joined him on the floor, almost close enough to touch him.

ASHAMED OF MY weak Arabic reading, I tried to make up for it by mastering everything else. After lunch the other kids would go outside and play basketball and I'd stay in the office, reading whatever the shelves had in English and answering Dr. Shafiq's phone. The office provided my first meaningful interaction with Sahih Bukhari, a definitive collection of hadith, *the* sayings and actions of Muhammad. Hadiths were second in importance only to the Qur'an, since the Qur'an was the Word of Allah, and hadiths were the words of Allah's final messenger.

Sahih Bukhari came in nine volumes. I was a few pages into the first one, expecting to plow through them like I did through Will Durant's books, when Iftekhar interrupted me.

"You should go outside and play," he said.

"There's so much I don't know," I pleaded. "They can go play basketball because they've been studying Islam their whole lives."

"Brother, what is it you're reading? Sahih Bukhari? You know why we read Sahih Bukhari?"

"To learn from the Prophet, sallallaho alayhe wa salam."

"To *do* as the Prophet did," he said. "Because in the Prophet, peace be upon him, Allah gave us a model for how to live in the world. Right?"

"Right."

"Well, brother, the Prophet liked to play sports and be physically fit. He enjoyed archery, horseback riding, and wrestling. So you don't have to stay in the office all day,

Mikail. Allah, subhanahu wa ta'Ala, gave you a body, not just a brain."

Outside I'd just stand by the Islamic Center's basketball hoop while the kids played. Eventually one of them invited me to take his place. I tried for about five minutes and then went back inside.

The next day I was reading Imam Ghazali's *Ihya 'Ulum al-Din* when Qari Saheb came into the office and pulled me from my chair, dragging me outside where the kids were playing soccer.

"Come, brother, come on."

"What?"

"You play."

"I was reading, I'm trying to—"

"Come, brother, you play. Mikail play."

"I can't play soccer."

"Your wife like, brother, she like strong man. Yes you play."

"My wife? I don't have a wife." He released my hand and ran off to join the game, his shalwar kameez flapping behind him, just chasing after the ball without having joined either team. I followed him in and almost got to the ball, only to have him knock me down and score a goal. The kids all laughed and cheered.

"Me, very old brother," he said, coming over to help me up. "I done, brother. You play." He walked out of the game and I stayed in. After that, I played outside every day.

Another time it was just him and me for Asr, the mid-afternoon prayer, at the apartment on a Saturday. I stood to his right, positioning my feet a few inches behind him to designate him as the leader. He pulled me over and switched us, putting himself at my right, and said, "You lead, brother."

"Me? No, Qari Saheb—"

"Brother Mikail lead, come on brother. Allahu Akbar, come on."

For the Qari, a walking Qur'an, to pray behind me, a know-nothing baby Muslim, was a minor disobedience of the Prophet's own words, but I trusted him. I looked at our feet and made the intention in my heart. Hands to my ears, *Allahu Akbar.* He put his own hands to his ears. *Allahu Akbar* served as a cue in the prayer, repeated with each movement. Whenever I said it, the Qari did what I did.

IFTEKHAR TOLD ME that a white family in the area had just accepted Islam: a husband, wife, and daughter who had their own farm. I replied with the usual *al-hamdulilah, mash'Allah*, and "may God continue to guide them."

"You should get to know the family," said Iftekhar, "and meet the daughter, insha'Allah." By then I had finally learned that *insha'Allah* meant "if God wills."

"How old is she?" I asked.

"Almost thirteen." The mom and daughter came by the Islamic Center on Friday and Dr. Shafiq set aside a classroom for us. After our introductions, he left and closed the door behind him. The mom wore all black, her blouse buttoned up to the neck; and she covered her hair with a turbanlike wrap. The daughter looked like a softer version of her.

We pulled up some tiny classroom chairs and sat facing each other. The mom did the talking for her side while the daughter studied a potential stain on her gray sweater. It was the same conversation that I'd had enough times with Muslims to skate through without effort—how I became interested in Islam, what really drew me to it, did I have a hard

time making the change—but I was still nervous. It felt like a job interview, which I guess it was.

"How did your parents feel about you being Muslim?" she asked. I knew that was coming.

"My mom's been totally cool," I answered. "She drives me to the masjid, buys me Islamic books, and never says anything against Islam." I hoped we could leave it at that.

"Mash'Allah! That's great, Mikail. That's a mercy from Allah to you."

She asked me what colleges I was considering. I told her that I hadn't really thought about it, though senior year was coming up, but I perhaps wanted to go to a Muslim country. "That could be a great experience," she said, "but remember this, Mikail: It's so easy being Muslim in a Muslim country. To be Muslim in Saudi Arabia, you never have to think; you just do what everyone else does. To be Muslim in America is a struggle; it takes a special person."

I walked them to the front door and watched the mother drive them off in a blue pickup truck, their phone number in my pocket.

"How did it go?" asked Iftekhar at Dr. Shafiq's desk.

"It was good," I said.

"Insha'Allah, you can marry her."

Then I felt a poking in my ribs from behind.

"She is very pretty, yes?" asked the Qari, smiling sweetly. "What her name, brother?"

"Maryam."

"You marry Maryam, brother." I turned away. The Qari laughed. "He marry Maryam, Iftekhar Saheb!"

"Insha'Allah," said Iftekhar, smiling too. Dr. Shafiq came in and had an exchange with Iftekhar in Urdu.

"Insha'Allah," Dr. Shafiq said to me, "you can start to talk to her, become friends with her."

"Insha'Allah," I answered.

"Mikail!" shouted the Qari. "Why, brother, you no marry Maryam?" He was only having fun with me now.

That night I dreamt about her. In my dreams I became her husband, carried her delicately to bed, and held her while she trembled. She was sure to be scared, I thought, but I'd be tender with her. Mukhtar had given the summer-camp teenagers photocopies of pages from some book about Islamic social life, with one of the bulleted points being "gentleness and respect is an essential part of the lovemaking process." And in one of the office hadith collections I had read the Prophet saying that whoever was gentle would have good in this life and the hereafter. I didn't imagine actual sex, just the act of putting her on the bed and reassuring her as she cried. Then I dreamed of building a mosque on her father's land.

a new hope

13

Something great was going to happen, I just knew it. Everyone treated me as a special investment that would pay off huge if properly protected.

"Islam needs to be taught in a way that people can understand," Iftekhar told me when we were alone at the Qari's apartment. "You could do better than any of us, because you know the culture and you know the youth. They're not going to listen to me, brother. But you come from the same background, and you are a nice-looking young man, you speak well, you don't have an accent . . . you can speak to them in ways that we cannot."

"Insha'Allah," I said humbly, but inside I was glowing.

At the end of the summer camp they held a banquet and I gave a speech. Mom was on the women's side of the room, sitting with Maryam and her mom. Before my speech, I went into the men's room and looked at myself, standing with my back straight and my chin up, staring right into my own eyes in the mirror. I had it together as much as anyone, I thought. It didn't matter what I was before or what anyone thought of me in Geneva—at the mosque I had respect and had earned it. None of the other kids gave their Islam the discipline that I gave mine, even if they had the advantage of Muslim families. I came in here on my own and did it all by myself; I was serious. My white shirt and red tie, the only traces of my DeSales life, held me in tight. For a moment I saw young Wesley held tight in his MP uniform, though it couldn't hold him forever. But I was different from him, I could see it. I wasn't crazy, and he never found Islam; it was darkness all around him and light around me. I went back to the banquet room to prove something to those people, even if they couldn't know what I was proving.

I started out all right, just explaining to the parents what kind of classes and activities the summer camp offered. Then I went off: "And in our high schools, we're hearing boys brag about how much beer they can drink and even girls bragging about their sexual exploits!" My tone became tough and I might have pointed my Malcolm finger. "That's what your kids are getting in that public school, and the Catholic school isn't any better, believe me. That's why we need Islamic high schools where we can hold onto *our* values. But al-hamdulilah, the Islamic Center has provided this camp for us to have a good summer with our fellow Muslims." It made me the star of the night, with all the kids' parents coming up to congratulate me and meet my mother.

Dr. Shafiq's son Mustafa came into the banquet area carrying a cardboard box of green-covered books: *Growth of Islamic Thought in America: Focus on Isma'il Raji al-Faruqi* by Dr. Muhammad Shafiq, fresh off the presses. Mom gave me $10 to buy one. I didn't know anything about al-Faruqi other than that he was Dr. Shafiq's teacher, but that alone made him something sacred to me. For Dr. Shafiq to write a whole book about this man, he must have regarded him with the same love and awe that I felt for Dr. Shafiq. The three of us were connected like grandfathers, fathers, and sons.

I asked him to sign it. He wrote, "To Br. Mikail with best wishes and prayers. May Allah guide you to the straight path. Work hard with patience and steadiness. May Allah bless you with success in this world and the hereafter (Amin). M. Shafiq." On the ride home I held that book with both hands, rubbing its cover with my thumbs. Sometimes I opened it to flip the pages and consider the work that went into filling each one. I stared at his name. Though I couldn't read it in the dark, the whole inside cover listed his educational background and publications. It was like squeezing a man's arm as he flexed his bicep.

Then I was back in Phelps with my last year of DeSales coming fast. I missed everyone at the mosque so much, and I missed that night of sad, magical good-byes so badly that I kept my shirt and tie on for the next three days, the sleeves rolled up and the tie loosened. It was like extending my last sliver of the summer as far as I could take it.

TWO WEEKS INTO senior year, Mom let me skip a Friday afternoon and drove me to the mosque.

"If we're going to keep doing this," she warned, "you have to do better in school. You have to get your work done."

"Okay, Mom." I almost wanted to, since I had already ingested Dr. Shafiq's book and learned that his teacher al-Faruqi used to scold Muslim students who got C's in classes taught by non-Muslim professors. It brought shame to Muslims, he said.

In the mosque I was surprised to find Iftekhar approaching the mihrab in Dr. Shafiq's old brown mantle to give the sermon and lead prayer. After jum'aa I headed straight for the office to get to him before anyone else.

"How is your mother?" he asked after our salams.

"She's good, she's outside."

"Mash'Allah. Say hello to her for me."

"Brother, where is Dr. Shafiq?"

"He is in Pakistan. He went back with his family."

"When did this happen?"

"A few days ago."

"Why did he leave?"

"I do not know, brother."

"When is he coming back?"

"He did not say."

"Is he coming back at all?" I asked. Iftekhar could see the growing alarm.

"Allahu Alim," he answered calmly. God is the Knower.

Dr. Shafiq was gone, Qari Saheb was gone, Mukhtar was gone. The kids from summer camp were all still in Rochester but they rarely went to Friday prayers, so they might as well have been gone. Iftekhar and Siddique were there but Fridays were so busy that I couldn't talk to them.

In November Mom took me to another jum'aa. It had been a few weeks since I last made the trip or even called, and I was sure that Dr. Shafiq would be back. He wasn't, and no one had news.

Mom was about to drive us home when Siddique came running out of the mosque and calling for me. I rolled my window down.

"Brother Mikail," he said, "next month I'm going to Pakistan."

"You too?"

"It's the program that I had taken part in last year, but this time I'm going as a coordinator, kind of a camp counselor thing. I am staying with the students in their hostel, assisting them, teaching when I can, whatever's needed of me, insha'Allah."

"That's great, brother."

"Do you want to go?" he asked.

"To Pakistan?"

"Al-hamdulilah! I'll talk to Iftekhar about it. No one as young as you has ever gone through this program before, but with your connections it shouldn't be a problem." I had connections? "Dr. Shafiq will be there," he added, "and Qari Saheb, and Mukhtar, and me. No problems at all, insha'Allah." Yeah, I guess I was connected.

Mom and I made another trip to Rochester to sit with Siddique and get all the information. He told us that it was a program for new Muslims running from December to February at the Daw'ah Academy, which was part of the International Islamic University, which was based at Faisal Mosque in Islamabad.

My airfare, room, and board were all provided for, and the Daw'ah Academy would even bestow a small stipend. Over the two months I would practice reading Qur'an, receive lectures from renowned scholars from all over the world, and experience life in an Islamic society. "Brother," Siddique warned, "I have to say this now: It is a different way of life there. You need to be prepared to see things that you have never seen before."

"Okay."

"Once you get off that plane, you'll be mobbed. Taxis, hustlers, cons, everyone looking for a rupee is going to run straight to you. Just say 'ji nehi' and keep walking. You'll see beggars—a *lot* of beggars, brother. The Hindu beggars cut off their children's hands and feet to get more sympathy from tourists. And you're going to see refugees. The Afghans have poured in, first from the Soviet invasion and then their own civil war. Somalis too, brother, plenty of Somalis."

"Is he going to be safe?" Mom asked.

"Oh, sure. It's not an election year."

I'D LEAVE SHORTLY before DeSales got out for December break, and stay in Pakistan through all of January. Fat Ed had no problem with shipping me off, but I had to get work from each of my teachers for the time I'd be gone. My French teacher gave me a thick stack of worksheets that never made it into my suitcase.

While talking to my art teacher, I heard two girls whispering behind me.

"Pakistan?" asked one.

"I thought he was just kidding with that whole Muslim thing," said the other.

"WHAT DO YOU think about the status of women over there?" Dan asked me at lunch.

"They have a woman prime minister," I said. "Benazir Bhutto. How many women have been president of the United States?" That had him.

"You're probably not even really going," he joked. "I bet you're just going to be at your house the whole time."

SIDDIQUE WOULDN'T BE coming until two weeks after me. I was flying with another convert—or *revert*, since everyone is born a natural Muslim and we only *revert* to our true religion—a black man named Charlie from Rochester, who had accepted Islam that summer and taken the name Siddique Abdul-Hadi. I called him Abdul-Hadi to avoid confusion with the original Siddique.

The night before leaving, I walked up the road to the overpass, watching cars and tractor-trailers on the interstate below me, listening to the *Star Wars* soundtrack on my headphones and feeling like Luke Skywalker again, like I'd finally make it off Tatooine.

I had never left Ontario County without Mom, but I wasn't worried about anything. Between Siddique, Abdul-Hadi, Mukhtar, Qari Saheb, and Dr. Shafiq, I'd never be lonely.

"I bought you razors," said Mom on the ride to the airport. "They're in the backseat; maybe you can squeeze them in one of your bags."

"Mom, I'm going to Pakistan. I don't need razors. I shouldn't even be shaving anyway."

We met Abdul-Hadi at the airport. Mom gave me a strong hug and told me to have fun. Walking down the ramp with Abdul-Hadi, I kept a secret hand in my pocket counting on zikr beads as I silently said Allah's Name. If I kept my intentions in the right place and remained mindful of Allah, He'd protect us on our way. This was supposed to be a holy mission on a scale grander than anyone at DeSales or Geneva or the whole Finger Lakes region could ever know. I couldn't help but think of Malcolm on his way to Mecca, sure that I'd return home with my own new vision for America, a better way for all of us.

Our first stop was Chicago, after which we'd backtrack east. For the two-hour flight I flipped through Sayyid Qutb's *In the Shade of the Qur'an*. It was while reading the short sura at-Tariq ("the Night Visitor") and Qutb's corresponding commentary that I came to my first epiphany of the trip: Allah designed for all things in the universe to fit together perfectly in His plan, and His plan included my reading at-Tariq on a December 13, 1994, flight from Rochester to Chicago. I didn't know the reason yet, but Allahu Alim.

Sayyid Qutb said that the shorter suras were like loud, hard knocks or shouts to wake up a sleeping person. I looked closer at the words. *By heaven and by the night visitor. Would that you knew what the night visitor is! It is the star of piercing brightness. For every soul there is a guardian who watches over it.* "Thus," wrote Qutb, "people are not left to roam about over the earth . . . without someone to watch what they do."

During our flight over the Atlantic Ocean, I made a point of silently repeating Allah's Name exactly twenty-five thousand times. Gazing out the window at night I saw tons of shooting stars and remembered reading somewhere that they knocked evil jinns out of the sky.

14 traveling through hyperspace ain't like dusting crops, boy

Our layover in Frankfurt was three
hours. I played the *Star Wars* soundtrack
on my headphones and watched people go
by, picturing them as characters from the Mos Eisley spaceport
cantina and myself as wide-eyed Luke Skywalker.

"Where's your visa?" asked the woman at the counter, our
passports in her hand.

"We don't need a visa," Abdul-Hadi told her. "Pakistan
doesn't require a visa from U.S. citizens."

"It's the Lufthansa policy," she said. "Lufthansa requires
it; we can't let you on without a visa." We were twenty minutes from boarding.

"What are we supposed to do?" asked Abdul-Hadi.

"You have to go to the consulate in Bonn and get a visa.
Then you can come back and you'll have standby tickets for
the next flight."

It seemed okay at first, because we were Muslims and could accept all things as coming from Allah. Standing outside the airport, we approached one of the yellow taxis and asked the driver to take us to Bonn, neither of us knowing how far Bonn was or how much it'd cost. I took the front seat, said Allah's Name a few times and fell asleep. When I woke up, we were at the consulate in Bonn and the taxi driver wanted more money than both Abdul-Hadi and I had put together. Apparently Bonn was over a hundred miles from Frankfurt.

I couldn't lie about how much I had, so I handed him the full two hundred dollars Mom had given me. He took it and left. Even if we secured our visas, we'd have no way back to the airport.

As we walked into the consulate, I made sure to keep my hands in my pockets as I counted secret zikrs on my beads. It was best to conceal such things. Otherwise, the Devil shaytan might suggest to me that my display of devotion had impressed Abdul-Hadi, and then I'd forget Allah but pray instead to be seen and praised by men. And that'd make me a munafiq: a hypocrite, liar, and religious faker. The munafiq was worse than anything, even an open worshipper of idols.

Inside the consulate was a giant wall-to-wall painting of the Ka'ba, the very center of physical existence, surrounded by pilgrims, and I knew I'd have to join them someday. That picture was another proof of Islam's transcendent brotherhood: The Ka'ba was in Saudi Arabia, and here we saw it proudly displayed in the Pakistan-Germany consulate. Muslims never thought of themselves as belonging to nations or races; we belonged only to the ummah, the worldwide Islamic brotherhood.

"As-salamu alaikum," I said to the consul, a dignified man with wavy hair and a nice suit. He shook our hands and returned the greeting. He was our brother too even though we were from thousands of miles away and had never seen each other before; I knew that from Malcolm. We sat before his desk, showed our letters that Mukhtar had written on our behalf for this sort of thing, and he put the stickers in our passports. "Islamic Republic of Pakistan," it said at the top. On the blank for "Purpose of Visit," he wrote "Daw'ah Academy." He stamped the visa with his official seal, reading "Embassy of Pakistan—Bonn" and a star-and-crescent in the middle.

"Someday, Allah willing," he said, "all of Americans will take shahadah."

"Yes, insha'Allah," I replied, unable to look up from my awesome visa.

"Did you hear about Michael Jackson?"

"No."

"He is Muslim." That story's been floating around for years. Maybe it's true now, Allahu Alim.

Outside the consulate, we had no taxi and no way to get out of Bonn, and our luggage was on its way out of Europe but I had no complaints. Allah provides, and Allah guides who He will. Things will work out as Allah wants them to, and Allah knows better than us. Anyway, wandering hopelessly in Bonn was still better than being stranded in Geneva, New York.

It got old fast. No one would help us. Nuns avoided eye contact. Policemen told us to hitchhike. Finally someone pointed us in the direction of the metro, saying that a train went by every half hour and passed right under the Frankfurt airport.

"How are we going to get on the train?" I whined to Abdul-Hadi.

"We'll sneak on," he said.

"Really? How?"

"I used to do it as a kid, it's no problem." So we got on the train. They threw us off at the next stop.

"But I'm going to die here!" I cried to the conductor. Abdul-Hadi kept his composure. They took down our names and addresses and said we'd receive bills for the stolen fare.

We stood and watched from this new station of wherever, lost in the middle of Germany as the train moved on without us. I paced back and forth, trying not to cry.

"Don't worry about it," said Abdul-Hadi. "I've done this a million times. Next train comes by, we get on and pretend to be asleep. They'll think that they've already checked our tickets."

"What if it doesn't work?" I replied, my voice trembling. "What if they throw us off again?"

"Well, by that point we're already a little closer to Frankfurt. Then we just hop on the next train and keep on doing it until we reach the airport." I felt safe with him. He had been through things; he knew what he was doing. He had that *measure more.*

The half hour until our next train felt like days. "Remember," said Abdul-Hadi, "as soon as we get on, take off your coat and bunch it up like a pillow and close your eyes." The train came, I did what he said, and it worked, getting us all the way to Frankfurt in the middle of the night. The next flight to Dubai would be in fifteen to twenty hours.

The airport was empty, allowing us a choice of benches to sleep on. Around four in the morning, I got up and left Abdul-Hadi to find a restroom and wash for prayer. Using my coat as a prayer rug, I made the obligatory rakats and also a few extra ones, and then I just stayed in sitting position on my coat, reflecting on where I was and why I was there.

I didn't know what time it was in New York but I tried

making a collect call to Mom and couldn't get through. Then I called my uncle Dan and told him what was going on. Hours later, after the airport became busy and loud again, I heard my name over the PA; they had someone on the phone for me.

"I only have standby tickets now," I told Mom. "I'm so worn out; I'm just ready to go home."

"Just wait it out, bud. See what happens. If there's room for you on the next plane, then you're good."

"I'm exhausted."

"I called Siddique," she said.

"What did he say?"

"Well, he didn't get to say much. I was screaming at him."

"Mom!"

"Hey, my kid's stranded in Germany. I let him have it. But he just listened calmly, never raised his voice at me. And then I asked him why he didn't get upset with me, and you know what he said?"

"What'd he say?"

"He said, 'That's not the Muslim way.'"

"That's true," I said, smiling.

"You're doing good, bud. Just hang in there."

"Thanks Mom."

ABDUL-HADI AND I took turns sleeping so that we wouldn't miss any announcements or changes in the schedule. It was too noisy to sleep well, so during my turns to stay awake I could barely keep my eyes open. And we were both starving because all of our money had gone to the taxi driver. To retain some sense of adventure and to stay alert, I put on my headphones and blasted the *Star Wars* soundtrack.

The screen showing arrivals and departures was behind us

so I had to keep turning around to see what time it was. Finally I turned to the middle-aged Middle Eastern man seated next to me and asked if he was flying to Dubai. He was. "I didn't bring a watch," I told him. "So I'll just get up when you do."

"Okay," he said politely. Then I lost it.

"I'm supposed to be on my way to Pakistan, but the airline required a visa even though Pakistan doesn't require visas from U.S. citizens, and we had to miss our flight and go all the way to Bonn, and I didn't realize how far away it was so the taxi took all our money, and we had no way to get back. We had to sneak on trains and now I just have a standby ticket and this whole thing could be a waste of my time. I've been sitting here for twenty hours with no food and I don't even know if I'll get on the plane that I was supposed to get on yesterday. We were on our way to a program for new Muslims at the International Islamic University in Islamabad, with brothers from all over the world to learn Arabic, read Qur'an, see life in an Islamic setting—I can already read the Qur'an; I know the alphabets but I'm just not any good at it, my pronunciation is awful, and I want to give it a flow like the Qari instead of just dragging through it. Most of all, I want to learn the language so I can understand the words, I know that English translations really don't do it justice." I looked at him and realized how much I had said and how fast and stupidly I had said it. "I'm sorry, I'm just real frustrated here."

"As-salamu alaikum," he said with a slight grin, extending his hand.

"Wa alaikum as-salam," I answered, taking it.

"I work for Lufthansa. I am Vice President of Operations in Dubai, but I am originally Algerian."

"Mash'Allah," I said.

"You will get on that plane." He bought us lunch and then

walked us over to the counter. "I am flying to Dubai," he told the blonde woman, "and these young men are getting on with me." She motioned to see my envelope full of creased and worn tickets, receipts, and forms. She looked it over.

"That's impossible," she said.

"Nothing is impossible," he told her, adding as he turned to me, "if Allah wills."

Before going to his seat in first class, he gave me his Lufthansa business card. "Call me when you arrive in Pakistan," he said. I thanked him profusely and promised I would.

I surveyed the seats around me. The demographics had visibly changed from our flight to Frankfurt. Across the aisle I saw two veiled women counting Allah's Name on a string of beads. We had not yet left the ground, but I was already out of the Western world.

THE CRAMPED SEATS made it hard to sleep; there was no room for my legs. After watching me contort into various unnatural positions, the man seated next to me decided to have mercy.

"I am going to go sit with my friend in back," he said. "You can stretch your legs." It didn't make much difference, since the armrest blocked me from enjoying the extra room, but I was tired enough to fall asleep anyway.

After I woke up, he came back and we talked. He asked what business I had in Dubai, and I gave him my whole story of accepting Islam and the invitation to study in Islamabad. "Youngest participant ever in the program," I made a point of telling him, "by at least five years."

"That is wonderful!" he exclaimed. "Oh, mash'Allah! America needs young men like you."

"All praise is due to Allah," I replied, stealing the words from Malcolm. "Only the mistakes have been mine."

"I want to write down something for you to remember: It is the name of a school that you might consider after you graduate."

"Yes, insha'Allah." Using an empty white envelope for scrap paper, he wrote ISLAMIC UNIVERSITY, AL-MADINA, and gave it to me.

"They could make you into a great scholar of Islam," he said. "Then you come back and spread the deen all over America." *Deen* meant religion.

"Thank you, brother," I said.

"I have something else for you." He reached into his pocket and pulled out a handful of German marcs easily amounting to hundreds of American dollars.

"I cannot, brother—"

"You must, brother. It's German money and I am no longer in Germany; it's useless to me." A flimsy excuse, since I had left Germany on the same plane. "And take these too." He put a pair of new leather gloves in my hands. "I am going from a cold country to a very hot country, I don't need these. You can use them when you go back to the United States."

And he gave me his card. Under his name it read, "United Arab Emirates, Department of Foreign Affairs."

It was night when we arrived in Dubai. All I'd see of the city were the palm trees outside the airport. Abdul-Hadi and I shared embraces and final salams with the two miraclemen who had come out of nowhere to keep us on the path, and then we all parted ways. Watching them go, I pulled myself back from thoughts of loving this world. Our short time on earth was supposed to be prison for believers and paradise for unbelievers, but sometimes Allah made things work out in such magical ways that you couldn't help but feel excited about being alive.

Abdul-Hadi and I found the airport's mosque—how awesome was that, first of all, that we were in a Muslim country where airports had mosques?—and made our prayers. I recited al-Asr with thoughts of our two helpers. In just three short verses, al-Asr tells us that by the "declining day," human beings are all losers and doomed, except for the ones who have faith and do good and guide each other to the truth. After leaving the prayer room, the entire airport felt like a mosque. I was confident that all I'd have to do was yell, "I'm a Muslim!" and everyone there would be my friend and invite me to their homes.

WE FIRST LANDED in Karachi, where the airport was crowded with people lining up to get out. From what we heard there had been shootings that day. After reaching Islamabad, we stepped out of the airport into a sea of men pressing from all corners with various offers, just as Siddique had said. We climbed into the nearest taxi, and I told the driver, "Masjidi Faisal."

On the way I must have spotted at least a dozen minarets poking up out of the landscape. For a second I thought that they looked like sharp erect penises but immediately scratched that; I was so happy to have finally arrived in the bosom of Islam. I was more alien in Geneva than here, I thought; here was where I belonged.

Our long Shahrah-e-Islamabad road ended right in front of Masjidi Faisal. I instantly recognized the mosque backdropped by the green Margalla Hills, just as Siddique had described. The mosque was huge, like football-stadium huge, and really did look like a spaceship with a rocket-minar on each corner and giant crescent-topped pyramidal dome in the middle, as though it could blast off into the clouds and carry its contents to paradise. Or it looked like a giant stone tent, almost.

Taking off my socks to wash for prayer was the best feeling in the world—another proof of the wisdom in Islam's details. Washing for prayer removes the *mental* dirt, and taking your time with it creates further distance between the prayer and whatever distracting stresses you faced. I washed my arms up to the elbows, ran wet hands over my hair, cleaned out my ears, rinsed out my mouth, and pushed water up my nose.

Then I heard the call to prayer blaring from loudspeakers placed on each minaret. It was the same voice from a thousand prayers in Rochester.

15 mein amriken musalman hoon

I ran upstairs, passing Allah's Name in colored tiles on the walls, to the outdoor courtyard and mosque entrance. The doors were locked so I pressed my face against the glass and blocked out the sun with my hands.

Inside it was all blue, which I had read in Jung was a universally holy color, the color that Hindu artists painted their gods and Christian artists painted the Virgin Mary's hijab, the color of heaven. At the far end of the gigantic room I could see the Qari with his back turned, facing Mecca as he performed the adhan. I realized that the stereotype of Muslims turning "east" to pray was no longer accurate, because the Qari now faced west. If Mecca was the point of reference, we were truly on the other side of the world.

"You," barked a guard in drab khaki uniform. I turned and saw him gesturing to me. "You, you." A rifle hung by its strap from his shoulder.

"Qari Saheb mera dost hai," I told him. Qari Saheb is my

friend. "Mein Amriken musalman hoon." I am an American Muslim. Mukhtar had taught me some Urdu that summer.

"You, no, you, you." He waved his hands in the direction I was supposed to move.

"Qari Saheb mera dost hai."

"You, you go."

"Qari Saheb mera dost hai, mein Amriken musalman hoon." Inside, Qari Saheb had finished the call to prayer and was on his way to the door.

"You, no," said the guard. I wondered if the Qari would make it outside in time.

"Mein Amriken musalman hoon," I repeated.

"No, no. You."

"Y'akhi," I said, calling him brother in Arabic. I didn't know how to say it in Urdu. "Acha," I said, *okay.*

"You, you—"

"I think you'd better move," said Abdul-Hadi.

"I'm okay," I said.

"YOU, YOU NO—"

And then the Qari opened the door, immediately surrounded by brothers giving their salams.

"Brother Mikail!" he shouted on seeing me. "Al-hamdulilah brother Mikail, as-salamu alaikum!"

"Wa alaikum as-salam wa rahmatullahi wa barakatuh, Qari Saheb!"

"I am happy man now, brother. How is your plane, good?"

"Al-hamdulilah," I answered.

"And Mom, how is your mother?"

"She is good, Qari Saheb."

"She Muslim?"

"Not yet, insha'Allah."

"And how is Maryam?" He smiled and poked me in the ribs.

"Good, Qari Saheb."

"You say Iftekhar, 'Brother Iftekhar talk to mother…Maryam, talk her mother, say I want to marry now, insha'Allah.' Yes, you say Iftekhar?"

"I'll see what he can do, insha'Allah. I don't know if that's what her mother wants right now."

"Why, brother?" He then took me by the hand and walked us inside. I found a place of my own and made sunna prayers with my backpack still on.

From our misadventures crossing time zones, I had no idea that it was Friday until the imam started his sermon. With my brain fried, I attempted to listen, still too ragged to even notice that he wasn't speaking English. When it came time for prayer, Qari Saheb stood up in the front row and repeated the call. Standing in line, I thought of how I might have looked, wishing that I could hover above the congregation and watch myself, the lone white Amriken Musalman praying with his brothers, accepted as a brother. After the group prayer I retreated to an open space and made my private sunna and zikr, closing my eyes to repeat Allah's Name under my breath. Then I sensed the presence of someone next to me. The mosque was wide open and half empty; he had no reason to sit so close. He was looking at me, staring even, projecting enough energy that I could know without opening my eyes.

Then he poked me in the leg. I turned and found the Qari, smiling like a schoolboy.

"Hello, brother," he said, trying not to giggle in the house of Allah. "As-salamu alaikum."

WAITING OUTSIDE FAISAL Mosque was a small gang of the women Siddique had warned me about, the beggars with footless children. Siddique had said that they would be Hindus, but these women wore burqas, the kinds with fabric grids covering their eyes. From under one a bony arm reached out for me.

"Lo-tee, lo-tee," she cried. Qari Saheb pulled me past them, leading Abdul-Hadi and me to brother Mukhtar. After another round of salams and hugs, Mukhtar directed us to the buses taking students back to their hostels. We boarded a short van packed with Malaysians, Indonesians, Filipinos, and Chinese Muslims, and sat behind the driver.

"You Muslim, brother?" he asked.

"Yes," Abdul-Hadi replied while I looked out the window.

"Mash'Allah, brother! You are here to study Islam?"

"Insha'Allah."

"Good, brother, good! You must study! Study, study, study! And you do a good job, insha'Allah!"

He dropped us off and we followed the other guys into the house. Inside it was so crowded that I couldn't notice any detail besides young men everywhere and crumbling walls— and a poster bearing Arabic script along with a machine gun hovering over an opened Qur'an. I felt a pit in my stomach and my eyeballs hurt. As I began to contemplate what the next two months could be like, a bus showed up and the driver called for us. It turned out that Mukhtar had sent us to the wrong hostel.

The new place was in a whole other part of town, surrounded by small mansions and new mansions under construction. Across the street lived a high court advocate whose house had marble columns and a steel gate, presided over by an attentive guard. Our hostel was surrounded by its own ten-foot-high concrete wall. Inside we had cooks and housekeepers and a room for just Abdul-Hadi and me with our own bathroom. Exploring upstairs we found the prayer room and then the balcony, which gave us a view halfway across town.

I leaned on the railing and looked out at Islamabad. Islamabad's only industry was government and its feeling was suburban, like an instant city. The collection of flat-roofed neighborhoods ahead gave no signs of action. They were silent and still, like a photograph, but the sun and dust and quiet colorless buildings blended together more like a painting. Minarets rose at aesthetically perfect places as though by design.

On the way to our room, we met one of our classmates in the program.

"I am Idris from Nigeria," he told us after trading salams.

"I am Mikail from America."

"Brother Mikail! You are an angel, right?"

"What?"

"Your name," he said, laughing. "Mikail is one of the angels? You look tired, brother. I'll let you sleep." Abdul-Hadi closed the door behind us and we chose our beds. Collapsed into mine, my eyes feeling like they had been sealed shut, I thought of the two miraclemen from our flight to Dubai—they put the truth of Islam in the world and made it real. I prayed for Allah to reward them. Any good that came from their help—whatever knowledge I picked up here, to whatever extent I grew in my Islam and the work that I'd do for Islam in America, whomever I brought to Islam, and whomever they in turn brought to the deen, and their children, and so on until the day when the mountains became like carded wool and we scattered from one another—would count as baraka, blessings, on their behalf. That was the Mercy of Allah: Even the smallest bit of good, done in Allah's Name, comes back to you ten thousand times.

When I woke up I tried calling them, but their numbers

didn't work. It made no sense. The Lufthansa brother's card gave four phone numbers and none of them worked. I couldn't help but wonder if the men were not even real men but some other kind of creature, mala'ika, angels, maybe, sent by Allah to help His sincere believers. They came in together, did their work, and together went back to the clouds.

I MET MORE students at dinner. Most of them were from western Africa, and there were a couple Ethiopians and South Africans. Two had come from Sri Lanka. There was a white Canadian guy who I tried hard not to see as a rival, and a Haitian, and a brother from Singapore. Over our beef, rice, and bread we shared stories of how we embraced Islam. One of the Sri Lankan brothers had the best story; his four-year-old son had just started praying in Muslim fashion for no reason, with no previous exposure to Muslims or anything.

"We should never say that we came to Islam," said an Ethiopian, "because that takes the power from Allah and puts it in our hands. What we should say is, '*Islam* came to *us*.'" It sounded right to me.

Before sunrise I was awakened by the call to prayer coming from upstairs, supported by accompanying calls from various mosques nearby. Abdul-Hadi and I made wudhu and plodded upstairs to join our brothers. After breakfast we rode the bus to Faisal Mosque for four hours of classes. The classroom had a monastic feel with bare white walls, stiff chairs, plain lecturer's podium, chalkboard, and nothing more besides a poster sitting on an easel at the front of the room, the "Muslim World" map, color-coded to show the relative prevalence of Islam throughout the world. North and east Africa, the Middle East, Pakistan, Afghanistan, the former Soviet republics in central

Asia, Bangladesh, and Indonesia were all dark green. Russia, some sub-Saharan African countries, India, and Malaysia were a lighter green. China and a few African countries were yellow, though China's Sinkang province was dark green. The rest of the world—Europe, the Americas, Australia, and South Africa—was pink and red, except for one light green sliver in South America and the Bosnian-Albanian region of Eastern Europe. Between classes I went over and stared at it up close, tracing my finger across the distance between New York and Islamabad, and trying to envision all of North America as light green, maybe dark green like Saudi.

Our school day started with an hour of Qur'an recitation, then an hour of Arabic, followed by a break and then two hour-long lessons from guest alims, scholars, who came from a dozen different countries just to teach us. The first came from Kuwait to lecture us about the learned men of long ago. With his heavy beard and robes, backdropped by the ugly walls of our classroom, it was easy to imagine us in their time, or at least having a direct link to them through this man and wherever he had studied. He told us about the founders of the various schools of law; they were great men and lived Islam on levels that we could never touch. He described the way that Imam Malik's face would change color whenever someone mentioned the Prophet, and how Imam Hanifah, upon hearing of a stolen sheep, refused to eat sheep for seven years—its average life span—lest he accidentally eat stolen meat. Imam Hanifah had also refused to work for a corrupt government, for which he was whipped ten times daily for eleven straight days, jailed, beaten, whipped thirty times more, jailed again, and forced to drink poison.

Then the alim told us about Imam Bukhari, whose famous compilation of hadiths bore his name. Bukhari memorized three hundred thousand hadiths in his lifetime, but even at the height of his fame ate only dried grass. On the road to Samarkand he longed for Allah to such a degree that he prayed for a departure from the world. "Ya Allah," he cried, "the Earth despite its grandeur is becoming narrow and troubling me greatly, so take me back to You." *That's balls*, I thought. Allah gave him the favor of illness and death on the eve of a holy day, Eid ul-Fitr.

The lectures finished just before Zuhr prayer, my favorite of the day because we made it at Faisal. Then we'd have time to walk around, socialize, or go to the gift shop, where I purchased a one-liter bottle of Zamzam water. Zamzam was a holy well in Mecca's same Great Mosque that housed the Ka'ba. It had first been found by the angel Gabriel (Jibril, we called him in Arabic), who unearthed it with his wing when Hagar and her son Ishmael (Ismail) were lost in the wilderness and dying of thirst. The well was rediscovered by Muhammad's grandfather and has been flowing ever since. To drink from it connected you not only to prophets but all Muslims in history, almost like ingesting the pilgrimage. In Malcolm X's autobiography, when he wrote "I drank from the well of Zamzam," he meant this water right here in my hands.

"That's the holiest water," said one of the African brothers when he saw my bottle. I nodded. "Really," he said. "Scientists tested the Zamzam water and found that it is so pure, more pure than any water on earth."

We made Asr prayer back at the hostel, and then Qari Saheb would come by to listen to our recitations over tea. The rest of the day was ours. I went on a lot of walks, mostly through the F-10 Markaz where Afghan kids would be out collecting garbage. The refugees lived on the other side of the Markaz in katchi abadis, mud houses with cow manure padding the outside walls for insulation. One afternoon I watched a little girl punch a boy for a plastic bottle. She cursed at him in raspy Farsi or Pashtu or Punjabi, I didn't know which, and she sounded like a sixty-year-old chain smoker.

When they saw me they yelled *Amriken, Amriken* and rushed over to pull on my arms. *One rupeya, one rupeya, lo-tee, lo-tee. Lo-tee* meant food, I learned, and one rupee was roughly three American cents. One boy who popped up from behind a corner looked exactly like a kid I knew back at Islamic Center Summer Camp, except this boy was starving and barefoot and his eyes looked ready to fall out of his head, while the kid in Rochester was wearing $200 Nikes and went to a Catholic school in the suburbs. One's dad was a mujahid who helped push the Soviets out of Afghanistan; the other's worked for Kodak or Xerox.

"Ji nehi," I said, pulling myself free and raising my hands out of their reach. They chased after me. *Lo-tee, lo-tee, one rupeya, one rupeya.* A girl up ahead stood in my way, six or seven years old with scraggly matted hair and the same raspy voice as the others. I pushed her; one quick hand and she was out of my way. They cursed and threw rocks at me as I walked out of the F-10 Markaz back into my neighborhood, crossing some invisible barrier that they wouldn't pass. Back at the hostel I sat in the living room and watched *Teenage Mutant Ninja Turtles* dubbed over in Urdu. Leonardo sounded just like the burly hit man from a Bollywood movie I had watched on the plane.

Then came verses from Allah warning those who mistreated orphans. They weren't new verses exactly; they had been in the book all along. They weren't even new to *me*; I had read them before, but when Allah finally wills that you linger on those words, they blow you away. The next day I

walked back to F-10 Markaz, that short sura now committed to memory, and ignored all the kids until finding the girl
that I had pushed. I waved her over to a shop and held the
door open. The others crowded outside to watch through the
window as I gestured with my hands that she could pick an
outfit and I'd buy it for her. She took a brown dress decorated
with sparkly things and toy jewels, went into the changing
room and came out wearing it over her dirty clothes. I paid
the cashier, who seemed glad to see us leave. Then the kids
followed me to a toy store. Leaving them outside, I picked a
soccer ball and paid for it. The money wasn't really mine; it
came from the Emirati brother on the flight to Dubai. He'd get
as much baraka for it as me, probably more.

"As-salamu alaikum," I said to the clerk.

"Are you Muslim?" he asked.

"Yes, brother."

"Do you know the 'Subhana Qallahumma'?" I had never
heard of it.

"No, brother, I don't."

"Then I'm sorry, but you are not Muslim."

"Ashadu an la ilaha illa Allah, ashadu anna Muhammadan
rasullullah," I told him.

"That is not it."

"I know that's not it, brother. I'm telling you the shaha-
dah. If someone says to you that there is no god but Allah and
Muhammad is the Prophet, then you cannot say he's not a
Muslim."

"Sir, I am sorry, but you don't even know the Subhana
Qallahumma, how can you be a Muslim?"

"Allah knows better than both of us," I told him, leaving
with the ball. I kicked it to the kids and then headed home with
light steps, my black shalwar kameez fluttering in the breeze.

the strongest man

16

"Qari Saheb," I asked, **"can you teach** me the 'Subhana Qallahumma'?"

"Okay brother." He walked me through it until I got it right. I still had no idea what the words meant in English or why we'd say them, but at least I could prove myself as a Muslim at the toy store.

"As-salamu alaikum," I told the clerk.

"Wa alaikum," he responded. I knew what that meant. *Wa alaikum as-salam* was how you returned the greeting to a Muslim; but when greeted by a non-Muslim, you left out the *salam*.

"Subhana Qallahumma wa bihamdika wa tabara gas-muka wa ta'ala jedukka wa la ilaha ghayruk," I rattled off in front of him, my eyes tearing up and my fists clenched at my sides. "Brother, I admit to not knowing it yesterday. I'm a new Muslim. I was born and raised in America with Christian parents, but al-hamdulilah, I have accepted Islam. And now

I've come here to study at Masjidi Faisal and better myself in the deen. Maybe I don't know as much as you, but that doesn't mean I'm not a Muslim."

"I am sorry, brother. I did not know." He seemed sincere about it.

"Al-hamdulilah," I said.

"Excuse me," asked a middle-aged man behind me, "but you are American Muslim?"

"Yes?"

"You . . . Farrakhan?"

"No, no," I answered, smiling.

ON FRIDAY WE went to the jum'aa bazaar, a giant flea market, after the prayers. Iftekhar had wanted me to find some kafans, funeral shrouds, to take back home. For my cousins I picked up some pretty jewelry boxes with elaborate designs on the lids. Throughout the bazaar I saw remnants of the Soviet war with Afghanistan: fatigues, gas masks, AK mag and grenade pouches, combat boots, berets, mess tins, green duffel bags, military flashlights, and big black bearskin ushanka hats with gold hammer-and-sickle insignias.

Some of the Africans and I watched a man slaughtering chickens. He'd hold one down with his foot, slit its neck, and toss it with the others on the pile, over and over, live chickens to his right, dead chickens to his left.

"He's supposed to say 'Bismillah'Allahu Akbar' when he does that," said my brother Luqman from Liberia. "Hey y'akhi, why don't you say 'Bismillah'Allahu Akbar?'" Luqman was a convert just like me, but had such a command of the religion that he could correct brothers who had always been Muslim. The butcher put his head down with shame and pointed at his chest. "He says it in his heart," Luqman explained, laughing as we moved on.

We never found the funeral shrouds, but I did fall in love. After spending the equivalent of ten dollars on three bronze coins supposedly from the Kushan period, I turned and spotted her in the billowy black niqab and could only see her eyes, but they were eyes like none I had seen in North America—perhaps because back home, women revealed so much that it was hard to notice their eyes. I looked once, turned around, and looked again and knew that was all I could have. The sin's in the third look, the Prophet told Ali when Ali was young like me.

Islam truly respects the power in being a woman, I imagined Siddique saying. He had never actually said that, but I thought it in his voice. In Rochester, Siddique had told Abdul-Hadi and me that in Pakistan he felt little to no sexual desire. After the first week or so it just goes away, he said, due to the lack of external stimulation. I understood and was already starting to feel it, even with this momentary infatuation—it was really only her eyes, nothing more. There seemed to be a decent chance that I could make it the whole two months without masturbating once, God willing.

ONE OF THE lecturers told us that masturbation was unnatural and a sin, but Siddique arrived in Islamabad at just the right time and gave me a better answer. "You're a young man," he said, "and life is full of challenges for the young man who wants to be Muslim—especially in America, brother. That's why you should marry early, to save you from trouble both in this world and the next."

"Is it allowed, though?"

"Brother, the Prophet, sallallaho alayhe wa salam, told Ali

that it was better to fast. But, you know, if it keeps you from fornicating, do what you gotta do."

They gave Siddique a room in our hostel. All of the students loved him. I bragged about how much time we had spent together in America and always tried to sit next to him at dinner. Walking with Siddique through the jum'aa bazaar or watching him wade through the beggars, I noticed how he looked at the world around him: his chin up, making casual turns of his head as though surveying his kingdom, gazing down on lesser men. And I wanted to speak like him. He had a deep and strong voice, sounding even stronger with his accent, and he'd emphasize just the right words.

"I'm sorry for my mother yelling at you," I told him.

"Al-hamdulilah, brother. She's your mom; she was really worried." Abdul-Hadi and I gave him the story of our two holy helpers from the flight to Dubai. "Your hearts were clean," said Siddique. "Allah provides for His servants." It led him to a tangent on how you'd need a certain amount of good in your heart to overcome evil. "Look at Jeffrey Dahmer," he said. "Remember how his teenage lover ran naked and screaming to the police, but Dahmer convinced them not to do anything? The cops put the boy right back in Dahmer's hands. Dahmer had evil power; but his lover, being homosexual, didn't have enough good to counter Dahmer's evil." It was like the dark side of the Force in *Star Wars*, I thought.

Siddique told us that since there were only four hours of class each day, we should use the spare time to get in shape. "For two months you're eating right: real beef, real chicken, real goat, rice, chapati bread, no garbage American food. It's a chance to develop yourself not only spiritually and mentally, but get some muscles on you. Fitness is sunna, brother." He reminded me that back in Rochester, he had wanted Dr. Shafiq to start lifting. You have to be strong in a land as hostile to Islam as America, and a land full of homosexuals too. "You can't underestimate them," he said. "They're as strong as men but they fight mean like women. And many of them take martial arts." He led me to a gym on the basement floor of a plaza in F-10. AMERICAN GYM, read the sign. On the glass door they had taped a poster of Arnold Schwarzenegger from his Mr. Olympia days. Inside they had wall-to-wall mirrors and posters of flexing Hulk Hogan, the Ultimate Warrior, and Mike Tyson. The long-haired lifter who worked there gave me a price that seemed out of my range, even though I hadn't yet figured out the exchange rate. "You should still do push-ups," Siddique told me outside.

AN ALIM CAME from Palestine with his round face framed in a black and white kifeyyeh, his big round eyes bugging out like golf balls. His name was Rushdie. First he taught us about the Protocols of the Elders of Zion, a secret document outlining the Jews' plan for world domination. "But Allah subhanahu wa ta'Ala is the best of planners," he said. I had read that in at-Tariq. "And whenever they disobey Allah subhanahu wa ta'Ala, He sends them a punishment. That is why Hitler came; Hitler was sent down upon them."

"How do we know that?" asked Idris from Nigeria.

"THE QUR'AN, BROTHER!" Rushdie bellowed as though he had been attacked. "ALLAH SAYS IT IN HIS QUR'AN!" He recited ayats off the top of his head in thick Arabic and gave us the verse numbers so we could look up their translation. It was in the seventeenth sura, Bani Isra'il (Children of Israel). Allah says that He gave a clear warning to the Jews, that twice they would be punished for their arrogance. So Allah sent Hitler; the proof was right there.

On Rushdie's last day at the Daw'ah Academy, he told us that to continue our studies of Islam and become alims, we should go to Palestine, since the best schools were there.

"There's nothing in Palestine but trouble," Siddique assured me, shaking his head. "If you want to be an alim, go to al-Azhar, go to Mecca or Medina, go to Malaysia or stay in Islamabad—you're at one of the biggest schools right here. I don't know what kind of school that brother's talking about, but insha'Allah it's not where you want to be."

We all knew that Rushdie was insane, but still I thought about death on battlefields. Islam had given me a healthy relationship to death. In America they believed in nothing after death, so all anyone wanted was to live long and look young for as much of it as they could. In America they carved up their faces and bodies with plastic surgery, lying to themselves and avoiding reality. A Muslim could see this life for what it is, and then death has nothing on him. What's the value of an extra ten or twenty years away from your Creator?

Of course Americans could not understand Islamic martyrdom. American comedians liked to joke that it was all about the reward of virgins in paradise. I couldn't really blame them for making that mistake, since Americans only cared about sex. If you said the word *sex* to an American, he wouldn't hear anything else. While I did think about the houris—their virginity grew back after you fucked them, endlessly reborn virgins for all time—to call them my inspiration would cheapen the cause. I had learned about Muslims oppressed all over the world, suffering and dying under an American-Zionist world order; what was so valuable about my own life that I couldn't give it up fighting alongside them? I loved my brothers enough to die for them; and perhaps, if the shaytan was whispering in my ear, I wanted them to know my name and remember my sacrifice with tears streaming down their cheeks. It should not have been so hard for Christians to understand: In this kind of Islam, we all had a chance to be Christ.

Every day after class we gathered in the living room and watched CNN International updates on the struggle in Chechnya. On days that momentum shifted in favor of the Chechens we cheered and gave each other high fives. It was so unbelievable, but that much more a glory of Islam, that these poor rebels with no resources or numbers—they had even less than the Afghans—could fight and maybe win their freedom from the giant Russian kafr empire. As they had for Afghanistan, brothers were coming to Chechnya from all over the Muslim ummah. Meanwhile, I was reading about Imam Shamil, the famous Chechen mujahid from long ago. And I was healthy and young and trying to make myself strong, doing push-ups as Siddique had suggested. One night I went to his room to talk about it.

He usually left the door open for us to come and ask questions. If the door was closed, it meant that he was trying to memorize Ya Sin, sura for the dead and dying which was almost a required knowledge, he said, since you never know when you will be in the presence of a dying person. This time the door was open only a crack—still open, *technically*—and I could hear his chanting. I gently pushed the door to establish that it was in fact open, and then knocked.

"I'm sorry, brother."

"No, no, brother Mikail. You look like something's on your mind."

"I think I want to go to Chechnya."

"And what are you going to do there?"

"I don't know." I looked at the floor. Even after some push-ups, I was in no place to suggest to someone like Siddique that

I had any value as a fighter. To stand before him forced the realization. "I was just thinking, insha'Allah, that while I'm here, so close, that I have the opportunity to help, you know?"

"Mash'Allah, it is great that you'd want to help your brothers, but you have more to offer than going to Chechnya."

"More than my hands? If we see wrong, we correct it with our hands first."

"Brother, whatever resources or talents you have, you can use them for the good of Islam. Most men have hands but not all of them have your brains. For someone like you to just go on the front line and become another body in a ditch is almost ingratitude towards Allah. He gave you a gift, and you'd be throwing it away."

"Yes, brother."

"Do you even know why you're here, Mikail?"

I looked at him and waited for the answer. "Why do you think that Dr. Shafiq and Iftekhar wanted you to see life in Pakistan? The community back home is eighty-five percent Pakistani, brother. So you need to learn this culture, pick up some Urdu, understand their humor, and get a tolerance for all the spices in their foods, insha'Allah, because Dr. Shafiq sees you as the future of the mosque."

I couldn't look at him, afraid that I'd smile.

"Insha'Allah," I mumbled, buying time with the generic response.

"They all place a lot of stock in you," he said. My insides tingled again. "And part of it might be that you don't look like the usual Muslim."

"What do you mean?" I asked, pretending not to know. Of course I knew. One of our lecturers had told me that in America, black converts were "a dime a dozen," but I was special.

"C'mon, brother," he replied. "You know, I was led to Islam through a search for myself as a black man. The Nation, Malcolm, all of that. But there's no pull like that for white people, and they don't see a lot of Muslims who look like them. Besides, with the Islamic Center so factionalized, maybe it's good for someone from the smallest group to be in charge."

"Factionalized? What do you mean?"

"The Pakistanis say it's their mosque because they're the majority. The Arabs say it's their mosque because it was built with their money. And the African Americans say, 'This is our country, we should lead the mosque.' Because there aren't enough white Muslims to threaten anyone, you'd almost be seen as neutral."

"Why did Dr. Shafiq leave Rochester?" I asked for a quick change of the subject.

"His kids, y'akhi. American culture was no good for them."

"That makes sense. I wish I could stay here."

"Dr. Shafiq loves Islam," said Siddique. "He could have been making six figures at a big school but instead ran a masjid for peanuts. Then he quit that to come back to a third-world country and raise his sons in the deen."

"Al-hamdulilah," I said, still thinking about myself and the great things I was meant for.

"Do you want to go see him?"

I jumped up like we could go right then.

DR. SHAFIQ LIVED in Peshawar, a considerable distance from Islamabad. To go would mean skipping a day of classes, but Qari Saheb and Mukhtar were going too.

Siddique wanted to get a haircut before we left. I went

with him. Waiting for his turn with the barber, he greeted the man on his right with the regular *as-salamu alaikum*. The man ignored him. "As-salamu alaikum," Siddique repeated, again getting no answer.

"Doesn't surprise me," he said, turning away from the man. "This is the land where racism began. You know about the caste system and all of that, right? The Aryan invaders set that up to keep from race-mixing with the black Dravidians . . . the entire foundation of Hinduism is white supremacy."

"Islam does away with caste and race," I answered. "Muslims don't see color."

"That's a lovely story, brother," he said sadly.

goat head soup

17

"It's a different world here," said Siddique on the way to Peshawar. "In Rochester I can drive with my eyes closed but here, brother, you need MOHSIN SHAH!"

"Yes brother!" shouted Mohsin Shah, our driver. The bus hit a bump and my head hit the ceiling.

"No pretty yellow lines dividing the road, brother! No traffic lights, no turn signals, no speed limits. You don't even need a driver's license, though they're starting to crack down. To drive to Peshawar you need a Pathan, right Mohsin Shah?"

"Yes, brother, Pathan good driver!"

"The Pathans are warriors," Siddique told me. "Mountain people, invaded over and over again through history. It made them strong. Strong people, right Mohsin Shah?"

"Yes, brother!" Mohsin Shah replied.

"If you tell Mohsin Shah that you like his hat," said Siddique, turning back to me, "he'll just take it off and give it to you. Pathans good people, yes Mohsin Shah?" Mohsin Shah again gave the affirmative. "You know, brother, Peshawar is Pathan country."

"Is Dr. Shafiq a Pathan?" I asked.

"Could be, but all I know is that he comes from a long line of scholars. His brothers were all alim or hafiz or qari, his father, his grandfather, and on down."

"That's a blessing."

"Just like Qari Saheb," said Siddique, pointing at him. "Qari Saheb's father is a qari, his grandfather's a qari, his brothers all qaris." Qari Saheb nodded. Siddique had been to Qari Saheb's home district, the valley of Swat. The most beautiful landscapes he had ever seen, he promised, and "nowhere in Pakistan will you find Islam practiced so honestly and sweetly, brother . . . the most gracious, hospitable people anywhere. If I were to ever leave the United States for good, that's where I'd want to live. I'd be a happy old man." I could barely fathom Swat as a real place, let alone the place that gave me Qari Saheb. It made me jealous that Siddique had gone there and met the Qari's father. "Just think of Qari Saheb," he said, "and everything that Qari Saheb is, and then think of him sitting at the feet of a man who looks exactly like him but with a longer, softer beard."

From there the conversation turned to Peshawar's local black market. Siddique said that in Peshawar you could buy anything—cheap VCRs, camcorders, even alcohol, smuggled from Russia through Afghanistan. "Heroin, opium," he added as an afterthought. "We're real close to Afghanistan—"

"Can we go over there?"

"Brother, it's all civil war now. You don't want to go there."

The bus hit another bump, and I spilled my books. "What do you have there?" asked Siddique. He picked up my volumes from the International Islamic University's library: the Sufi classic *The Conference of the Birds* and the Dhammapada, the Penguin edition with Buddha on the cover. "You should stick to the Qur'an," he told me. "While you're in Pakistan surrounded by expert readers of the Qur'an, you should take that opportunity to improve your reading and your Arabic."

"What do you think of Sufism?" I asked. The Sufis sought a more direct experience of Allah, and I couldn't fault them for that, but I wasn't sure if I could call them Muslims. Sometimes it seemed like they thought they were prophets.

"For where you're at," said Siddique, "it's like playing with dynamite. If you're not far enough on the path to know what they're really saying, those books will lead you straight out of your religion." He switched topics by asking me how I liked the bidets.

"They took some getting used to," I answered.

"It's actually sunna to squat, did you know? That was how the Prophet did it."

I wanted to be like him so badly, if there was a sunna way to piss of course I'd want to know it. But the Prophet's sunna was also Siddique's sunna, and I wanted to be like Siddique too.

WE FIRST SAW Dr. Shafiq's youngest son, Mujtaba, in front of their house with a cricket paddle. Mohsin Shah pulled up and Siddique called out to him in Arabic.

"Kay fahallukum?" he asked Mujtaba.

"Ana bikail." Mujtaba seemed vaguely intimidated by Siddique, which I remembered from our days in Rochester. He led us down a cement walkway around the house, opened a gate and there was Dr. Shafiq sipping tea at a round table, chickens in the grass around him. He wore a white shalwar kameez and brown pakul hat.

"Mash'Allah!" Dr. Shafiq exclaimed, jumping out of his chair and causing the chickens to scatter. "Brother Mikail," he said at our embrace, "how are you? Are you enjoying Pakistan?"

"It's amazing," I told him.

"Very good, good," he said. "Insha'Allah, you might come back after you finish high school." He then issued commands in Pashtu to his son, who left and came back with tea for all of us. Dr. Shafiq said something else, and immediately Mujtaba asked, "Brother Mikail, would you like to play cricket?" I knew what was happening; Dr. Shafiq wanted to discuss my future with the other men: my education, my wife, the life they would plan for me. My posture straightened as I walked with Mujtaba to the field. He was only a couple years younger than me, but I saw myself as closer to his father's position than to his.

"How do you like Peshawar?" I asked him.

"I like it, but Mustafa doesn't because nobody plays basketball here."

A circle of kids waited for us, some holding paddles. Mustafa jumped out from among them to embrace me. Someone handed me a paddle and said that I'd be up first.

"I don't know what to do," I said. Mujtaba showed me how to hold the paddle.

"When you hit it, run here," said Mustafa, standing near the pitcher.

I swung for the fences and connected. Everyone screamed for me to run straight ahead. Then they told me to run back to where I had been before. Then I had to run back. Then back again. And again.

"Hurry, hurry!" screamed one boy. "Our score is much less!" I kept running back and forth in a straight line and noticed all the guys laughing. I had no clue how many times I was supposed to run, but figured we were well past it.

"Keep running!" another one shouted. I played dumb and kept going, giving them a funny story—*once there was this dumb Amriken and he didn't know anything about cricket*—

After the game, Mustafa and Mujtaba went inside to help their mother prepare dinner while I joined the men in the backyard. Dr. Shafiq introduced me to three scholars from his school, each with a long black beard (one with streaks of henna), glasses, a white shalwar kameez and his own style of headwear: one in white cotton kufi, one in black Jinnah cap, and the third in a gray pakul. Dr. Shafiq gave them a quick rundown of my journey to Islam. They replied with the usual recognition of Allah's Will, and one even said that it was his honor to meet such a special young man. Siddique leaned back in his chair with his arms crossed and a proud father's smile.

"It's an honor for *me*," I replied, "to be sitting with men of knowledge. The Prophet, sallallaho alayhe wa salam said that the ink of the scholar was holier than the blood of the martyr."

"Listen to this young brother," Dr. Shafiq told them. "You see this brother Mikail, he reads very much."

"What have you been studying lately?" asked the scholar in black Jinnah cap.

"Well, I read in the Qur'an how every nation has had its own messengers sent by Allah subhanahu wa ta'Ala, delivering Islam in its own language." They nodded. "Also in Sahih Bukhari, I read that Allah has sent over one hundred thousand prophets to mankind, peace be upon all of them. I was wondering, then, if Buddha, Confucius, and Lao-Tse could have been some of these prophets, only to have their messages distorted later on as the Christians did with Isa, alayhe wa salam." I had already posed the question to Iftekhar back home, and expected the same answer from these brothers, but knew that I'd impress them with my consideration of such things.

"Allahu Alim," he said. "Allah knows best. There is no way for us to know such things in this age."

"Brother Mikail," said Dr. Shafiq, "at one time, this area was the center of Buddhist knowledge."

"Really?" It was hard for me to conceive of Pakistan as having a non-Islamic history, or even a past relationship with India.

"The Daw'ah Academy takes the students on field trips to see Buddhist ruins in Taxila, but I do not know if they are doing it this year."

"This year it's Lahore," Siddique interjected. "They see the forts and Masjid Badshahi."

"Very good," said Dr. Shafiq. "They will like that, insha'Allah."

"It is better for them," said the scholar in the pakul.

"See how brother Mikail has a very good mind?" Dr. Shafiq asked. "See how he asks these questions?" Everyone said *mash'Allah* or *al-hamdulilah*. "At the masjid in New York," he continued, "in summer program when other children were playing outside, brother Mikail stayed in the masjid all day, reading and asking questions."

"Are you planning to be a scholar?" asked the alim in the pakul.

"Insha'Allah," I answered.

"Where are you planning to study?"

"I don't know; there are so many great schools."

"Malaysia has the most dynamic Islamic University," said Dr. Shafiq. "They do good things there."

"I was thinking about Mecca or Medina, insha'Allah."

"What branch of knowledge most interests you?" asked the scholar in the kufi.

"I am not sure yet."

"Tafsir, fiqh, ilm ul-hadith?" Qur'anic commentary, Islamic jurisprudence, or traditions of the Prophet.

"You should learn the Arabiyya," said the one in the Jinnah cap. "Study fiqh in Medina, insha'Allah. They need qualified jurisprudents in America."

"Go to Saudi, yes," said Qari Saheb, "learn the Arabiyya, become hafiz, marry pretty Maryam."

"You have the brain for it," said Siddique, "if you can stay focused on what you need to do. Stick to the Qur'an, that's the basis of all knowledge." He turned to Dr. Shafiq. "Brother, there's a school in Virginia that will pay his way. If he goes through their program they'll send him to Saudi and provide for everything."

"I know that school," said Dr. Shafiq. "They would turn him into a terrorist."

I didn't want to leave Dr. Shafiq in Peshawar, but he assured me that he'd soon come to Islamabad and teach my class.

"You marry Maryam," repeated Qari Saheb in the bus as he tickled my sides.

IN ROCHESTER I had heard an Egyptian brother complain, "Dr. Shafiq is not an imam, he's a philosopher." It took a while for me to understand how that could even be a bad thing, but I preferred him over the madness of Rushdie reading Hitler in the Qur'an. When Dr. Shafiq came to Faisal Mosque he gave thoughtful lectures on the parallels between religions.

Hinduism and Judaism, he told us, were not truly "world" religions since they were named for specific places or nations and made no effort at converting outsiders; however, they both gave rise to reform movements, Buddhism and Christianity, that emphasized compassion over ritual and law and spoke to all of mankind. Buddhism and Christianity seemed to be valid in ways that their parents were not, and more in common with Islam.

Dr. Shafiq was only in Islamabad for two days. Siddique, Abdul-Hadi, and I accompanied him to the bus. I was alternately spacing out and focusing on random things: a chicken walking in the dusty road, a convulsing Sufi on the ground with rupees in his lap as he rocked back and forth, a veiled woman haggling over oranges—the orange of the oranges standing out for me as the only color there somehow. Faced with too much to process, my cognition was shutting down. Dr. Shafiq noticed.

"This is our life, you see?"

Then he got on his bus and went home.

I looked out the rear window of Mohsin Shah's bus the whole way out of that market.

"He'll come back to Rochester," said Siddique. "The community needs him too much and he loves them too much. You'll see him again."

"Oh, I know," I said, trying to be tough.

AS SOON AS we arrived at the hostel I went right back out and walked with nowhere to go. *Maybe I'll find a mosque*, I thought; there were mosques all over town, and to pray only at Faisal or the hostel put me in kind of a bubble. Anyway, Islamabad itself was a bubble and kept me sheltered. Everyone told me that Islamabad wasn't the real Pakistan, it was too safe and synthetic and mainly populated with government people—if you want to see the *real* Pakistan, go to Karachi or Lahore or even neighboring Rawalpindi. I had been to the Rawalpindi bazaars; Siddique still joked about how I had stood frozen in front of a pile of skinned goat heads, the flies swirling around them, unable to say a word. "In America, people like to pretend that their food doesn't look like that," he said. "They just pick up their plastic-wrapped meat at the supermarket, clean and with no eyeballs. They're disconnected from reality, brother."

I found some Afghan kids and handed out rupees to hear them recite Qur'an. They stood straight for me with their feet together, folding their hands in front of them to recite as though in prayer. They didn't know the names of any suras but if I said the opening words, they could give the rest. I tried to ask them where I could find a mosque. "Masjid," I said, assuming that any Muslim would know the word in Arabic. They looked at me blankly. "Mosque," I said, opting for the English. Then I said the Arabic word for prayer, salat, while raising my hands to my ears. I also tried it in Urdu—namaz— but that didn't work either. I didn't know how to say "mosque" or "prayer" in Pashtu or Punjabi so I imitated a muezzin with his hands to his mouth—*Allaaaaaaaahu Akbar!*—my voice cracking during the long *a*. The kids then took me by the hand and we ran together.

There was no Saudi money behind the construction of this one and it didn't wear the name of a king. It was just the size of someone's house; its cold floor was covered with old fraying mats, and it had only a single grimy faucet for wudhu and no real doors. I walked in with the boys and performed a short prayer, two rakats out of respect for the place. When I sat up from my prostration, one of the boys placed a straw kufi on my head. Because the Prophet had prayed with his head covered, my prayer now had the benefit of sunna. The mosque was slowly filling for Asr. My Afghan brothers and I joined the congregation in the last row.

I GAVE THE kids some extra rupees for their help and kept walking. Within a mile of the hostel I found a small crowd assembled around a real live dancing bear. The show was put on by two men, two boys, and a small malnourished dog with its ribs sticking out. One of the boys beat on a little drum, causing the trained bear to stand on its hind legs and dance with little sidesteps, and the dog to freak out and chase its own tail. The other boy rushed back and forth to collect rupees from the pavement.

I imagined Dr. Shafiq saying, "This is our life, you see?" The sky was starting to change color. Soon it'd be dinnertime at the hostel but I wanted to stay outside. I wasn't eating much anymore; they gave us the same meal three times a day, just meat, rice, bread, and tea, and it had me losing interest in food. Besides, Ramadan was coming up, my first full Ramadan, and I wanted to train myself to deal with hunger.

I could hear a man wailing on the next street over. It sounded almost like a call to prayer, but not really. It was pained and desperate. I followed the sound until I found a Somalian refugee walking slowly down the middle of the empty street with infant son in one arm and a walking stick in his other hand. He and the baby were draped in what reminded me of the mosque's ratty prayer mats. His stick tapped the road and he'd cry out his story as though making a sad song. Tap, cry, tap, cry. I turned around and went the other way, thinking in Siddique's voice: *In America, brother, people would only feel sorry for the dog and the bear and maybe the boys, but forget to look at the men. The men are hungry and miserable too. Life is hard for everyone here.*

I came inside after dark and prayed Maghrib by myself. Afterward I stayed in sitting position for a long time and thought of everyone: the boys, the sad dancing bear, the crazy starving dog chasing its own tail, the wailing Somalian man with his baby. Not asking for anything specific or even knowing what to ask for, I just *remembered* them to Allah.

I couldn't say anything about it to Abdul-Hadi or even Siddique. It just cheapens days like that to prattle on about what amazing things you saw and how you reflected on them. They only grow in meaning when you keep them inside yourself; when you think instead of talk. Besides, I couldn't be sure that it was really so amazing or if I was just being a dumb kid from America who had never seen *real* life, the way it was for most people on the earth. But Siddique knew that I had been out and told me that the Prophet, sallallaho alayhe wa salam, said, "If you knew what I know, no one would walk alone at night." If I needed to go outside again, he said, he would go with me.

18 drops of hellfire

We were trudging up Daman-e-Koh, one of the Margalla Hills behind Faisal Mosque—Idris from Nigeria, Hasan from Ghana, Luqman from Liberia, and another Luqman from Singapore—and found ourselves trapped in branches covered in three-inch thorns, so tangled together that they all seemed to be from the same tree. I wondered what kind of creatures those thorns were meant for—one of the brothers back at Faisal had warned us about wild boars, but Siddique stifled him since there'd be no pigs in a Muslim country. *Maybe monkeys*, I thought, then considered what I would do if we encountered one.

By the time Luqman from Liberia found a path, I was covered with scratches and bits of twig and had thorns stuck in my clothes. Since we always spoke of Islam as sirat ul-mustaqeem, the straight path, I tried to get deep about it and make the whole ordeal into a parable: While I thrashed around in the thorns and thought I'd have to fight through it, Luqman from Liberia kept his head clear and his eyes open and found the way for us. He was a sturdy Muslim: the most advanced reader of Qur'an, though he never bragged, and carrying the weight of a civil war back home, though he never complained. Siddique was right: To be a great scholar, I'd have to find some focus and discipline that I didn't have on my own.

From the top of Daman-e-Koh, all we could really see was Faisal Mosque at the foreground, with the rest of Islamabad disappearing in a bluish white haze—it almost looked like water, like the mosque was an island or a futuristic submarine that had surfaced, its minarets as torpedoes or water-to-heaven missiles.

When it came time for Asr prayer, Luqman from Liberia taught us how to make tayammum, the ablution when no water was present. With our jackets spread in front of us for rugs, brother Idris from Nigeria gave a loud adhan in case there was someone else in the hills.

Our backs to the city, we stared out at the endless green hills, and I thought of climbing down the wrong side to fight my way through thousands of miles of thorns and see where it would go—Afghanistan; Kashmir; the Himalayas; maybe Sinkang, the Muslim province of China? Maybe Swat, the pure valley that produced Qari Saheb? My poor awareness of Pakistan's geography put Swat everywhere that I couldn't reach.

Exhausted, dirty, and scratched but on a trail, we at least had an easier time walking down Daman-e-Koh than climbing up. At the hostel I slumped into the living room couch and turned on the television. American pro wrestling was on.

Two nearly identical men with curly black beards, crisp white jalabs, and white kufis came in and sat down. We gave salams and they shared exchanges in Urdu.

"He wants to see this when he comes to America someday," said one of them, turning to face me.

"What's that?" I asked.

"This here, the . . . fighting."

"Wrestling?"

"Yes, brother."

"Hulk Hogan," said the other one. "Macho Man. Andre."

"Andre the Giant?"

"Yes," he answered, stretching out his arms to convey girth and height.

"Andre is dead," I told him. His friend explained it to him in Urdu and he said something back.

"He wants to know if Andre was Muslim."

"I don't think so, brother. I hadn't heard anything about it, but Allahu Alim."

"Mash'Allah," he said, "every soul must taste of the death. Even the biggest and strongest man, even giant man, brother. All of the muscles and the fame, none of it stops the death." It sounded like he read from a script.

"Yes, brother," I said.

"Even the Prophet, sallallaho alayhe wa salam, he had to die. He was not as the Christians portray Isa, alayhe wa salam, you know; the Prophet, sallallaho alayhe wa salam, he was born naturally and died naturally." Allah bless the man for wanting to teach, but did he think I didn't know this stuff? "Umar, radiallaho anho," he continued, "refused to believe that the Prophet was dead. He said, 'If anyone says Sayyedna Muhammad, sallallaho alayhe wa salam, is dead, I will chop off his head.' But Abu Bakr, radiallaho anho, told him and the people, 'He who worships Muhammad, sallallaho alayhe wa salam, let him know that Muhammad, sallallaho alayhe wa salam, is dead. He who worships Allah, subhanahu wa ta'Ala, let him know that Allah, subhanahu wa ta'Ala, is alive and cannot die.'"

"Al-hamdulilah, brother," I replied. He kept going, lecturing me like I was a Christian or at best a ten-year-old at the

Islamic Center Summer Camp. "Islam is the perfect way of life; everything in Islam makes sense . . . like the way we wash for prayer, you know, we call this wudhu and it has good reasons behind it . . ." They were members of a group called the Tablighi Jamaat, which had started some eighty years before in British India. Their idea was that after centuries of interaction with Hindus, Muslims no longer knew their own religion; so they went on the road teaching simple things to whoever they met, just getting down the basics.

It seemed like a good idea; when people asked Tablighis why they never tried to teach Islam to non-Muslims, they replied that you can't go around converting others until you have mastered the deen yourself. There were so many things in the day-to-day practice of Islam that Muslims took for granted, little beautiful things like thanking Allah for clean water. Even when it's little-kid stuff that you already know, it never hurts to listen, since Allah puts so much wisdom into His religion that the well really has no bottom.

Soon it would be Ramadan, the brother told me, and I should thank Allah for the blessing of fasting in a Muslim land. After providing a long-winded explanation of the spiritual and physical benefits of the fast, he asked if my parents were Muslim.

"No," I answered.

"They need to accept Islam, insha'Allah. You must be very gentle with them, brother, and show the truth of Islam through your kindness and good deeds. If they do not accept Islam, insha'Allah, there is no hope for them."

"What about someone with mental illness?" I asked.

"If someone through disease cannot have a good mind to make his own decision, brother, and he does not know reality, then insha'Allah, Allah, subhanahu wa ta'Ala, is the Most Merciful."

"Mash'Allah," I said. "You know, brother, my mother is not Muslim, but she has been supportive of my efforts to learn and practice Islam. She has never said a word against Islam. She drove me to the masjid where I accepted shahadah, she drove me to the masjid for jum'aa prayers and for a summer program where I studied Islam, she bought me books, she bought me prayer rugs and kufis, and she allowed me to come here to Pakistan to live among Muslims and improve my reading of Qur'an. She has even sent me some money while I was here. She has done as much for my Islam as any Muslim."

"I'm sorry, brother," he said softly. "If she does not become Muslim, it does not matter. She will burn in the hellfire, insha'Allah."

THE TABLIGHI BROTHERS spoke delicately and sweetly, no matter what they were saying. And every other thing out of their mouths was *insha'Allah*, if God wills. Repeating them to myself in all English, Tablighi statements became harder to accept: If God wills, your mother will burn in the hellfire. Why would God will that? The hadiths said that Allah's mercy overwhelmed His wrath, that He had a mercy we could never comprehend.

That night I went to Siddique's room and asked him about the Tablighis.

"Wonderful brothers," he said. Whenever he shook hands with Tablighis they'd leave little gifts in his hand, zikr beads or a vial of musk. They had nothing, but whatever possessions they came into, they parted with almost immediately. On their exit from this world they'd leave nothing behind but their continuing baraka, the blessings for their good words and deeds adding up forever.

"They told me that my mother would burn in hell," I said.

"Brother, let me tell you something. The Prophet's uncle Abu Talib never accepted Islam in his lifetime. He was a good man, never harsh to the Prophet, sallallaho alayhe wa salam, as his other uncles were, but he died a kafr. He died out of Islam. And Allah's mercy to him was that in Jehennam, the fire would only touch the bottoms of his feet and cause his brain to boil."

"Okay," I said in my own soft holy Tablighi voice.

"Brother, you know that the Prophet's mother died when he was a child. And Allah, subhanahu wa ta'Ala, would not allow the Prophet, sallallaho alayhe wa salam, to pray for her."

"Okay," I said again.

"You can pray for your mother while she's alive. But if she dies out of Islam, you can't help her. That's just between her and Allah." So I knew what I had to do. I couldn't argue with people who had given up all of their possessions and devoted their lives to teaching Islam. Mom had saved my life, and I'd save her soul.

THE SECOND DAY of Ramadan, I went with Luqman and Idris from Nigeria to a mosque where the Tablighis crashed. We sat on the floor to break fast together, twenty of us on either side of a long spread covered with sweets, and started with dates in the practice of the Prophet. While we ate their food, the brothers told us simple things about Islam.

The Tablighis invited us to go on the road with them, even if for only ten days. I wanted to. I could live like this, I thought. What a life it would have been, going from town to town and sleeping in mosques to rejuvenate this deen, becoming the hero in others' stories of Muslim kindness.

The stars were out when we left the mosque. A Tablighi

brother pointed out Venus and told me the story of Harut and Marut.

"They were two angels who came down to earth and fell in love with a beautiful woman named Zuhra," he said. "But when they approached her, she would have nothing to do with them unless, she said, 'you drink alcohol, worship an idol, or commit murder.'"

"Astaghfur'Allah," I said. God forgive me.

"Of course these angels refused. But when they came to her again and she gave them the same conditions, they decided, 'Okay, drinking alcohol is the least of three evils; we can do that much.' But when they got drunk, Zuhra convinced them to worship the idol. Someone passing by saw these angels performing shirk, and so they killed him. And this woman rose into heaven and became Venus." It didn't make sense to me; angels did not have the free will to sin, and how could a human ascend into heaven and become Venus? It sounded like jahiliyya, pre-Islamic ignorance, lingering on in Muslim dressing, but I didn't want to cause trouble.

He smiled at me. "It's not true, brother," he said. "It's just something that people have made up."

"It sounded suspicious," I replied. After making our final farewells, he pulled me back from Luqman and Idris from Nigeria and discreetly handed me a pen.

"If I had enough for your friends," he said, "I would give each of them one. But this is all I have, and you are the youngest, so I want you to have it." I took the pen, and we embraced one more time. "Remember me in your prayers," he asked.

SIDDIQUE TOOK ABDUL-HADI and me to break fast at the home of a retired colonel—we called him Colonel Saheb—whose son worked for Kodak in Rochester and whose grandson Jehangir I had met at the Islamic Center Summer Camp. Colonel Saheb picked us up in his compact car with a chauffeur.

"There's so much cultural baggage from the caste-minded Hindus," Siddique would tell me later, "people here want to flaunt their money as much as anyone." Aoudhubillah, he'd say. I take refuge in God.

The seating arrangements for dinner placed me between Colonel Saheb's two gorgeous teenaged daughters, neither of them in proper hijab but simply in long scarves resting on the backs of their necks. Colonel Saheb sat directly across the table from me. "He's a strategist," Siddique would explain later. "He wants to see where you're looking."

Before dinner, the colonel's wife asked me to say grace. I hesitated. Muslims don't say *grace*; we eat in the Name of Allah and that's it.

"Maybe recite al-Fatiha," she suggested. I looked at Siddique but his eyes gave no answer. It was my call. Making it clear in my niyya, intention, that I was only respecting my hosts and intending no deliberate innovation in Islam, I went ahead and said it.

"These upper-class people are educated in London," Siddique told me at the hostel. "They go to these rich English kafr schools, pick up kafr ways, and then come back here to mix it all up."

"And their daughters dressed like Hindus," I added.

"That's right, brother." He laughed. "I knew you'd notice that, you're a young man. You want to see real Islam, you have to go to an Arab country. Go straight to the source. Here it's too diluted."

The Tablighis were right, then. And that night I jerked off, Allah forgive me. I thought about Colonel Saheb's daughters and pumped it out, then stared at my load in the bidet. A few weeks' worth, it was a big load and especially thick, clinging so hard to the porcelain that it took more than one flush. That's why we have hijab, I told it.

✪

MORE OBVIOUSLY THAN ever, I needed to get married. The Prophet had said that marriage fulfilled half your religion, and I understood. The only two things I ever really thought about were Islam and sex, but without a legal means to reconcile them, they pulled me in opposite directions.

I had a monster between my legs that wouldn't sleep. Masturbating only gave it peace for a short time.

It made perfect sense to me that saints from the early centuries of Christianity would chop their dicks off, but Islam wasn't into that. We did not follow a celibate Christ but a Prophet who loved women—he used to have sex with every one of his wives every single night, I had heard or read somewhere. It was perfectly natural, even a blessing, that I wanted women. I just had to get one the right way.

I called Maryam's mother. At first it was hard to talk to her because of the delays, but once we got accustomed to it, I told her that the brothers were suggesting that I get married.

"Brother Mikail, are you ready to support a family? Are you prepared for the responsibilities of a husband?"

"Uh, I guess not."

"You should probably give it some time, then." But she put me on the phone with her daughter anyway.

"As-salamu alaikum!" said Maryam. It sounded like she was excited to hear from me.

"Wa-alaikum as-salam," I answered, with a tone that I thought was kind of smooth.

"Hello? Hello? Mikail?"

"Yes, I'm here."

"Hello?" Her voice had a nervous urgency, like it really mattered that we didn't lose our connection.

"There's a delay," I told her.

"Oh, sorry."

"That's okay," I said.

"What's it like over there?"

"It's amazing, al-hamdulilah. There's so much to tell you that I don't know where to start."

"How's your Arabic coming along?"

"It's tough," I answered. "Nobody here speaks Arabic, so I leave the classroom and don't have any way to practice. I've actually picked up more Urdu and Punjabi and Pashtu."

"Arabic's not easy, mostly for the grammar," she said with authority. "But Mom got me through Arabic 1 and I'm starting to get comfortable with it." *Arabic 1?* She was five years younger than me, and I was studying Arabic in a mosque in Pakistan, but she could still embarrass me if she wanted.

"I'm learning a lot, though," I assured her. "Our lecturers come from all over the world."

"That's great! I wish I could go." That was the first time I noticed the absence of women in our program.

She told me to stay safe, and it made me feel like I was doing something epic for her sake. Like she was standing at the foot of a mountain and watching me climb, knowing that I'd retrieve a treasure from the top and bring it down for her.

After masturbating for the first time in so long, I had to do it a few more times and then decided that I could abstain for the rest of my time in Pakistan. Sometimes I thought about Maryam, but thoughts weren't sins, not really; and besides, insha'Allah, she would be my wife someday. I also thought about Colonel Saheb's daughters, but it was their fault for not covering, or Colonel Saheb's fault.

BREAKING THE FAST was different at Qari Saheb's house. His porch was crowded with young boys kneeling before Qur'ans on wooden rehal stands, running their fingers over verses. "That is what I like to see," said Siddique. "Every one of these kids is future hafiz. They'll have it all down by the time they're ten."

"Insha'Allah."

"Did you ever hear of how Qari Saheb became hafiz?"

"No."

"When he was a boy, his father woke him up every morning for salatul-Fajr, then made him climb up on the roof and recite all the Qur'an he knew before he could come down for breakfast. After breakfast he sat with his father and memorized more. As years went on, he had to spend more and more time on that roof every morning until eventually he was reciting the whole Qur'an."

Qari Saheb's children brought us our food. At the end of the meal, Qari Saheb presented me with a beautiful plaque of that special sura Ya Sin, black letters on gold and covered in glitter.

"Insha'Allah, brother Mikail," he said, "next time I come Rochester, you have all Ya Sin memorized." I wanted to. There were hadiths suggesting that if a Muslim read Ya Sin at night to seek Allah's pleasure, Allah would forgive his sins and remove the dismay of the hereafter. As we were leaving, Qari Saheb brought his wife out to meet us. Her hijab was on right, with not a lock of stray hair. We gave polite greetings of *assalamu alaikum*.

"Did you see, brother?" asked Siddique on the way home.

"What?"

"We met his wife, y'akhi. That means a lot to a man like the Qari. We're like his family now. You're an uncle to his kids."

The next week we had dinner with an Amriken named Dawud whom Siddique had met during his last stay in Pakistan. On the walk to his apartment, Siddique tried to teach me how to defend myself through the use of pressure points. He'd grab my arm, pull me close, and then push a knuckle into my temple, making my legs give out. Then he invited me to try on him, taking my hand and placing it at the exact same spot on his head. I drove my knuckle into his skull as hard as I could, but it didn't do anything. "That's not it," he said. I kept trying. He repositioned my hand but still I couldn't hurt him.

Dawud was something special, he told me. "People back home say that if you don't like America, you should just leave, but this brother did just that. He grew up in the Bronx, embraced Islam, and couldn't handle living among the kafrs anymore, so he just left. He came here and married a Somalian refugee woman, al-hamdulilah, and now he studies at Faisal." Dawud was the opposite of so many Pakistani brothers, said Siddique, who left their lives in the bosom of Islam only to make big money as doctors or engineers in the United States.

Dawud opened his door to us in a green jalab. His beard was just long enough to be contained in his fist, the length preferred by the Prophet. A giant curtain divided the living room so that his wife could serve us without being seen. A plate of food would slide under the curtain to Dawud, who then passed it to one of us.

"I have a great deal of respect for you brothers," he told us. "You're the ones living the struggle. Me, I couldn't take it, these girls showing off . . . well, brothers you know what they show off. At school, at work, wherever you go, there's no avoiding it."

"It's not easy," I said. Before leaving we exchanged addresses. Dawud said he would write to us if God willed, and he promised that we'd see each other again, "if not in this world, the next." Siddique had a glow about him for the rest of the night, which made Dawud seem that much more impressive; like the idea of Qari Saheb having a father, or Dr. Shafiq's relationship to Ismail al Faruqi, it was hard to believe that Siddique could look at a man the way that I looked at Siddique.

COLONEL SAHEB'S WIFE was the principal of an all-girls private school in Rawalpindi and asked me to come give a talk to her students. Upon my arrival, she brought me to the teachers' lounge and introduced me to her faculty. None of the women wore correct hijab, just that same flimsy Indian scarf on their shoulders with their hair uncovered. "It's great to be living in a Muslim-majority country," I said with a smile. I wondered if they caught the distinction. *Muslim-majority.* I wouldn't call Pakistan itself a "Muslim" or "Islamic" society, not anymore. The women didn't know how to dress and the government had no real respect for Islam; not even Benazir Bhutto wore hijab, not really—her scarf revealed her hair and neck and could easily slip off the back of her head. Siddique told me that the people in Swat demanded the appointment of a qazi, an Islamic judge, so the government sent them a qazi without a beard! That's what happens when you follow a woman and call it Islam.

The colonel's wife had me sign their guestbook. I gave my signature under that of a man named Imran Khan, who she explained was the "Michael Jordan of Pakistani cricket." Then she led me to the morning class. They were all teenagers and wore a uniform consisting of a white shalwar kameez, gray sweater, and blue blazer. No hijab or even one of those scarves. Some of the girls were pretty.

"This is brother Mikail Muhammad," she told them, "and he is an American Muslim studying at the Daw'ah Academy in Faisal Mosque. He's going to talk about his experiences coming to Islam and living in Pakistan." There were maybe a hundred girls there, and she just put me in front of them, a boy who could lust and jerk off into his bidet with all these girls in his head. I stood at the podium, and one of the girls came up to adjust the microphone for my height.

"As-salamu alaikum," I said, petrified. They returned the greeting in perfect unison. "I'm, uh, honored to be here . . ."

I began clumsy enough, but they were well trained, bursting into applause every time I hesitated. I started to smile and even make eye contact with girls in the front rows. By the end I was getting performative, anticipating their applause and playing off it.

For the afternoon class, there would be no awkward starts. "AND CHRISTIANITY CAN'T SAVE AMERICA, BECAUSE THEY HAD THEIR CHANCE!" My finger was stabbing the air in front of me. "WE HAVE ALL SEEN WHAT CHRISTIANITY CAN DO! IT WAS CHRISTIANITY THAT PUT SHACKLES ON THE FEET AND THE HANDS AND THE NECKS OF AFRICAN MUSLIMS AND BROUGHT THEM TO THE AMERICAS IN CHAINS! IT WAS CHRISTIANITY THAT TURNED MY COUNTRY INTO A NATION OF DRUNKS AND PROSTITUTES! CHRISTIANITY COULDN'T GIVE PEOPLE WHAT THEY NEEDED! CHRISTIANITY LEAVES LITTLE BOYS NOT KNOWING WHO THEIR FATHERS ARE, AND LITTLE GIRLS NOT HAVING MOTHERS WHO CAN TEACH THEM HOW TO BE WOMEN!"

The girls were frozen. "THAT'S WHAT CHRISTIANITY HAS DONE TO AMERICA, AND THAT'S WHY AMERICA

WILL FALL UNLESS IT CAN SEE THE SOLUTION, THE ONLY SOLUTION, THE ONLY WAY OF LIFE: ISLAM, AL-SIRATUL MUSTAQEEM, LAID DOWN FOR US BY RASULLULLAH SAYYEDNA MUHAMMAD, SALLALLAHO ALAYHE WA SALAM."

Of course they clapped again, but this time it came stiff. The principal thanked me, then took the podium to remind her class that "Muslims do not condemn other religions."

On the bus back to Islamabad I wondered what had happened. It was now obvious that I could never be an alim, since my having any kind of knowledge or authority would only cause harm to the deen. I was smart enough and passionate enough to read all day, sure, but couldn't ground myself as my teachers advised.

Speaking to those girls, I could have used a soft voice and gently corrected errors at that school, and I could have been like a Tablighi renewing Islam for Muslims. Instead I was angry like Rushdie, speaking from negative places. You could give me something beautiful and perfect like Islam but still I'd ruin it. The Qari laughed and played all the time, but people would see me and ask why Muslims couldn't smile.

Elijah Muhammad had told Malcolm X to beware of adulation: Those cameras were more dangerous than any narcotic. First they chase you, but then you chase them. Malcolm was rightly guided and never let the cameras deceive him, but me? All it took for me was a speech at Beaconhouse School for Girls. Their applause made me feel like I had a power over them, like they were giving me the rope to pull them where I wanted. What if I had more than an afternoon with those girls, what if they gave me that every day and their applause just piled up in my brain—how far would I go? I could have ended up like David Koresh, whose Branch Davidians had burned up with him two years ago. Or Charles Manson, or Wesley

Unger; I could have been Wesley. I *was* Wesley, of course I was. My father, like Allah, subhanahu wa ta'Ala, was closer to me than the vein in my neck. When Reverend Calvin Unger told little Wesley Calvin Unger that the Devil would get him someday, he was right: Satan did get him, but it was the Devil in our blood, and it got me too.

Returning to Faisal Mosque, I sat on the grass in the shade of a minaret and dwelled on these things for a long time. The Prophet had called the best of men he who retreated to the mountains to save others from his evil. Perhaps the best I could do for Islam and my own soul was to climb up the Margallas and live there with the wild monkeys.

I found Luqman and Idris standing by a weird shrine thing on the mosque property. I didn't know what it was, but the sight of it always made me uncomfortable.

"It's the tomb of some local saint," Luqman guessed.

"These people need to learn their Islam," I said with no life in my voice. "Muslims aren't supposed to have saints and shrines; this is some Sufi nonsense." I didn't really know much about Sufis other than that some broke a lot of rules and tampered with religion. There might have been a secret reason for it beyond our understanding, or it might have been a simple corruption of Islam. Allah knew best. But the whole Faisal Mosque now struck me as a corruption of Islam. It was funded with Saudi money but designed by a Turk, and Turks were so desperate to be thought of as white Europeans that they had all but forfeited Islam. I looked up at its giant brass crescents topping the minarets and the point of the dome; what did a crescent have to do with Islam? The Prophet never put crescents on his mosques or chose the moon as a symbol for his community. If the Prophet was alive and came to Islamabad, he'd mistake Faisal Mosque for a temple of moon worship.

And look at the flag of Pakistan with a star and moon on it—you didn't see moons on flags in the Middle East where people stayed true to Islam: no moons on the flags of Saudi or Egypt or Jordan or Syria, or Iraq or Kuwait or Libya or Bahrain, Qatar, Yemen, Oman, Iran, or the Sudan.

Years later I'd learn that the shrine wasn't even for a saint but a general, Zia ul-Haq, who was president of Pakistan from his coup in 1977 to his death in 1988.

ALL OF MY energy went into staying clean for prayer. Farting or going to the bathroom violated wudhu, so I tried to do them less often. I heard stories about great Muslims who would worship Allah nonstop through the night, performing morning prayer with the same wudhu as the previous night's Isha prayer. It seemed like something to shoot for, but the spicy food made it hard not to fart. I'd even feel it bubbling during a prayer and clench up to hold it in. A few times I couldn't tell if the gas left my body or not; better safe than sorry, I'd withdraw from the prayer to redo my wudhu and start the salat over. It was embarrassing when praying in a group.

Then I started to feel an urge to urinate while in prayer and sometimes I'd focus on the flexing of my urethra. I read that while passing by two graves, the Prophet heard the men tormented inside, and he said that one was being punished for his calumny; the other for not properly cleaning his private parts after pissing. That was why the Prophet squatted to piss, and why the scholars called it makrooh, detestable, for us to stand; standing increased the chances of splashing on yourself. Eventually I would have sensory hallucinations of peeing my pants—the tickle in my urethra of just a single drop slowly easing out of the hole, but still enough to invalidate my prayer. Then I'd back away from the jam'aat, watching brothers discreetly step over to fill the gap I left behind, and retreat to the bathroom. Pulling down my pants and feeling around in my underwear, I found nothing. I was dry. But then I'd wonder if I had missed the drop, so I'd go right back in and search again. Before renewing my wudhu I'd linger over the bidet for a long time, feeling that tickle in my urethra and waiting for whatever was inside to come out. I'd shake my penis, pull it and squeeze it from the bottom up to the head like a tube of toothpaste to get the last drop.

Then I washed my penis because it was the Prophet's way. Bathrooms in mosques or Muslim homes provided a water jug for that reason. But then my next examination in the bathroom would reveal a tiny wet circle where my tip touched my underwear, and I couldn't know if it was urine or the water from my washing. I even wondered if I had hallucinated the wetness—was my genetic disposition to schizophrenia finally kicking in? So I took to praying with folded napkins in my pants. After prayer I raced to the bathroom and made sure that the napkins were not visibly wet.

"Brother Mukhtar," I asked him after classes, while my brothers milled around the mosque. "I have a question." The way I explained it sounded academic, though I was ready to cry and couldn't look at him.

"Allah is merciful," he assured me. "Insha'Allah, if it is a medical condition, it is not your fault." So I tried to forget about it but still knew that on the Day, our genitals would testify to Allah about our deeds. It was hard not to imagine a giant, veiny penis standing between me and the gates to paradise, blocking my way, ready to fall and crush me if I came any closer.

going home

19

We still had to buy funeral shrouds for the Rochester community. Siddique went with us to the jum'aa bazaar because he said Americans had no sense of bartering, we'd just accept whatever price we were given. To help with something like that would look good on his resume in the hereafter; death was serious business. Siddique told me that merely attending a funeral prayer earns you a qirat, and he who stays through the burial earns two qirats.

When the Prophet's companions asked him to define a qirat, he told them, "rewards as big as a mountain."

THE FINAL WEEK of the program was all good-byes. Every day someone left. Brothers from the same country usually left together. One day it was the pair from Sri Lanka, then the

Ethiopians, then the South Africans. Siddique went home before Abdul-Hadi and me, leaving us nearly alone at the end.

Everything became a last time: my last time walking through F-10 Markaz with the Afghan kids, my last lesson with Qari Saheb—he was conscious of it too, going easy on me since my reading was as good as it could ever get there. Our last time in Faisal Mosque was for taraweeh, the special late-night prayer in Ramadan. I liked the way that the mosque looked at night, all lit up, and I liked the way that I felt inside, like we were putting in overtime with our religion.

When it finally came our day, I sat on the concrete wall surrounding our hostel, my overstuffed bags on the ground, looking across the street at the high court advocate's miniature palace and to my right towards the Markaz. Since I had so much to bring home, including my liter of Zamzam water and a full nine-volume set of green Sahih Bukharis, I wore four layers of clothing just to make room in the bags. Mohsin Shah pulled in, and Qari Saheb hopped out of the bus; he was coming with Abdul-Hadi and me to the airport. He didn't do that for everyone. And he held my hand for the whole ride.

"Be good man," he said before we boarded, kissing me on the cheek. I swung my overstuffed bag on my shoulder, and he watched us disappear into the gate.

From Islamabad we went to Karachi and from there to Bahrain, where we saw what we could of life in an Arab country without leaving the airport. Then came a bitter layover in Frankfurt, and I couldn't get on the next flight soon enough, vowing never to step foot in Germany again. I was actually happy to get off the plane at JFK and step foot on American ground again. Then it was Rochester, where both of our moms were waiting. Abdul-Hadi and I shared a good Muslim brother embrace, and then I left him with the funeral shrouds, heaving my bags back to my old world.

On the ride home I didn't say much. Mom assumed that I was just exhausted, but I was really formulating a strategy; she needed to see the truth of Islam, but I needed to be careful in how I showed her. My arguing and preaching never brought anyone to the deen. If I could keep Islam soft and approachable and show her that we weren't all crazy and militant, she could come around, if God willed.

Pakistan was slipping into the past. I already felt like it had been decades ago. New bits of information like the snow on the ground and the lights on the highway were entering my brain and pushing out the last two months. Perhaps with sensory deprivation I could keep the adventure fresh—if I closed my eyes and refused to inhale, I could hold onto the sight of Faisal Mosque and smells of jum'aa bazaars—

Then I saw our house again and the same driveway and the same door and then the same kitchen, and then my own room, and I just sat on my bed staring at things, trying to remember that two months ago, these things and this room were my life. From my reading of Joseph Campbell's *The Hero with a Thousand Faces*, I knew where to place myself in the quest: Having attained the Ultimate Boon and returned from the unfamiliar world back to the familiar, it became my duty to share the Boon with mankind—or at least with Geneva.

AT DESALES I was treated like Neil Armstrong coming back from the moon. Fat Ed mentioned my return in the morning announcements, and the kids even seemed happy to see me. They passed my pictures around in every class and asked lots of questions. I had a debriefing with the guidance counselor, who expressed his concern for my health. My face looked gaunt, he said; I was a skinny kid to begin with, but had lost at least fifteen pounds.

Mr. Harris invited me to speak to his freshman history class. I put together an outline and talked about Pakistan for forty-five minutes, focusing on the religious differences between Islam and Hinduism and the need for an Islamic state to be free from Hindu-controlled India. When it came time for questions, only Mr. Harris raised his hand.

"What are your thoughts on Bangladesh?"

"I didn't go to Bangladesh," I whimpered. That was all I could say. One of our lecturers at Faisal Mosque had taught us the history of Pakistan without one word on Bangladesh— formerly East Pakistan—or on the Bengali war for independence from Pakistan that left millions dead and hundreds of thousands raped, Muslims on Muslims.

MY FIRST TIME back at the Islamic Center of Rochester, Iftekhar hugged me and suggested that I go into the masjid and make a nafl prayer. After my salat we sat in a corner and I gave a full report of the last two months. "Al-hamdulilah," he beamed. "Brother Mikail, you are doing well, insha'Allah. We are all proud of you. And soon, insha'Allah, you will be graduating from high school."

"Insha'Allah," I repeated.

"It is time to think about what you want to do. If you wish to continue your studies of Islam and become an alim, Dr. Shafiq and I would be happy to give you anything you need. Letters of recommendations, support from the community— anything, insha'Allah."

"Shukrun," I said humbly. Then I said "shukria." They

both meant "thank you" but I didn't know which was Urdu
and which was Arabic, or which I should even say to Iftekhar
since he grew up speaking Urdu but Arabic was the language
of God and true Muslims. "Brother," I said, "my mother wants
me to go to art school."

"Art school?"

"Yeah, there was this representative from an art school
who came to DeSales, and my art teacher wanted me to apply,
and then I told my mother about it, and she thought it was a
good idea. I used to draw a lot. But what I want is to go back
to Pakistan, or Malaysia maybe, and I was thinking about
Saudi—"

"Here is what you do," he said. "Respect your mother.
Respect your mother's wishes. This art school, where is it?"

"Pittsburgh. The Art Institute of Pittsburgh."

"And it is a two-year school or a four-year school?"

"Two years."

"Okay, you go to art school for two years out of respect for
your mother. Then you pursue Islamic studies, insha'Allah."

Iftekhar's brother walked into the mosque and gave me a
happy salam.

"So what is your plan?" he asked.

"It looks like I'm going to art school."

"Very good, brother. We need more Muslim artists."

"Insha'Allah," I said.

"Muslims can be artists, you know! People think we cannot, but al-hamdulilah. There have been many great Muslim
artists."

"Yes," I said.

"We just cannot do the, you know, the animation."

"The what?"

"Brother, Prophet Muhammad, sallallaho alayhe wa salam,

he says, do not draw the living things or you will be tormented by them in the Jehennam, the hellfire. Allah, subhanahu wa ta'Ala, will say, 'Give life to that which you create.' But no one can give life but Allah, subhanahu wa ta'Ala."

"Right," I said.

"Have you seen *The Lion King*, brother?"

"No, I haven't."

"It is so beautiful, Mikail, I bought it for my daughter. Too bad we cannot make our own."

He then went into his theory that *The Lion King* revealed America's war with Islam. The hyenas represented Iraq, he said, since the hyena army marched like Iraqi soldiers, and in the background of one scene he saw a star and crescent.

DURING SPRING BREAK I took a bus to Berkeley Springs. One of Wesley's sisters picked me up and brought me to her house. She and her husband owned a trucking company with a fleet of eighteen-wheelers. I fell asleep in their living room and was later awakened by the psychic tension of another human being staring hard at my face. I opened my eyes and saw Wesley. Once I realized who it was, I shouted, "Dad!" with an ease that might have surprised both of us.

"You are a quiet man," he told me in his truck.

"Yeah, I think I am."

"The quiet man knows, yet does not relish, the absolute truth."

"Okay."

"You ever notice how uncool queers are? So uncool, they call themselves gay."

"Yeah," I said with a slight laugh.

"They can't keep quiet, and they cannot control the quiet

man. In fact they fear him and try whatever to make him talk. You know what I mean?"

"I think so."

"Just walk away from them; it's better for you."

"I will."

"I see you as someone who reads a great deal."

"Definitely," I said.

"Reading is good, but the uncool queers love to talk about how much they read and quote whomever. The cool, quiet man reads but never does that."

"Yeah, that annoys me."

"And should the quiet man step out, away, be gone forever— there are at least ten men to which the women who loved him will step after he is gone, and the quiet man knows it."

At his house he spoke about my mother. "Here's what I want you to tell her: If a man makes a woman do something simply because she is a woman—something as a woman she would not do except that he makes her do it, because she is a woman—she is not guilty for it; he is."

"I'll tell her that."

"And you tell her that a woman can repent for a man's sin if she wants to, but that does not mean that he's forgiven by God the Father so that he can do it again."

"Okay."

"Listen here: There are many things about your mother that I can say, honestly; I am the only man who truly knows them."

Staying with him meant missing prayers during the day, but I made them up after he went to sleep. I still wasn't sure how he felt about Islam. I had told him about Pakistan, but he only asked if it had been positive or negative. Positive, I answered. He said that he saw me as an artist and writer, but warned that if I stayed Muslim, I would never be published.

When it came time for me to go, Wesley gave me a novel that he had written, *The Hangman*. It was actually only the outline of the story, though it filled a nine-inch-thick stack of yellow legal paper, more than fifteen hundred pages covered with his horrible handwriting. "The story deals with the psychology of the Mafia," he said. "You can use it to teach yourself how to write. And if you ever want to put your name on this story and sell it, I won't claim credit."

He put me back on the bus with his outline for *The Hangman* held together by thin brown rope and wrapped in two clear grocery bags. The rope cut into the edges of the paper. I wondered how I appeared to the people around me, sitting here with this giant armful of beat-up papers clearly the work of illness: probably like I had wanted to look a couple years ago, when I walked up and down Exchange Street with my bus station story.

"HOW WAS IT?" asked Melissa in front of DeSales.

"What?"

"Pakistan. You *did* go to Pakistan, right?"

"Yeah, I did."

"I'm going to write about you for the school newspaper."

"Okay."

"Can I call you?"

"Sure," I said. It'd be a good chance to educate DeSales about Islam.

After the phone interview she wanted to see my pictures, so I let her come over. Mom was at one of her jobs. We sat together on the couch while I gave commentaries on each picture.

"What's that?" she asked, pointing at the Badshahi Mosque

in Lahore. For some reason she leaned into me when she asked. It wasn't necessary.

Then I moved toward her and I saw her lips open; she knew and was ready and soon enough was in my lap, and I had her breasts in my hands.

"We can't do this ever again," I said, looking away from her. She fixed her shirt and ran out the door. I didn't see her face but still knew that she was crying.

After she was gone I made wudhu and prayed. It was around the time for Maghrib, which consisted of three required rakats and two optional ones that you could do for love of the Prophet. I did the required part and then started praying for forgiveness in two-rakat cycles, two, two, two, two, and it kept on building, the guilt snowballing with it—I had to keep on praying and paying myself back, I was bad and *so* bad because I knew it and went for it with full intention. I allowed myself to enter into conversation with this girl who had tried to tempt me once before, and then I spoke to her on the phone—to teach Islam in the DeSales newspaper, who was I kidding? And then I let her come over, knowing full well what evil she'd awaken in my thoughts, knowing that if she gave me a chance, I'd go for it.

I thought of Maryam, who'd never let a boy's hands in her shirt but someday would give me everything, me and me alone. And she was probably thinking of me at the precise moment that I grabbed Melissa's boobs, somewhere a hundred miles away or so on the far side of Rochester, dreaming of me and our life together, our first night together. I felt less wicked than pathetic, just a loser who kept failing again and again and always for the same reason, always led by the dick even though I had read the warnings in all the hadiths.

In a way it was Melissa's fault, I thought, but then I caught

myself—*that's the shaytan trying to convince me that I'm innocent, he's trying to turn me away from a sincere repentance*—
she was accountable for her part but it didn't lessen mine.
As a man and Muslim, I was her protector, but now I had
molested her and possibly given a bad impression of Islam.
Maybe I ruined the deen for her and she'd never accept the
truth, in which case her sins and disbeliefs would fall on my
head; I'd have to repent for her entire life of whoring around
and/or praying to statues of Jesus, drinking wine and calling
it his blood and so on.

The prayer went for hours. Sometimes I was fast with the
words and movements and other times I prayed slowly, in correspondence to how I felt the guilt. I savored that hurt and
counted my rakats, but feared my intention; was I doing it
out of a sincere fear of Allah, or was I only bragging to myself
about how far I would go? Maybe I shouldn't count, I thought.
But anyway I made a total of three hundred rakats.

We spoke once more on the phone. I felt that I owed it
to her.

"Islam sets up protections against this kind of thing," I
said.

"Protections against me caring about you?"

"A man is like an animal, and he treats women like animals. I would end up taking advantage of you, and I'd treat
you like a dog."

"I'm not a little kid, Mikail." It stung when she called me
Mikail, like she was rubbing it in. "Who's the virgin here? It's
not me." That startled me but I regrouped fast.

"Besides all of this, I'm kind of engaged. Did you know
that?"

"Who are you engaged to?"

"She's from the community. She embraced Islam with her

parents. The brothers at the masjid introduced us, and we've been talking."

"How old is she, Mikail?"

"Well, she's gotta be thirteen by now—"

"You poor, poor things," she said before hanging up.

AFTER THAT I graduated. Wesley had asked for an invitation, and I sent him one, but he never showed up. I wasn't expecting him to and didn't really care. I walked across the stage in my blue cap and gown with gold tassel, and Fat Ed shook my hand like he meant it and gave me the diploma. And then DeSales had nothing on me for the rest of my life.

Dan held his graduation party on the night of Mike Tyson's comeback fight after serving three years for rape. Tyson had supposedly followed the Malcolm X template, converting to Islam in prison and taking the name Malik Abdul Aziz. I couldn't be too sure since he came to the ring with new tattoos on his arms, and tattoos were forbidden in Islam. They were images of human faces no less.

"Who's that supposed to be?'" asked one of Dan's friends.

"Arthur Ashe and Mao Tse-Tung," Dan answered.

"Who are they, like Muslim people?"

The fight went less than two minutes before the other guy's manager threw in the towel. In his postmatch interview Tyson gave the shahadah in English and I got goosebumps. It made me wish that I had watched the fight with Muslims, especially Qari Saheb, who had met Muhammad Ali, and we could have shared in Mike Tyson.

out of step

20

After the triumph of my return wore off, it seemed that everyone at DeSales still saw me only as the screwed-up kid who threw himself on the floor, wrote letters to Charles Manson, and saw a shrink on Wednesday afternoons. Graduation marked the end of that character. In Pittsburgh I'd be reborn with no past at all; I could even introduce myself as Mikail Muhammad and that would be all they knew. I brought my black shalwar kameez, my long white jalabiyya, my green and white kifeyyeh scarf, and some kufis and bought a long strip of black fabric at Wal-Mart to make my own Ayatollah-sized turban.

The Art Institute of Pittsburgh made me fill out a roommate compatibility survey and placed me with two other kids who checked the "nondrinker" box: a punk-rock kid from Washington, D.C., and a jock who came from somewhere in the Midwest.

"So you don't drink because of your religion?" the punk guessed from my gigantic turban and shelf of leather books with Arabic titles.

"Yes," I said, "I'm Muslim."

"That's cool," he said. "I'm not religious, but I'm straight-edge. You know about straight-edge?" I shook my head. "I don't drink, do drugs, or have promiscuous sex."

"That's cool," I said back. The punk gave me a quick education on straight-edge, which had grown out of D.C.'s hardcore scene and treated alcohol with a near-religious militancy that I could appreciate. He had lots of stories about going to shows and seeing horrible things in the mosh pits, but had a sense that the victims deserved their fates for not "respecting the scene."

"If you go in there, you have to be ready," he said. "You have to know what it's about. In D.C. they don't fuck around; they'll slice your chest open."

"This is gonna be the shit," he proclaimed of our future. He said he had a job lined up working for his uncle when he finished at Pittsburgh, making $90,000 a year drawing underage Japanese cyborg girls who fought space aliens with phallic tentacles that wrapped around them and shot sperm everywhere. It was a whole genre, he said.

Though I had no intentions of drawing ninja sex mutants, there were still religious questions regarding my presence in art school. I called Maryam's mother and asked her if I could draw living things. Would the pictures come alive and torture me in the hellfire?

"Mikail, first of all, what's the intention of the rule? Why aren't we supposed to draw living things?"

"Because only Allah gives life," I answered.

"Look at the historical context. In pagan Arabia, people

made paintings or statues to worship them. That's why the Prophet forbade those particular people in that time and place from having images. If you draw a picture of your mother, is your intention to make an idol of her? Do you believe that her soul lives in the picture?"

"No."

"Okay. Second, Mikail, you should think about those hadiths. You know, there were no tape recorders back then. By the time Sahih Bukhari was compiled, all of the concerned parties had been dead for generations. How scientific is that?" I had never thought about it; what a religion scholar would call "oral tradition," a lawyer would call "inadmissable hearsay"—hadiths were basically hearsay. "Mikail," said Maryam's mom, "Sahih Bukhari is not the Qur'an. They don't carry equal weight. There's a philosophical purity and simplicity that you'll find in the Qur'an but not always the hadiths." I had read hadiths saying that if a fly lands in your drink, you should dip it to make sure both wings are submerged.

She put me on the phone with Maryam. My dynamics with the family were changing. When we first started, I'd have a long conversation with the mom and then a few minutes of chitchat with the daughter. I talked about the same things with both of them—sometimes having the exact same conversations, with Maryam repeating her mother's lines verbatim—but now noticed that I spoke more with Maryam. We were also starting to talk about things besides Islam, which meant that she had to speak her own words.

"Have you ever shot a gun?" she asked.

"No."

"I have. Dad made sure that I knew how to handle one. We have a gun in every room in the house. There's a little pistol behind the toilet." It had less to do with anything Islamic than the family's rural American conservatism; her farmer dad with bushy red beard was as comfortable in a green and yellow John Deere hat as in a white kufi.

Though we still said good-bye with Arabic greetings of peace, ending phone conversations now felt flirty, with a tease of romantic suspense that seemed borderline haram. I had only seen the girl twice and had forgotten what she looked like, but remained sure that we were building something.

We were building something, I thought. But I forgot what she looked like.

THE MOSQUE IN Pittsburgh had a more serious feeling than the Islamic Center of Rochester. The building itself was a converted old church with crumbling plaster and peeling paint and rats in the walls, but the brothers had heart. Every Friday night we slept over, using the masjid as our refuge from the clubs and parties and all the bad things out there, the bad things shaking their breasts at us in the street. Since it was in a bad neighborhood and I walked there alone, the punk let me carry his big knife. On my way I used to hope for someone to jump out and kill me, and then I could say to Allah that I died on my way to His house.

The only brother I got to know well there was a lanky white guy with huge bushy beard, the kind I wished I could grow. He called himself Musa. Once I went with him to another mosque in town, the official-sounding "Islamic Center of Pittsburgh," but it had none of the spirit of what we called *our* masjid. The Islamic Center was in the university part of town and filled with doctors and engineers who didn't really care about Islam, we were sure—they sent their kids to Catholic schools, wore prohibited silk ties, and attended office parties where alcohol was served and the sexes mixed freely. It made me think of the Islamic Center of Rochester in a different way; everyone there worked at Kodak, Xerox, or IBM and wanted their religion easy. Maybe there was a serious mosque in Rochester too.

Musa complained about the Islamic Center in the car, respectfully stopping the Qur'an tape whenever one of us spoke.

"And look at their bank accounts," he said. "They love Islam so much, but do you think they're banking Islamically? You think they're not collecting tons of riba?" Riba was interest, prohibited in Islam; Mom had agreed to pay my Pittsburgh tuition out-of-pocket because I objected to getting interest loans. "It's hard being a Muslim in America," said Musa. "A *real* Muslim, anyway, who wants to give Islam everything he has. I'm not going to be here much longer, insha'Allah."

"Where are you going?"

"Egypt, brother. They don't play with religion there, insha'Allah."

I didn't say anything so he kept on going. "Islam in America, y'akhi, just you watch. It's going to be so watered down, insha'Allah. People want to assimilate and be half Muslim, half American. It's not right."

I WORE THE turban in class. I thought it made me look extra serious. Students behind me had to move their seats to see around it.

During mechanical drawing class a black kid walked by my seat and saw the Qur'an on top of my books.

"Wait a minute, the Qur'an? But you're *white!*"

"I'm Muslim," I replied.

"A white Muslim? I was wondering when I saw you. We

gotta talk." He approached me again after class. He was a Christian, but his dad belonged to the Nation of Islam and believed that all white people were devils. This kid took the Nation of Islam to represent orthodox Muslim doctrine, but seeing me changed everything.

Each day we'd walk across the yellow bridge together, talking religion. "Why do Muslim women cover their hair?" he'd ask.

"When you see pictures of Mary, how is she dressed?"

"Oh, man, I hadn't thought of that."

I had an answer for everything. *But don't you allow a man to have more than one wife?* Yes, but statistically there are more women than men in any society, and then you must consider that women have a longer life span, men go off and die in wars, men are the traditional providers, and there are more gay men than lesbians. Besides, men in so-called monogamous societies have more women than anyone, they just don't marry or do anything for them, or at best they practice serial divorce. Polygamy protects women.

Why can a Muslim man marry a Christian woman, but not the other way around? Because in traditional societies, the man ruled the household. A Muslim man would have Muslim children and a Christian man would have Christian children.

His name was Oscar when we started talking, but within two weeks he changed it to Asad Latif. I witnessed his shahadah and had him repeat it as Dr. Shafiq had done with me. When we prayed, I recited whatever short sura he was trying to memorize, as Qari Saheb did when I was learning al-Kauthar. And I tried to be his Muslim hero, to make him want to be a part of me like I wanted to be part of Siddique.

Sometimes we'd skip class on Fridays for jum'aa, but couldn't do that every week. Usually we dipped out of class to have our own two-man jum'aa in the hall, and I'd deliver a short sermon I had prepared just for him.

Soon he confessed that he was in love with a Muslim girl that he knew back home, but she wouldn't have anything to do with him when he was a Christian. Her name was Madinah. He showed me a huge colored-pencil portrait of her that he had done in high school.

"You really shouldn't be drawing this girl," I told him.

"But you said we could draw people if our intentions were good."

"Brother," I said, imagining myself to sound like Siddique, "just because it's not idolatry doesn't mean your intentions are good. This girl is physically beautiful to you, and you have these feelings for her that are not appropriate because she's not your wife. She is someone's daughter, someone's sister, and someday she'll be someone's wife—maybe yours, insha'Allah, but Allah knows best."

He knew what he had to do. I watched as he dangled her over his sink and lit the match.

PITTSBURGH WAS THE closest I had ever been to living in a big city, so to encounter mentally ill people on the street made for something exciting and new. Pittsburgh had some good ones. There was a Christian preacher who'd stand on the corner and scream his fire and brimstone at the art school kids. In my Muslim gear I must have been a refreshing change of pace from the pierced-and-tattooed punks he was used to seeing. "MUHAMMAD'S NOT GONNA SAVE YOU!" he shrieked when I came by. "YOU KNOW THAT, RIGHT? ALLAH IS NOT THE GOD OF ABRAHAM!" I let him have his fun.

❂

DURING THANKSGIVING BREAK I went to the Islamic Center of
Rochester and met Brother Jonathon, their new white kid.
We were the same age and he even came from Phelps. He
changed his name to the Arabic version but kept his dad's last
name, calling himself Yahya Edington. He was awkward and
humorless, even worse than me.

"Where are you at in your Islam?" I asked him.

"I don't know what you mean," he said.

"What are you doing right now?"

"Just reading, you know, learning Arabic, insha'Allah."

"Mash'Allah." Everyone fawned over him; he was the new
star. He wanted to go to an Islamic institute near Washington
and become a scholar of shari'a law, and Iftekhar got him
accepted into the same Daw'ah Academy program that took
me to Pakistan. I gave Yahya my address; he'd write a letter from Islamabad saying that he met more brothers who
remembered me than he could even name.

I'd only learn how Yahya Edington turned out because he
ended up on the national news. He studied engineering at
Syracuse University and then went to Fordham University
School of Law, later becoming a patent lawyer in Connecticut.
A decade after the last time I saw Yahya, police would arrest
him for stabbing his neighbor to death. He had wrongly sus-
pected the man of molesting his daughter. The judge gave him
twelve years.

slayers of husayn

21

During winter break, Dan came home from his first semester in Binghamton, and we met for coffee. He told me that all of his friends were Japanese now and he couldn't relate to white people anymore. He sounded like he had learned a lot.

"The nation-state is a dying construct," he said, manipulating his hands as though molding the idea like clay. "We're stuck in this nation-state paradigm, but it's only a construct, it's not *real*, and we could just as easily shift to another construct, one not drawn with geographic and ethno-tribal divisions." I got the first part of it, but he kept going and became hard to follow. I drifted in and out. "So let's call 'culture' the values, norms, institutions, and artifacts," I'd hear him say, and then lose him again.

Dan had already moved light-years ahead while I was wasting my time in art school. In January I went back and lasted a week before calling Mom and having her come get me.

"If you're sure this is what you want to do," she said on the phone, "then I'm with you." So I packed up all of my things and rolled up my Islamic posters.

"I'll see you again," I told Oscar/Asad, repeating what Dawud had said to me in Pakistan, "if not in this world, the next."

"You're really going to be a scholar?"

"Insha'Allah."

"Wow, a scholar." I left him thinking that.

I got my letters of recommendation from Dr. Shafiq and Iftekhar. The plan was Malaysia, but first I needed to raise some money. If Allah wanted this path for me, I thought, He'd make it easy. Then Tom called. We hadn't spoken since our DeSales graduation, but, mash'Allah, he asked if I wanted a job.

"I'm a janitor at Hobart," he said. "I work overnights and we have a temporary position open. You'd be by yourself most of the time, which I know you like, and it's only a six-hour shift."

Tom's crew worked the huge library where I had once tried to steal the Penguin Koran, vacuuming and shampooing the floors, cleaning the bathrooms, wiping down desks and tables. "It's great," he told me. "I just take random books off the shelves and walk around reading." Once he found an encyclopedia of Marvel comic book characters and was able to walk out the door with it because the alarm was off. "It's even better if your crew works the dorms. At the end of the year you can take anything the kids left behind. They don't even care—some rich cocksucker's mom buys him a big TV for his room, and he just leaves it."

My crew worked the student cafe in the neighboring Scandling Center. I had to bring my own books to read. We

did get free leftover cakes and unlimited soda from the fountain, but I'd give longing looks out the window at the library.
There were probably books in there that could help me in
Malaysia, I thought. I would not have tried to steal from
it again—I was a Muslim and stealing was wrong—but if I
could just spend my 11 PM to 5 AM shifts in there, with half
the lights off and nobody else around, I'd bury myself in new
knowledge every night.

Scandling was lame. The other guys in the crew all knew
each other already and I was too into my own mental adven-
tures to even try and get in with them. One of those guys, a
touchy NASCAR fan named Al, showed me how to do everything and then left me alone while he did another section of
the building. I had to pick up all the chairs and put them on
top of the tables and move the tables so that I could vacuum
every inch of the carpet. It took forever. Then I mixed chemicals in a wheeled yellow bucket and mopped the slate floors
in the kitchen and halls. The worst part was the bathrooms;
everyone in Geneva hated the Hobart and William Smith students as stuck-up rich kids ("The school gives every incoming
freshman a Jeep Grand Cherokee," Tom joked) and I had to
get up close to their feces. Hobies and Smithies lived like sav-
ages. Seeing how they smeared their shit everywhere, I wondered what the condition was like inside their clothes. Filthy
kafrs—these guys probably bought new Abercrombie boxers
every week because they didn't know how to clean their assholes. The girls' bathrooms were even worse because they also
had bloody napkins to play with. The bleach I used to clean
the toilets would leave white stains on my clothes, eventually
becoming holes and tears, but after a while I splashed the
bleach on purpose. For Allah's Sake I'd happily destroy my
clothes and clean up rich kids' shit; this was my jihad. If it

could put me on a plane to Malaysia, al-hamdulilah, I'd wipe the Hobies' asses for them.

My ruined T-shirts might have made me look noble and self-sacrificing, but I was still lousy at the actual work, moving too slow when rearranging the tables and chairs and spending too much time reading. Then I poured the wrong chemical in the mop water and ruined the floor.

"Look at this," said Al. "You fucked up the slate."

"What's wrong with it?"

"Look at it!" His voice got high at the end, like he was really losing his composure over the dumb slate. The chemical had apparently left a slight film, but I hadn't paid enough atten-tion to know what the slate looked like before and couldn't tell the difference.

Al didn't like me, but he became more forgiving after Tom told him a story.

"Hey Al," he said as they punched out their time cards. "How's it going with the new guy?"

"He's a fuck-up," Al replied. "He fucked up the slate."

"Go easy on him, Al. He's been through a lot."

"Yeah? Like what?"

"Don't tell anyone . . . but his dad is Charles Manson."

"*The* Charles Manson? No shit?"

"No shit, Al. His mom was a member of the Family, and she used to have conjugal visits with Charlie at San Quentin."

"Oh, man." Al was polite, even gentle with me from then on. I laughed when Tom told me why.

We worked as everyone else in Geneva slept. After my shift ended I walked down the middle of the empty streets, feel-ing like the last man alive. Nan and Gramps left their door unlocked for me. I'd wash up, perform my Fajr prayer, and maybe stay awake long enough for Gramps to get up and

make me pancakes. Then he set out some blankets for me on
his couch, and I went to sleep while he read his little book
of Catholic prayers. Ramadan came and I *technically* fasted,
since I ate at night and slept through the daylight hours, but it
didn't feel like it counted. I also missed the afternoon prayers,
Zuhr and Asr. I'd make Maghrib, the early evening prayer,
and then Isha, the nighttime prayer, before leaving for work. I
kept track of missed prayers in a notebook, planning to double
up with every Zuhr or Asr until I cleared my balance; but as
I worked five nights each week, the salats piled on and I fell
far behind.

Preparations for Malaysia went beyond saving money. I
had to ready myself spiritually for the mission, but any hope
for that was going down the tubes. Siddique used to talk about
the prayers as an exercise for our iman, our faith, and he was
right; slacking on the program left my spiritual muscles weak.
All I could do was make the short du'a before opening a book:
Rabbi zidni ilma, "Lord, increase me in knowledge." I needed
that too: There'd be no hot-shotting in Malaysia; it wasn't
Islamic Center Summer Camp. I'd be thrown in with students
who had spent their whole lives in madrassahs, learning the
deen. To hang with them I'd have to hit the books hard.

The books I brought to work were mainly from the Shi'a
perspective. I hadn't yet made a serious examination of Shi'a
Islam, though it came up in my scattered readings and the
histories of places like Iran. Our Islamic history classes in
Pakistan made no mention of Shi'as, as though they never
existed. When I asked Dr. Shafiq and Iftekhar, they did their
best to brush the matter aside. "Oh, it was just a political
issue," they'd say. "There are no sects in Islam. It's nothing for
you to worry about." Siddique, however, said that some Shi'as
did in fact deviate from *real* Islam. I had asked Qari Saheb

what he thought of Ayatollah Khomeini, and he answered, "Good man, brother, but Shi'a," as though being Shi'a disqualified someone from being a complete Muslim.

The Sunni-Shi'a split began with the death of Muhammad, who had not only been a prophet but also head of the Islamic State. Though Muhammad was Allah's final messenger to mankind with none to come after him, his passing brought on a struggle for temporal leadership over the community. The question was first tribal and political, but turned religious over time; the supporters of Muhammad's son-in-law and nephew Ali became the Shi'as, and their opponents became the Sunnis. And with that, there was no longer such a thing as only *Muslim*; you had to specify what kind of Muslim you were, which half of Islam you belonged to.

I knew that much already, but we—the Sunnis—made it all sound so painless, a minor disagreement between friends. Sunnis even recognized Ali as fourth of the "Rightly Guided Caliphs," providing a neatly wrapped resolution that should leave everyone happy. My new Shi'a books had a different tone. First I'd scrub Hobie and Smithie shit off the toilets and walls, then take a break and read how Abu Bakr had denied Fatima, the Prophet's daughter and Ali's wife, her rightful property— a village called Fadak—by citing a quote of Muhammad, previously unknown to her, that prophets cannot leave inheritance. And then the Sunnis went to Ali's home to demand that he pledge allegiance to Abu Bakr, in the process trampling pregnant Fatima under a door. When Ali finally ascended to power, he was challenged in Islam's first civil war by Ayesha, Abu Bakr's daughter and the Prophet's widow.

I learned that, after Ali's martyrdom, his son Hasan sought to end the conflict by waiving his claim to power. They killed him anyway. Then I read an entire book dedicated to Hasan's brother Husayn, who was brutally slaughtered by Yazid's forces at the battle of Karbala. Every page gave a horrible detail: Husayn stabbed and cut up, chopped apart and trampled under the enemy horses, his head stuck on a spear and his body left to burn and stink under the hot sun. As the book explained, Husayn knew that he'd suffer all of this and went through it for our sake, giving his life to save Islam. I cried for him like I had for the Prophet's daughters, as though crying pulled the bad things out of me.

I had been taught to revere that first generation. The Prophet had said that they would be the greatest Muslims of all time, seconded by the generation immediately after them, and then the generation after that, and the generation after that, each a little weaker in the deen than the one before it, until the final days when one could not tell the Muslims from the kafrs. I stood on the far end of a declining history, sixty generations removed from the blessed companions of the Prophet, sixty degrees weaker in my faith. But now I learned that for politics, the owners of that Golden Age would kill the Prophet's own family and rip Islam down the middle forever. And here I was, fretting over missed prayers.

I began to understand why Sunnis wished that Shi'as did not exist. For Sunnis, the keepers of what has become "orthodox" or "standard" Islam, the presence of dissenting opinion kills that myth of Islamic unity, the ummah. But there was no such thing as the ummah, at least not since the day the Prophet died. It had always been sects and factions and war.

Those fuckers, they ruined it for me; my great Muslim heroes, the pious forebears, stole the whole religion out of my hands. If they were the starting point for Islamic history, the tradition now looked like fourteen centuries' worth of turds heaped on a diamond.

✪

IN THE SPRING came pilgrimage season and Eid al-Adha. The sacrificing of goats had originated with Abraham, who was ordered by God to sacrifice his own son. We believed that the son was Ishmael, though the Judeo-Christian tradition said it was Isaac. The story went that Abraham had his son in position and was ready to bring down the knife, when suddenly God provided a ram to be killed in his place. I already had a mental image of men putting knives to their sons' throats, but it wasn't for God. What if Abraham was just a Morgan County schizophrenic? But I took these doubts as signs of my own failed submission. Things like emotion and intellect, they too are limited and temporary. When I die, there's no brain left for me to question or challenge God, but God is still there. God alone is master of all things, Rabbil'Alameen, Lord of all the Worlds. Once you really know this, you should trust in God no matter how fucked it sounds.

I had no money and wasn't the head of a household, so I didn't have to slaughter anything (nor did I have to pay zakat, the Islamic charity; instead, I qualified as a recipient). I hated being exempt from religious duties; it meant that I was still a boy. Siddique was a full man, required to do things and carry out the law. He let me go with him to Maryam's family's farm, where I watched him and her father pick out a goat.

Everything had to be done right. Islam had rules for sacrifice that made it humane. You weren't supposed to kill the animal in front of other animals, and the actual killing was done in such a way that the animal died as soon and painlessly as possible. I had no idea how to do it, but Siddique had experience and a sure hand. We laid the goat on its side. Maryam's father held it down. Grab its legs, he told me. It was little enough that I could take its front legs in my left hand and its hind legs in my right and keep them from thrashing around.

Siddique took his big knife, said the proper words and then pushed the blade into the goat's neck—just a little push, and then the knife was inside it. The goat cried and tried to kick. The blood spurted hard, the point being to cut a certain artery and get it all out. The kicks slowed down as blood covered the barn floor. The goat stopped crying. Siddique was perfectly hard about it but still merciful, giving no signs that he took pleasure in such things. Finding the experience unpleasant only made me glad that I had taken part; these were just things that had to be done, and men did them. Inside the house, Maryam was making me brownies; I liked to imagine myself as her shelter from the ugly facts of death and blood, but she had grown up on the farm and saw things like that all the time.

I didn't tell Siddique about my crisis with Islamic history. It had me doubting everything—just given the nature of history and oral tradition, how well could I know the Prophet? But you can't admit to feelings like that. If Catholicism was a religion of guilt, Islam was one of shame. It reached a point at which I couldn't stand to be around Muslims anymore, for fear that they would see through me. When you're around a true Muslim you can sense it emanating from him. I had felt it around others, as well as its negative equivalent coming from bad men like Rushdie back in Pakistan. If I stood before true Muslims, they'd feel the weakness in my heart.

We had a word for religious fakers: munafiq, hypocrite. On the Day of Judgment they'd fare even worse than open nonbelievers. Afraid that I'd be one if I prayed among men at jum'aa, I only went to the mosque at night when I could be alone. On weekdays the Islamic Center's office would be occupied, usually by Iftekhar, but after the second afternoon prayer they left and locked the doors. One of the Egyptian brothers had given me a key. I could show up at any time of night, hang out for a few hours or even sleep in the mosque (with my head in the direction of Mecca), and sneak out just before the first prayer of the new day, before Iftekhar or Siddique showed up.

Alone I would pray, sometimes in the mihrab where the imam would stand, and for a required prayer such as Maghrib or Isha I even turned on the microphone and delivered a loud adhan. Sometimes I'd turn on every light in the building, but other times kept it dim and used just the lights over the mihrab or in the back of the room. There were nights when I left all the lights off and made my prayers in the dark, the only illumination coming from cars on Westfall Road, their headlights shining through the windows to glide across our walls.

Mom bought me a portable word processor. To carry it made me feel like Wesley. I'd bring it inside the mosque and plug it into the same outlet as the mihrab microphone from which Qari Saheb gave his adhans and Dr. Shafiq delivered khutbahs, and I'd sit on the prayer rug and write. Having just read Ray Bradbury's *The Martian Chronicles*, I wanted to create an Islamic version with Muslims in outer space getting existential about themselves, Muslim astronauts arguing religion on Pluto and such. Most of it came out corny.

I wasn't always by myself; sometimes on a Friday night I'd find a brother secluding himself in the mosque, or even a traveling jamaat of Tablighi-type brothers coming in off the road in need of a place to sleep. It was never anyone that I knew, but they always had something positive to tell me, some sweet hadith about the rewards of coming to the mosque at night or the blessings of paradise. One brother, an African American convert in white robe and pointed beard, loaned me a special brown leather-bound volume of stories about the Prophet. It smelled of his musks and oils. I kept it in my car to return to him someday, but he never came back. Another, a South Asian engineering student from the Rochester Institute of Technology, came around a few times and we got to know each other. His name was Nadeem and he was just a few years older than me.

"There are much worse places to be on Friday nights," he said, like the brothers used to say at the Pittsburgh mosque. And at night was when you found the "real brothers," he told me, "because you know, everyone comes to the masjid on Friday. The ones who come at night, when they will not be seen, those are the ones who really have it in their hearts." So I really had it? I didn't feel like I had it and hurt only more for him saying that. It was like I had conned him in some way.

Nadeem had lots of stories about prophets and saints of old. Most of the stories seemed Islamically credible, but some veered towards the borderline unacceptable side of Sufism. He had one about this pious man who strove to attain the greatest houri, the virgin of all paradisical virgins. The man had to pass through different stations, and the whole thing ended up an allegory of what he was doing in his own heart or in his nafs, his soul.

I had my own houri right there on earth. On nights that I was alone, I'd call Maryam with the kitchen phone and talk for hours, over time becoming comfortable enough to talk about sex.

"Islam isn't antisex," she said. "It's fun; it's good." I knew that she was only parroting things that her mom had said, most likely in the mom's exact words. "That's the benefit of having a prophet who married; Muslims are never taught to look at celibacy as holy."

"How do you think you would like it?" I asked.

"What do you mean?"

"I mean, like positions."

"Maybe with the man on top, or me on top."

"Yeah, me too," I said.

When she said *man*, I knew that she meant me, the only man who would ever know her that way. For a moment I feared that I was being inappropriate in a mosque, but then rationalized that while the physical structure, the "Islamic Center," *contained* a mosque, its kitchen was only a kitchen.

Another night Nadeem told me that story about the Prophet saying to respect your mother three times before you respect your father, and it had me ready to flip out because I had been so mean to Mom. Even worse, I had been mean to her in the name of Islam, since she wouldn't meet the conditions for my respect. I left Nadeem in the mosque and went outside to walk by the pond.

Sitting beside the water in the dark, watching traffic lights zip down the I-390 on the other side, I thought of Wesley conceiving me with rape, though I was sure he never saw it as such. A man cannot rape his wife, right? Marriage is implied consent forever. It's yours; you bought it. We had stories about the Prophet saying that the angels curse a woman who turns away her husband; in that case, it's almost a mercy to rape your wife instead of leaving her to Allah's displeasure. Wesley might have thought that he respected motherhood, since he kept my mother in the house to protect her from all of the wicked men of the world.

Back in the Islamic Center, I called Maryam. Her mom answered the phone.

"As-salamu alaikum, Brother Mikail!"

"Wa alaikum as-salam."

"How are you these days?"

"Good, good . . . I'm sleeping in the mosque tonight."

"Mash'Allah!"

"You know that thing in the Qur'an where it says an adulterer can only marry another adulterer?"

"Yes, uh-huh?"

"I've decided that it's wrong."

"Well Mikail, there's a very good reason for this ayat. You see, back in—"

"No, there's no reason for it. I don't care what happened back then or how things were back then."

"Mikail, you can't understand the Qur'an without looking at the time and place that it was—"

"Bullshit!" My intellect had shut off. All I wanted to do was save my mother from myself, which I apparently aimed to do by yelling *bullshit* at Maryam's mother. "If this is supposed to be the universal message, we can't answer every tough question with, 'well, back then it was like this.' The Prophet, peace be upon him, he married Ayesha when she was what, six years old? And he was fifty years old at the time. What do we say to that?"

"Well, Mikail, in seventh-century Arabia, it was normal to—"

"And what about killing apostates? The Qur'an says there's no compulsion in religion, but if someone leaves Islam you can chop off his head?"

"Mikail, in the political climate back then, they had to—"

"Fuck the political climate," I blurted. Siddique had already explained it with "political climate," since forsaking Islam would amount to treason against the Islamic State.

"Are you doing okay, Mikail?"

"I don't know. I'm having a hard time."

"Mikail, that's why it's called 'submission.' Submission isn't easy. We're not supposed to do it blindly. The truth is there, and we have to use our brains to find it. Look at it with a scientific mind, Mikail. You're smart; I know you're smart. These things are here for a reason. We all really like you, Mikail, but you know, your picture isn't on our wall yet, so I don't want you to feel any pressure there—"

What was that supposed to mean? I hung up on her and walked into the prayer hall to lie down on my stomach, my head pointing to Mecca, my arms and legs outstretched as though I had fallen from the sky, crashed through the roof, and landed that way. I could see Nadeem on the other side of the room, hunched over his Qur'an. He might not even have noticed that I was there.

DURING THE WEEKENDS, most brothers only came to the mosque around the times of required prayers, sometimes not even then, so I could treat it like my own house. The kitchen provided leftovers from huge Pakistani banquets, but they were usually too spicy for me to handle. Sometimes I found curry and wrapped it in big discs of bread. I'd also walk downtown and bring back groceries, always stopping at the Hindu-owned store where I could measure the status of my Islam with a look at their statues and paintings. I had to be Muslim, I thought, since I could never be anything other than Muslim; I couldn't get into monkey gods or blue-skinned man gods any more than I could get into Jesus.

Still, postcards of Hindu temples made me think about the mosques I had seen. The first time that I stepped foot into the

Islamic Center, I didn't know how to read Arabic and couldn't know what the wall decorations said. Now I knew. On one side of the mihrab hung a plate bearing Allah's Name. The plate on the other side read *Muhammad*. We claimed that Muhammad was only a man, but did we really believe it? Could we say that Muhammad was ever wrong? The Qur'an itself said so, when Allah scolded the Prophet for his rude treatment of a blind man, but Muslims didn't seem to engage the full depth of that verse. I had heard Muslims say that the Prophet only made mistakes deliberately so that we would not worship him—though to believe this was actually a kind of worship. There were even hadiths saying that Muhammad would intercede for us on the Day of Judgment, almost like a *savior*, another Christ.

SIDDIQUE WAS RIGHT; I should have become grounded in the deen before exploring off the map. But I had no discipline and read recklessly, falling to the autodidact's curse: hopping around from book to book, moving sideways instead of upward, encountering strange ideas without any preparation. I learned about Rabia al-Basri, the female Sufi saint who said that she loved Allah so much, it left no room for anything else—no love for Muhammad, no hate for the Devil. That stuff was like playing with dynamite, Siddique told me.

While reading Attar's *The Conference of the Birds* in Pakistan, I had stumbled upon the verse "Forget what is and is not Islam." It looked bad, but Attar was a lover of Allah and inspiration for Rumi, Sufism's greatest poet-saint. For him, forgetting Islam could not have meant forgetting God. Could I then have God without religion? For all that I was giving up—and I *was* giving it up; I could feel Islam slipping away—what did I gain?

It hurt so bad, sometimes I just sat in the mihrab and cried. Maybe I wasn't a Muslim. I didn't know what I could bear witness to anymore. Siddique had once said that if you lost your faith, you never had it. But I knew that I had it: At some point it was real and I believed it with all my heart, sincerely enough to induce sensory hallucinations of pissing my pants, enough to pray three hundred rakats for kissing a girl, and enough to want to die in a ditch in Grozny. Where did it go, and did it even matter?

I TOOK ONE of my blue-covered Saudi Qur'ans and walked out to the cornfield behind Mom's house. The dirt had been tilled and combed into rows. To avoid stepping on seeds I walked between the rows. I walked until I was far enough from the houses and road to be the only person who could hear my voice.

I dropped the book in the dirt. It landed on its spine and fell open.

"La ilaha illa Allah," I said. There is no god but Allah, and I still meant it with all my heart.

My jeans unzipped, I reached in and pulled out my penis, dangling it high above Allah's Qur'an. There was a tickling tension in my urethra, my body's hesitation to submit to my command, but finally I let go and rained down on the pages. After something like that, could I still call myself a Muslim? I no longer agreed with the question, but the sacrilege did strike me as a highly Islamic act, like the Prophet smashing idols. The Prophet hoped that we'd never make an idol of him, but what if we did? Were we supposed to smash *him*? How many Muhammads had there been, and how many Qur'ans? How many Islams and how many Meccas? They come and go, meaningful only for a speck of time, but there's only one Allah.

Allah owns all of it; Allah stays long after they're gone. No one will ever have the guts to see it this way, I thought, but Real Islam is when you love Allah enough to say "La ilaha illa Allah" and then piss on His Words. Then I walked home and left the book behind.

Some people would think that what I had done was worse than rape or murder, since the Qur'an was more sacred than the human beings who read it. I couldn't get into that any-more. Allah was more merciful than anything in His creation, but we painted Him to be a real hard-ass. For my crime, I was surely bound for the worst parts of the Fire, but it just seemed so absurd now: the angels watching me pee, recording my deeds so that Allah could *get* me, burn my ass good. There were also men who'd give me that fire in this world, since the major schools of fiqh agreed that you could kill Muslims who crossed the bounds. If that's the kind of Punisher Allah you want, have fun with Him. Have fun making yourself miser-able. The Allah that I wanted was more like a mom.

That night I dreamt that I was at Kauthar, Allah's pond of milk in paradise, with Muhammad, his son-in-law Ali, and his grandsons Hasan and Husayn. No one said a word and none of them had faces. They held me there by the white lake-fount, their bodies intersecting each other as they wrapped around me with eight loving arms. Maybe it was good-bye, but in their arms I couldn't feel afraid.

22 in the name of vince mcmahon

Tom loaned me a tape of that spring's WrestleMania, the first one I would watch since the Ultimate Warrior dethroned Hulk Hogan six years earlier.

The World Wrestling Federation called WrestleMania XII the "blast-off" of its "new generation" led by Bret Hart and Shawn Michaels. Compared to the bulky Hogan-types of the 1980s, Bret and Shawn were small (steroid scandals in the early 1990s had rendered huge muscles problematic), but they had their own heroics. Instead of praising the "largest arms in the world," announcers now said that it wasn't the size of the dog in the fight that mattered, but the size of the fight in the dog. Bret and Shawn would take on all the monsters and suffer awful beatings, but somehow find ways to get through it and win.

Bret's gimmick was basically his lack of gimmicks. He just went out there and wrestled, treating it like a real sport.

Shawn acted like a male stripper, dancing to the ring in sequined vests, leather chaps, and little biker hats. First he threw off his hat and played with his long, dirty-blonde hair, then wiggled out of the vest. While unzipping the chaps on each leg, he'd bend over and stick out his ass; then he gyrated his hips and undid the buckle in such a way that simulated masturbation. His tights were covered in broken hearts, with HEARTBREAK KID emblazoned across the rear.

The World Wrestling Federation was building up Shawn as its next big star, his ascension climaxing with a championship win at WrestleMania. The hype around the match portrayed him as having dreamed of winning the belt ever since he was a twelve-year-old boy. This was Shawn's chance to make his dream come true on the biggest night in wrestling, and we were all supposed to wonder if he could really do it. Meanwhile, there were implications that Bret Hart objected to the direction in which a man like Shawn would take the sport, that he saw Shawn's dangling earrings and sequined vests as cheapening the championship. Bret was placed in the role of the wrestling traditionalist, defending the hard old way against Shawn's glittery youth rebellion.

Their difference made the story, even in the way they came to the ring. Bret simply walked down the aisle, all business like he was really on his way to a fight. Shawn descended from the roof of the arena on a cable, soaring over the crowd while the speakers pumped his entrance music (which he sang himself):

> *I think I'm cute*
> *I know I'm sexy*
> *I got the looks*
> *that drive the girls wild*

I got the moves
that really move 'em
I send a chill
up and down their spines
I'm just a sexy boy
(sexy boy)
I'm not your boy toy
(boy toy)

His vest and chaps were sparkling silver, his tights a virginal white with gold and silver hearts. He also wore little white gloves with hearts on them. His hair was in a ponytail.

The match itself was treated with a great deal of seriousness, with the referee explaining the rules to both men beforehand and then ceremoniously holding up the belt for the crowd. The "new generation" stars would perform with more genuine athleticism than the oiled-up bodybuilders-turned-wrestlers of WrestleManias past, flying through the air and executing high-risk moves. In his prime, Hulk Hogan rarely went beyond twenty minutes, but Bret and Shawn kept it going for more than an hour. The match finally ended when Shawn kicked Bret in the face and covered him for the three-count. As the crowd popped, the new champion sat up and put his face in his hands. The referee handed Shawn the belt, and he just knelt there, holding it in front of him in disbelief, then collapsing over it and putting his forehead to the mat. It looked like an Islamic prayer. *He's making sujdah*, I thought. Scrunching his eyes shut and trying to make tears, Shawn slowly stood to his feet and kissed the gold. Then the referee raised his arm to make it official, and the fireworks exploded above them. The ref snapped the belt around his waist and then Shawn stood there alone and bewildered in the middle of the ring, while Vince McMahon on play-by-play declared, "A TWELVE-YEAR-OLD BOY'S DREAM HAS COME TRUE!" and twelve-year-old girls in the crowd held up HEARTBREAK KID signs with hand-drawn hearts.

IT MADE SENSE to put the belt on Shawn Michaels; the little boys that grew up on Hulk Hogan in the 1980s were now entering their twenties without any sexual confidence. We needed a new idea about men to wrap around ourselves, so enter Shawn with his long hair and tattooed bicep, dancing and stripping, in love with his own body. I got a CD of the wrestlers' theme songs and played Shawn's on loop, mastering his routine in the living room while Mom was at work. Mastering Shawn's trademark nip-up—when he'd be lying flat on his back and spring into the air, landing on his feet—I felt the same as when I memorized the ayats from *Malcolm X*, like I had captured some part of the Heartbreak Kid and was a step closer to being him.

Not everyone liked Shawn Michaels; even if you admired what he did in the ring and secretly admired his swagger, it's hard for a guy to cheer a man who shakes his hips and plays up to the teenybopper girls. Tom took me to his friend Roger's house to watch the big pay-per-view matches, and those guys all thought that they could kick Shawn's ass themselves.

"Shawn's a little faggot," said Roger's brother Terry.

Shawn was defending his championship against Vader, a four-hundred-pound beast that the announcers compared to a mastodon. Vader looked like a real-life brutal tough guy, like a football player or bouncer or maybe just a truck driver who could handle himself. If Vader was fighting Shawn in a bar, no one would ever bet on the Heartbreak Kid. You couldn't even root for Shawn; he was too pretty. "Look at him," scoffed Terry as Shawn slipped out of his chaps. "What a fag."

"He doesn't shave his chest anymore," I said. I had intended to mock Shawn but lost my nerve halfway through and couldn't deliver it as a joke.

"Do you like him better that way?" asked Tom. Everyone laughed.

Besides Shawn, my favorite new star was Mankind, who looked like he had never seen a gym in his life but had made a name for himself by legitimately destroying his body in the name of entertainment.

Wrestling had become much more violent since the glory of Hulkamania, and Mankind would go the extra mile to make it look real—doing stunts that resulted in injury even when done right. He was thrown through tables and burned with flaming branding irons and dented chairs with his head. During a match with Vader in Germany, Mankind lost a portion of his right ear. In a Japanese "king of death matches" tournament, he had his face stomped in thumbtacks and his arm sliced open on a bed of nails. For the tournament final, the ring ropes were replaced with barbed wire and small explosives occupied each corner of the ring. By the end of it, Mankind's face was so bloody you couldn't recognize him.

As far as I could see, Shawn Michaels and Mankind were the two best wrestlers in the world. They weren't the best because they were giants (I was taller than both of them) or blessed by the lab with drug-enhanced muscles—it was what they made of themselves, going farther than anyone else. Shawn Michaels was the best because he worked his ass off; Mankind was the best because he was willing to kill himself. I saw something to admire in both of them.

"I THINK I'M going to be a wrestler," I told Mom over dinner.

"Okay," she said, not even asking what happened to Malaysia. Nor did she mention that I was only 170 pounds and had been threatened with failing gym class every year at DeSales.

"There's a school in Elmira," I said. It was about two hours south of Geneva, most of the drive running along Seneca Lake.

"You should probably get a job. If you get a job, you can do anything you want."

In her ten years at the battery factory, Mom had worked her way up from the assembly lines to the offices. She helped me get on the three-to-eleven shift, mixing powders into a container and then cooking them. During breaks I'd go to her empty office and just sit at her desk with the lights off, hiding from the world for fifteen minutes at a time.

I never spoke to anyone at the factory. Soon enough they noticed my constant daydreaming and self-imposed exiles and began to single me out. There was a tag team of gargantuan women—one reminding me of a bleached-blonde Andre the Giant; the other short but wide like a wall—who liked to pick on me.

"Hey Mike," said the wide one, "have you ever had sex?"

"I don't know," I mumbled without looking at her.

"We can help you out, you know," said the blonde Andre. Then they laughed.

They had a prank in which the blonde Andre would call my name, and then I'd look up to find the wide one flashing her breasts.

"Don't be afraid," the wide one would say. "That's what they look like."

There were some cute girls there too, but they worked in another section. I could only glance at them through a window on my way to the vending machines. If there was anything I could have said to them, I didn't know it; I was too far behind to understand how any of that worked. In the years that other guys were learning how to talk to girls and impress them, I was staring at the floor and saying prayers. And here I was now, having skipped a few years of social development, convinced that flirting and sex only happened through the use of magical formulas and secret passwords that I would never decipher.

During a shift when I was walking away with my soda to Mom's office, I heard one of the cute girls say to the other, "That guy creeps me out." They might not have been talking about me, but I decided to quit the job anyway. My next job was at the shampoo factory in Geneva, a gymnasium-sized room filled with noisy machines. The shampoo smell choked me. Standing on one of the lines, watching plastic bottles go by, I zoned out, thinking about Iftekhar and Siddique—did they notice that I hadn't been around? Did they wonder what I was up to? I hoped that they just assumed I made it to Malaysia and was living with good brothers, immersing myself in my studies, maybe married to Maryam. And then I thought about Maryam. Had her mom found another Muslim boy for her? How were all of the good Muslims going to remember me?

"You'll get used to it," said a middle-aged woman with an old smoker's voice. "We all do." Not me. It was only my first day, but during lunch I walked to Nan and Gramps's house and never went back. I spent the rest of the afternoon watching soap operas. In two weeks they sent me a check for half a day of work.

Then I went to the Manpower hiring agency and told them

that I wanted to work construction. I had no experience or skills in that area, but it was at least a man's job with some character, not like working in a factory with old women. Manpower got me a job at the outlet shopping center in Waterloo, building what would become a Levi's store.

"MIKE!" shouted the foreman every morning. "MIKE, YOU GET ANY PUSSY LAST NIGHT?"

"Not last night," I answered, hoping he at least believed that I had gotten pussy some other night.

"YOU DIDN'T? WHAT'S THE MATTER WITH YOU?" He then turned his attention to Wa, a fifty-year-old Vietnamese man who spoke little English. "HEY WA! YOU GET ANY PUSSY LAST NIGHT?"

"Yes," Wa replied with a big smile. The foreman and Wa had known each other for years. Their company came up from Virginia to do the Levi's job. The foreman said that I reminded him of his own son back home.

"How old are you, Mike?"

"I turn nineteen in September."

"Shit, my boy's almost your age. He's sixteen and gets more pussy than you'd believe!" I believed it. His son could have been a nice kid but now I wanted to break his jaw.

The foreman had a hard time finding things for me to do, since I didn't know how to do anything. First he had me sanding drywall. When that was done he gave me some four-foot-long screws to screw into the fixture over the main counter. I had to stand on a ladder and somehow balance this gigantic screw above my head to turn it in. The foreman watched me struggle and drew the expected conclusion: "Shit, Mike, you're not getting enough pussy!"

I only felt useful when we had something heavy to lift or push and all the guys had to join in, but I knew I wasn't strong.

As just another pair of hands, I could hide in their strength. Other than that, all I ever did was sweep the floor and take out garbage. The outlet mall had a parking lot the distance of two football fields, so I'd load up a dolly with trash and push it to the dumpster on the farthest side. Then I'd ride the dolly back, coasting across the parking lot. It felt like I was crossing Seneca Lake. When you only swept a floor for ten hours, you needed to eat up time. "WHERE THE FUCK IS MIKE?" yelled the foreman.

I was still proud to look at the store and know that I had played a part, however small, in keeping society going. After the Levi's was finished, I worked at the future Esprit just a few stores away, but during my first lunch decided that I was sick of construction and went home. I soon found a job stocking shelves at the toy store on the far side of the parking lot, quit after a few weeks, and was then hired at the Gap back on the same side as the Levi's. I stayed at the Gap through my training period. As soon as they expected me to know what I was doing and be responsible for things, I bought some dumb shirts on my employee discount and quit.

After all of this work I had some money to bring to the United States Wrestling Federation school in Elmira. The school ran in a former storefront with the windows all covered in newspaper. I timidly pushed open the door and then saw it, the ring, a real-life ring right in front of me, an altar enclosed in red, white, and blue ropes. A bunch of guys around my age in sweats and sneakers, a few in real wrestling boots, stood on the apron outside the ropes and watched the trainer toss a kid around. A couple of them appeared to be built and one was just fat, but none of them looked like wrestlers on TV.

I just stood there, not saying anything and no one

acknowledging my presence, while the trainer coached a kid through a suplex.

"It's easy," said the trainer, running his hand through his curly black mullet. "I'm not really doing anything. You take your own bump, and I just guide you over." They stood facing each other, their right arms draped over each others' necks. The trainer put his hand on the kid's hip and said "one . . . two . . . go." He then bent his knees and fell backwards while the kid went into the air, making it look as though he had been thrown. The impact was loud. You could hear the real wood and metal under that mat; it was no trampoline like some people thought.

The kid stood but the trainer just sat up and looked at everyone. "Remember when Mankind beat the Undertaker and all those druids came out in black hooded robes?" he asked them. "Well, I was the last druid on the left. You can tell because at one spot the robe moves and you can see the red boot, same boots I have on." Then from a little side room emerged a round, balding man, who I assumed to be the owner. We had spoken on the phone. Before getting into wrestling, he might have been a salesman of some kind, I wasn't sure.

"Hi, you must be Michael," he said, extending his hand. "I'm Bob."

"Nice to meet you," I said, giving a firm handshake to show that I was stronger than my skinny arms would have him think.

"Why don't you come on into the office and we'll talk." He led me into the room from which he came and sat behind a cluttered desk. Bret Hart's action figure stood atop a stack of papers.

Bob asked me what I wanted to do.

"I'm not sure," I said. "I've thought about wrestling, but

maybe I'd be better in the creative part of it, you know, behind-the-scenes type stuff."

"Well, you have to break into the business for that. You could start as a referee; they get to take bumps too." He said it as though I had never watched wrestling before. He passed me a clipboard with things to sign, absolving him of any liability in case I broke my neck. I gave him $50 for a down payment, agreeing on $100 every following week until I finished my training. Then I could be a certified referee and work his shows in front of real crowds.

Bob brought me back out and said to get in the ring. I jumped onto it like the guys did on Saturday mornings, then bent over to step through the ropes.

"Wipe your feet on the apron first," said the trainer. "It's just a thing for respect."

"Okay," I said, making sure to wipe them good though it was purely a symbolic gesture, since the dirty white mat was already blemished with years of boot scuffs, blood stains, and duct-tape patchwork. Then I stepped in with my right foot first like it was a mosque.

"Nice to meet you," he said. "My name's Frank."

"I'm Mike."

"Oooh," he winced after our handshake. "Firm, man."

"Thanks."

"No, no. You don't want that in this business. When you're applying for a job at the bank or something, have a firm handshake, sure. You look like a real go-getter. But if you shake *my* hand like that, I'm thinking wow, this guy's gonna be stiff! If you're stiff, I'm not going to trust my body in your hands. That's how accidents happen and people get hurt. You want to be real loose, like this." He gave me his hand again so I could notice how slack it was.

"Oh," I said.

"That's just something about the business. Now let's see you run the ropes." He showed me how to do it in three big steps. They had a much smaller ring than the ones on television. Frank said I ran the ropes faster than anyone he had ever seen, which kind of embarrassed me but I couldn't stop smiling. "Okay, now here's the basic bump." He tucked in his chin and threw his feet out, landing flat on his back with his arms spread to absorb the impact. It reminded me of falling on cue at DeSales. He showed me how to lock up collar-and-elbow and do armbars into hammerlocks and reversals. "Go easy," he said. "You don't need to really twist my arm; we're working together here. And you don't need to stomp your feet so much."

After that I refereed some practice matches. Frank stayed outside the ring and played the part of an evil manager, distracting me so his man could choke the other guy. I had seen enough wrestling in my life to know what to do.

Before leaving for the day, Bob ordered pizzas (I picked off the pepperoni) and soda and said that anyone who wanted to could spend the night there. Frank immediately said that he would stay. I understood that he was setting the proper example; this is how you pay your dues, by living in the ring, just as Nadeem told me that I'd find my real brothers in the mosque at night.

Frank sat on the edge of the ring apron with a slice and told us which wrestlers were assholes in real life and who the cokeheads were. He had some funny stories about hanging out with Superfly Snuka, but then told us that Snuka had supposedly killed his girlfriend in a hotel room. Then he revealed the terrible truth that Andre the Giant wasn't actually seven foot five, but closer to six ten, which for a wrestling fan was like learning there wasn't a Santa Claus. And WrestleMania III didn't draw more than seventy or eighty thousand people, impressive enough, but not the ninety-three that Vince McMahon claimed. As he went on with stories, I grew comfortable with Frank and the guys. When we talked wrestling, I never ran out of things to say. Only when the subject turned to beer or girls did I get quiet, having nothing to offer on either.

That night I slept in the ring. None of us had pillows and our backs hurt from our earlier bumping. Only slightly matted, wrestling rings were not made to sleep in. Lying on my back, I looked over at the bottom rope, a steel cable wrapped in padding and blue tape. Reaching out and grabbing it, I felt the tension as I pulled. These men were my new brothers, I thought. As in the mosque, we cemented our bond through a language of initiation which also kept the outsiders out. My favorite wrestling insider term was *kayfabe*, which meant "fake" in a variant of old carny talk. Frank said that all the lingo came from wrestling's days of carnival strong men at the start of the twentieth century. "I don't know half of it," he said. "Old-school guys like Pat Patterson, they can have whole conversations in carny talk, and I won't even know what they're talking about."

All brotherhoods had terms for the ones outside, like *kafr*; they helped us define ourselves as the ones inside the ropes. We referred to ordinary fans as *marks*, which again went back to the carnival strong-man cons; and even if we were marks too, we hoped for initiated status through our payments to Bob.

Before falling asleep I looked at the mat, noticing an old red stain nearby and wondering who it came from. It was fun to imagine an important historical figure like Bruno Sammartino or Killer Kowalski so that I could make the claim of sleeping in their blood.

On my way home the next morning, I stopped at the toy store in Horseheads Mall and bought a Shawn Michaels action figure. I never went back to Elmira. To keep it up meant handing Bob a hundred bucks every week, and that meant having a steady job. Besides, brotherhoods always let you down. It was a lot easier to just stay at home and watch wrestling tapes.

23 history of the egyptian wrestling federation

"Look at this bitch," said Tom in the magazine aisle at Wegmans, swimsuit issue in hand. "You can see her camel toe." I shot a glance and then turned away. "Are you gay?"

"No. Why would you even say that?"

"Because I've never heard you say a thing about girls for as long as I've known you."

"I like girls," I assured him, "I just don't talk about it."

"What's your problem?"

"I don't know, maybe the Muslim thing." Hanging out with Dr. Shafiq and Iftekhar, I never had to say "look at those tits."

"You need to see a fuckin' porn, that's what you need."

"No, that's not what I need."

"What are you afraid of?"

"Nothing, it's just a waste of money I don't have."

"I'm paying. You have no argument."

"You can buy it for yourself," I compromised. "I'll just tag along."

Neither of us knew our way around Rochester, so it took a long time to find Monroe Avenue, home to the city's sex industry. Tom told me to keep my eyes open for an old-time movie marquee reading "Show World," but he found it first. As he parked the car, I noticed an old friend walking out of the front door with a plain brown magazine-size paper bag in his hands.

Nadeem! The RIT engineering student who used to sleep at the Islamic Center, the one who told me about the greatest houri in paradise. I jumped out of the car.

"Nadeem!" I called behind him. He didn't turn around. "Nadeem!" He kept walking. I ran up and shouted to him. He stopped and turned.

"Hello," he said.

"As-salamu alaikum, brother! I haven't seen you in forever!"

"Wa alaikum as-salam, how are you?"

"Al-hamdulilah, Brother Nadeem. How are you doing?"

"Oh, I am not Nadeem. I am Nadeem's brother."

"I didn't know that Nadeem had a brother in town."

"Yes, yes. I heard you calling, 'Nadeem! Nadeem!' and I thought, 'insha'Allah, is someone calling my brother? So I turned around."

"I'm sorry, then."

"No, no, mash'Allah. Have a good night, brother."

I watched him continue down the street. It was Nadeem; I knew it was Nadeem.

When he used to speak to me in the mosque at night, telling those wonderful stories, inside I would feel like the biggest munafiq in the world. Now I wondered if he felt that way too. Did either of us deserve it?

Since we were under twenty-one, Show World wouldn't let Tom or me in, so we drove back home and watched wrestling tapes. After sitting through the first three volumes of the old *Best of the WWF* series, we walked outside with a carton of eggs to the overpass, where we bombed trucks on the I-90.

"So are you eating bacon again or what?" asked Tom.

"No," I said.

"Are you still Muslim?"

"I don't know."

"If you could have the body of any wrestler," Tom asked, "whose would it be?"

"Shawn Michaels," I said without hesitation. "He's built, but you know, not overly muscular. Like he could go to the beach and not look like a steroid freak."

"On some level," Tom replied, "you're in love with Shawn Michaels."

I COULD PRETEND to be Shawn Michaels when alone in my mom's house, but it didn't help with girls in real life. My entire sexual experience amounted to that drunk New Year's Eve girl who scared me with her pubic hair, my failed betrothal to a twelve-year-old Muslim convert, and Melissa from DeSales, whose breasts had presented the first major challenge to my religion. During one of my night visits to the Islamic Center I wrote Melissa a letter, giving congrats for her graduation from DeSales and promising that I had experienced some major changes in my life. Basically I was saying that if she still wanted to make out, I was good to go. Back in Phelps I walked up to her house and put it in her mailbox.

She came over the next day and gave me a big hug as I opened the door.

"I wanted to say good-bye the right way," I told her.

"It's never good-bye with you."

"Where are you going in the fall?"

"Manhattanville College. It's in Purchase."

"Where's that?"

"By the city. What are you doing? Weren't you going to Indonesia?"

"Malaysia. I kind of forgot about that."

"So what have you been up to?"

"I don't know. I still hang out at the mosque, but—"

"But what?"

"Melissa, I'm going through some stuff, and I don't know where I'm headed, but I really like you."

"I like you too," she said, almost whispering.

"Really?"

"Of course." And as stupid as that, we kissed again, and soon she was in my lap with my hands back in her shirt. Then she stopped and shoved my hands away. "Did you know that I'm a goddess?"

"What?"

"I'm a goddess. I'm an ethereal goddess."

"I don't know about that."

"I am."

"Well, you know, um, I'm Muslim and we don't—"

"I am a goddess," she asserted, her hand under my shirt, her fingertips grazing the edge of my jeans, teasing but never going in. Then she brought her hand over the surface, sweeping across my erection. I couldn't say a word. "I'm a goddess," she said again.

"You are?"

"Yes, yes I am."

"Okay."

"Talk to me about beauty," she said.

"What do you mean?"

"Talk to me about beauty."

"Guys can't, you know, while things are—"

"No, *you* can't." She smiled, climbed off of me, and stood up. "You'll be okay, Mikail." She kissed me and said she had to go. It felt like a cinderblock was hanging from my scrotum. When she left I tried to jerk off, but my balls hurt so bad that I could only cradle them in my hands like a crying baby and wait it out.

After the pain wore off and I could masturbate again, I recognized what she had done. *There is no god but God*, I had said in Arabic at least half a million times in the last three years, but here this girl rubbed my dick and I called her a goddess. That was all it took for me to commit shirk, the worst sin in all of Islam, the one sin that makes you no longer a Muslim. Melissa was Zuhra from the Tablighis' story, hot enough to bring down angels. And she played the pussy game that Wesley had warned me about.

I saw her a few times at the end of the summer, and we made out some more, never advancing past a mauling of her breasts, though once she ran her hand over my lap again. It was brief and over clothes but still more than I could handle. I asked her what she thought of the size. She said it was perfect, big enough but not frightening. There was one time, she claimed, she went down on a guy and his thing was so thick that she couldn't even get her mouth around it. And there was another guy as long as her forearm and as big around as a soup can. "You don't want it that big," she assured me, but I kind of did.

We'd be watching a movie and she might drape her leg over mine, which caused me to tremble so hard that I had to run away. "What are you afraid of?" she asked, though she knew. Of course she knew, and she loved it. Sometimes she invited me to play with her breasts and then stopped everything to ask a question about Islam. "Mikail, how were the hadiths collected?" Then she'd smirk as I tried to recollect myself. "Mikail, what does Islam say about homosexuals?"

"Well," I answered, "the Prophet said to kill the one who does it, and kill the one he does it to. So I don't know, I guess that's about it—"

"You should start chopping heads, then, 'cause you're looking at a dyke." There was no way that I could find the appropriate response, so I just smiled and faked a laugh.

Besides the fact that she had been with two girls, she could boast of superhuman powers of fellatio. "At least that's what they say," she disclaimed.

"They do?" I asked, hoping for details.

"Well, I learned from a gay guy, so it makes sense. Gay guys give the best head."

"Do you . . . *like* it?"

"Sure, I love it. But sometimes the end result tastes like chlorine and sunflower seeds."

"Really?"

"Haven't you ever tasted yourself?"

"NO!" I shrieked in defense, supporting myself with another fake laugh.

Before she left for school, she gave me a nine-tailed whip. A cat-o'-nine-tails, she called it, with a smile suggesting that it had some subversive use beyond my comprehension. I brought it to the mosque at night. Reading that Shi'as would grieve for the Prophet's martyred grandson Husayn by engaging in various self-injurious behaviors, I wanted to whip myself. *Ya Husayn, Ya Husayn*, I cried while flinging it over my right shoulder, wishing that I could see how pink my back was getting. The pain forced me to switch sides and whip the left. At one point I remembered that this was the same place where Mom drove me to become a Muslim and where I had learned Islam at the feet of Dr. Shafiq, Iftekhar, Siddique, Qari Saheb, and Mukhtar. I felt partly ashamed, but then only astonished that things can go so far from where you started.

IN NOVEMBER I rode a bus with Tom to New York City to watch the Survivor Series, one of the World Wrestling Federation's biggest annual shows. In the main event, Shawn Michaels lost his championship to a big freak named Sycho Sid. The Heartbreak Kid's dream had been shattered, but I was over it by the time we walked out of Madison Square Garden. Shortly after our trip I called Melissa, who had come home for Thanksgiving, and a minute into our choppy conversation blurted out that I loved her.

"You *love* me? How can you love me, Mikail?"

"If it weren't for you, I'd be married to a twelve-year old."

"You wouldn't have married that girl, Mikail."

"I might have, but no matter how crazy I was, you stayed with me. Remember that time you were jogging?"

"Yes, I do. You've grown up a lot."

"All because of you, Melissa! I love you."

"I love you too, Mikail." She said it. She loved me, and now I had a girlfriend. She asked me to come over. We made out a little and then she said that she was tired, so I went home and stayed up all night thinking about her.

She went back to school. Her first night home for winter break, we went to Denny's. She ordered coffee and I got chocolate milk. We sat there for a couple hours. "Mikail," she said, "did I ever tell you about my collection?"

"Your collection of what?"

"Boys. I have a collection of boys."

"How do you collect boys?"

"Different boys, you know, they all have their own functions. There's a boy at school who's like my heart, I guess. He's the one who's good for hugs. And there's Jeff, have you met Jeff? He lives in Geneva."

"No, I haven't."

"He has long hair, plays the guitar . . . I thought you met him."

"What's his function?"

"He's like the penis, I think. That's the only way to say it. Sometimes I need that too."

"Oh."

"Except that it's not always good with him. Last time he wanted anal, and—"

"Okay, Melissa."

"I've probably had anal about a dozen times, but I don't like it."

"It doesn't seem pleasant."

"But you're the brain, Mikail. You're the only one who can challenge me intellectually."

"Really? That's cool."

"I'm serious. Mikail, are you okay? Are you sad?"

"No, I'm okay. I really love you, Melissa."

"And I love you. What are you doing tomorrow night?"

"I don't know."

"Let's spend the night together. I don't mean that we have to do anything, but maybe we will. But let's just be together anyway."

"That sounds good."

"I'm going out tomorrow, but I should be back home by ten. You give me a call, and then I'm all yours."

The next night I kept calling her house and getting no answer. Maybe Jeff wanted anal again.

The guy at school who was her heart didn't know about me or Jeff, and couldn't have handled it. Jeff the penis didn't know about me or the guy she hugged at school, and maybe wouldn't have cared because he was the one doing the fucking—but regardless, *I* was the only one that she ever told about the collection, because only my love was selfless and true. On nights that I got to see Melissa, she told me about Jeff and the dirty things he did to her, and I listened without complaint. I approached our relationship like religion; if I suffered patiently and kept the faith, I would be morally entitled to some kind of reward.

THEN GRAMPS DIED. Nan had already gone and he made it barely a year without her. When he was in the hospital I promised him that I would get baptized in the Catholic Church if he wanted me to. I remained as far from the Church's teachings as I had ever been, but it just seemed like a nice thing to do after all the shit that I put him through. When the Monsignor—the same one who looked at me when he mentioned the "terror of Mohammedism" during Mass—came to give Gramps his last rites, Gramps asked him to baptize me right there so that he could see it.

"Well, that's a very serious thing," the Monsignor replied. "I'd have to talk to Michael and make sure that he's ready and understands what it means." But Gramps passed away before the Monsignor could be fully convinced. It had me hating religion for a while—not just the Catholic Church, since I would have been just as much a prick at another time.

I couldn't see where my life was going. I was a madrassah dropout, wrestling school dropout, creepy virgin, compulsive masturbator, quasi Shi'a self-flagellator, WWF-tape collector, unemployed, and unmatriculated. It didn't seem like I had much reason to wake up the next day. My only real friend was Tom from DeSales. All the Muslims were gone, except for a pen pal in Cairo. He was more than ten years older than me and sent me Muslim books, real basic stuff that you'd send to new converts though I had converted years ago. I never revealed my changing status with Islam, but I sent him pictures of me in the wrestling ring from Elmira, and he thought they were cool.

I asked him if they had professional wrestling in Egypt and he did not understand what I meant. He wrote back that Egypt had an Olympic wrestling team, and they watched televised wrestling from Europe.

Maybe this was my great purpose, I thought. Allah was the best of planners and had a reason for things working out as they did.

"Mom, I'm going to start a wrestling federation in Egypt."

"Okay," she said.

"I have an investor lined up in Cairo, and we're going to talk to TV people there." My pen pal didn't quite understand what I had in mind, but he said the government-run TV might be into "free" or "Romanian" wrestling, whatever that meant.

"Do you think wrestling will work over there?" Mom asked.

"Better than American football. Wrestling's not an alien sport with weird rules to explain, it's just a good guy and a bad guy fighting in a ring. Everyone in the world understands it." In Pakistan nobody cared about the Super Bowl but we watched the World Wrestling Federation, and even Tablighis knew who Andre the Giant was.

I also knew enough of Muslim culture to tinker with the formulas for my audience. The WWF had been pretty xeno-phobic at times, exploiting white-trash patriotism with char-acters like Nikolai Volkoff, who sang the Soviet national anthem before his matches, and the Iron Sheik, who waved an Iranian flag and spit at America's mention. The foreign-fanatic heels made great foils for American heroes like Hulk Hogan and Sgt. Slaughter (who would eventually turn his back on the fans, becoming an Iraqi sympathizer during the first Gulf War). I could employ those same concepts in Egypt: with villains in blue and white, wearing the Star of David and carrying Israel's flag to the ring, and champions who fought them in defense of the entire Muslim world. My pen pal in Cairo liked the idea, saying that we could recruit wrestlers at the local gyms, boxing clubs, and martial arts dojos, and he even knew someone who worked in television. It wasn't hard to get lost in another fantasy image, this time of the Vince McMahon/Don King/P. T. Barnum of Cairo, Great American Promoter—for some reason self-exotifying in a giant cowboy hat and all-white suit with a black rope tie and shiny belt buckle like Boss Hogg from the *Dukes of Hazzard*. In Egypt I could end up rediscovering Islam, I thought, or maybe I'd just go through the motions of being a pure Sunni but still keep my inner torture, or maybe I'd play the role of normal American and pretend that I had no relationship to Islam at all. If I portrayed myself as ignorant of Islam, eventually I could stage a dramatic conversion and put that into the wrestling storylines; but I pulled away from those thoughts because it would make me a munafiq.

With two VCRs connected by a cable and the same shitty old TV I had since seventh grade, I created training videos for my wrestlers. *Volume 1: Pre-Match Histrionics* just showed the opening moments of various matches throughout different leagues and time periods. I wanted my wrestlers to see the theatrics that establish character and set the stage for a match: walking the walk, gesturing to the crowd, staring down your opponent. Then came the second volume, *Post-Match Histrionics*, which showed the other end of the story, the twenty-minute Hulk Hogan posedowns.

To save money for the trip, I got a job working with developmentally disabled adults, riding the vans that took them to their day programs. They all had files about them that I had to read. There was one woman who spoke incoherently each morning about soda pop and liked to scratch her arms, covering them in twenty years' worth of white scars. I read in her file that forceps had been used in her delivery. There was another who liked to rock back and forth and only had use of one arm, which she would bite or use to hit herself; when she was just a baby in her crib, her father punched her in the head. Riding the bus through town, I'd just look at them and wonder why they were in their seats and I was in mine.

Since I was working and the plan seemed serious enough, Mom helped with the money to order a custom championship belt from a guy who made them for real wrestling leagues. My belt looked just like the design that the World Wrestling Federation had been using since Macho Man's tournament triumph in 1988, with a winged eagle in the center plate; but where the WWF belt said WORLD, mine would say EGYPT, and the globe behind the eagle's head would be replaced by an outline map of Egypt. The side plates had King Tut and the Sphinx.

I remembered the old fantasy league that I ran in Canandaigua Junior Academy with the dice, record books, character cards, and epic wrestling stories like "Dream Match." The champion of my seventh-grade fiction, Flyin' Brian Pillman, was based on a real wrestler. In October 1997, the real Brian Pillman died in his hotel room. The official cause of death was atherosclerotic heart disease, but there was rumor of prescription drug abuse.

I wanted Tom to know. He had gone off to college some three hours away, so I called his dorm room.

"He's out," said his roommate.

"Could you just let him know that Brian Pillman died?"

"Okay," said the kid with a new solemn tone, probably thinking that Brian was one of Tom's hometown friends. Tom never called back. He had a whole new life up there, wherever he was. A month later I had to tell him about the Shawn Michaels vs. Bret Hart rematch from Montreal—"the craziest shit ever," I told his voicemail, but that and three other messages went unanswered. We did meet up at the Geneva Denny's when he came home for winter break, and he suggested that I join him in college.

"If I got in, you could get in," he said. "You couldn't have done worse at DeSales than I did."

"I don't know; I might have something going on."

"Like what?"

"It's kind of insane."

"Everything you do is fuckin' insane; your dad is Charles Manson."

"Yeah, well . . . I might be starting a wrestling federation in Egypt."

"Right on," he said.

"No, seriously. I have a plan."

"Okay, what's your plan?"

"I have an investor in Cairo. I'm going to save up and go over there and teach the bare minimum. I mean, I don't really know how to do all the moves but they can get by with fake punches and kicks. There's no WWF-style wrestling in Egypt so there's nothing to compare them to."

"Jesus Christ, you really think it could happen?"

"I don't see why not."

"How far along are you in your plan?"

"I've already paid for my belt."

"Your belt?"

"Yeah, it's a real belt, like four hundred dollars."

"Holy shit!" he exclaimed, his face lighting up as though the whole thing finally hit him. "You got a fucking *belt*?"

"It looks like the WWF belt, except it says 'Egypt' on it."

"Jesus Christ. I'd bet that's the only reason you're doing this, so you can have your own belt."

That same week my pen pal in Cairo wrote to say that he wanted to get married, which would unfortunately kill off any funds for the Egyptian Wrestling Federation. I threw the *Pre-* and *Post-Match Histrionics* tapes under my bed and tried to forget the whole thing, though the belt was still on its way— maybe getting my own belt *was* the only reason. If nothing else, I could at least be buried with it under a tombstone read-ing WRESTLING CHAMPION OF EGYPT—UNDEFEATED.

24

the furious cock

"You don't drink or smoke," said Tom, "so you'll probably be alone all the time."

SUNY CANTON WAS a two-year "Agricultural Technical College." The school's logo was a cornstalk growing out of an open book. Set deep in the wilderness of New York's North Country region, I couldn't fathom anyone being there and not feeling lonely. Driving the nearly two hundred miles to Canton, it was hard to believe that the town had existed all this time, right here in the same state, without my ever hearing of it.

Tom's written directions led me away from the heart of the town, past the end of its sidewalks, to an isolated island of green fields and drab tan and gray buildings encircled by an empty road. I parked in a quarter-full lot and followed the signs to Mohawk Hall to sign in for my room.

TOM WAS RIGHT; all anyone ever wanted to do was forget that they were in Canton, and getting wasted seemed the easiest way about it. So while they snuck whole kegs into the dorms and toweled their doors, I sat in my room staring at the wall (which I had decorated with Qari Saheb's Ya Sin plaque and a framed photograph of Andre the Giant). My only means of access to Canton society were Tom, who lived in what kids called the "Marijuana Intensive Suite" and thus interacted with everyone, and my car, which all of his friends seemed to need at some point. I was always giving rides into town for missions to the poorly stocked video store, to the poorly lit supermarket, or to McDonald's. During one trip, Tom's roommate Rob took out his knife and made a bong from an empty chocolate milk carton. He left the knife behind and I left my doors unlocked; the next time I gave people a ride, they noticed that someone had used the knife to rip up my backseat. "That's Canton," said Tom.

"You see that girl?" asked Rob, pointing out of the window as we drove off campus. "That's the Blue-Lipped Nut Face."

"Why's she called that?" I asked. Tom and his friends had previously called her "Ritalin Girl."

"I hooked up with her one time, and she wore blue lipstick, and I nutted on her face."

We were all obsessed with sperm, or at least its value as a way to mark things. The idea might have entered our Canton culture through Rob's praise of porn legend Peter North, who was famous mainly for the volume of his ejaculations. Rob's favorite part of any Peter North film was anticipating his "money shot," the moment at which he'd destroy a young woman's face with semen. "Look at that shit," gasped Rob.

"She's fuckin' blind now." Females were just another part of the surrounding environment in need of vandalism.

I guess it was the same principle at work when Rob decided to play "beef ravioli baseball" in Heritage Hall's third-floor lounge. My job was to underhand-pitch the full cans of ravioli and he'd swing for the fences with his aluminum bat. Every time he connected, the can would explode. Ravioli got everywhere and made that whole wing of Heritage smell, which we took as a proof of conquest. Whatever it meant to ejaculate on someone's face, we had fulfilled on the campus itself.

Tom bonded most easily with guys who, like us, saw themselves as aliens in Canton. "These fuckin' townies," Rob sneered. "Look, it's like this: If you were born north of the I-90, you have no future." He said it with all the weight of an official fatwa coming from al-Azhar. The I-90 cut New York State in half, running through Albany, Syracuse, Rochester, and Buffalo. Mom's house back in Phelps was south of the road by about one hundred yards. Rob had come from Rochester and told stories about how he used to crack people's heads open with baseball bats. One of these days, he promised, he'd bring us all to Rochester and to a video store on Monroe Avenue that doubled as a whorehouse. Rob said that he was going to try out for porn sometime, but only seemed semiserious about it.

Their suitemate Jim had come from Middletown some six hours south, where he sang in a punk band with his high school friends. He was hefty and strong, not only from lifting weights with the football players but also from his job back home, something involving lumber. His dad got him the job. Jim's dad was a cop, which made it that much funnier when he drew anarchy signs on everything.

The way that Jim spoke about it, punk almost sounded like a new religion. It boasted the same uncompromising individualism I had found with my roommate at Pittsburgh, but Jim's favorite bands romanticized his Irish roots and the immigrant experience with pub anthems about drunk fights and labor unions. One day in class I spotted black-marker graffiti on my desk reading, MY DAD'S A WORKING-CLASS HERO—IS YOURS? and recognized his handwriting. I wrote under it, DISABLED VETERAN.

Walking around on campus, Jim would spot me a hundred feet away and start belting out drinking songs at the top of his lungs: "IT DOESN'T TAKE A BIG MAN TO KNOCK SOMEBODY DOWN—JUST A LITTLE COURAGE TO LIFT HIM OFF THE GROUND!" His band back home had opened a few times for his heroes, the Dropkick Murphys. When drunk, he'd sing the Murphys anthem "Boys on the Docks," throwing his arm around me and slapping my back, the bottle still in his other hand. One of those nights he looked at me and said, "You know Mike, when you die someday, there's a special place waiting for you. You're one of those guys, I know it." I felt like it could be true because he had said it. From then on I started borrowing his punk CDs and helping out with his radio show, just hoping to capture some of whatever he had.

Their suite's living room was always dark, lit only with strings of dim Christmas bulbs lining the walls. They had decorated with fairly typical college-boy stuff: Rob had a poster stolen from a porn shop, advertising a film starring Peter North and Anita Blond. Jim hung up old fliers for punk shows and a *Trainspotting* poster (because heroin addiction was cool if you had a British accent). And there were bottles everywhere, empty bottles lining windowsills and the tops of dressers like trophies. On their front door Rob had put a sticker of the beskirted woman icon that you see on restroom doors. He stuck it so that the figure's crotch went over the peephole, and then he cut away enough of that part to still see, so it looked like he was staring out at the world from inside a vagina. *Fisheye*, he called it.

They were always wasted. Beer and weed still made me uncomfortable, though I didn't know why. I didn't really have a religious objection anymore, but they just seemed ugly and stupid. Maybe if you go through your high school years without ever getting drunk or high, you missed the chance for it to ever make sense.

Tom would wander in from sad Canton parties, his eyes red and hair messed up, sweating for no reason and unhappy with the way things were going. We'd storm through the dorm halls tearing down fliers and leaving all the photocopied campus nonsense on the floor. Back in his room I'd watch him make drunken phone calls to Jim's radio show and request the bands that Jim had gotten us into—NOFX, Swingin' Utters, the Descendents, Subhumans, Angry Samoans—and drunk Rob would wave his arms around and preach about how we were all different but that it was okay.

"Schutt, you know what kind of guy you are?" he'd ask. "You're the kind of guy who'd go down on a girl and then go to class the next day without ever washing his face." It had to have been a joke because the self-professed "Cunnilingus Monster" knew that I had never gone down on anyone, and in fact found the idea of being face-to-face with a vagina completely terrifying.

"Nah," Tom countered. "Mike's not that guy; he's all religious and shit."

"You're religious?" Rob asked, his quarter-open eyes widening for a moment.

"Yeah he's religious," Tom answered for me. "He's fuckin' Muslim."

"No way. Mike, you're Muslim? How the fuck are you Muslim?"

"It just kind of happened," I said. "I used to be real crazy about it."

"Can you speak it? Can you speak Islamic?"

"I can say a couple things in Arabic."

"Do it, man. Say something in Islamic." So I started to rattle off a short sura of the Qur'an and Rob could barely contain himself. "Fuckin' Christ, man! You're *really* Muslim! What the fuck, you're like a human parlor trick!"

THEY ALL HAD funny girl stories and gave the girls of their legends funny names. Rob had his Blue-Lipped Nut Face. Tom told me about a girl who let her boyfriend jerk off in the middle of Oreo cookies before putting them back together and feeding them to her. He called her "Jizz Gomper." I had a girl named Lisa who the guys called "Googly-Eyed Bitch." After ten seconds of making out with her, I tried what Rob called "the Move." It was actually three moves. First I pulled her hand toward my junk. If she was okay with that, I'd unzip and bring it out. Then came the third and most risky maneuver, putting my hand on the top of her head and nudging her down.

"I might have chlamydia," she said.

"Really?"

"Yeah."

"If you have chlamydia, can you give head?"

"I don't know," she replied. So I had her call the school health hotline, and they said sure. After that it was a steady supply. I was still too gynophobic to ever touch her below the waist, but she gave me what I wanted. Sometimes I'd lie back and take it; other times I threw her down and pulled her hair and tit-fucked her, finishing with Peter North facials to make Rob proud. Gobs of my unborn children landed in her hair, in her eye, up her nose, in her ear. She'd swish it around in her mouth, let it dribble down her chin, rub it into her skin, lick it up wherever it went. Sometimes it didn't even seem like she was really a person, like our hook-ups were just one step above me masturbating alone. For our level of emotional intimacy, she could just as easily have been an underwear catalog.

She was fun for a while, and I was happy to add my own anecdotes to the Canton folklore, but one night in postejacu-latory clarity I pushed her away and knew that it was over. Staring at the ceiling, I announced that I couldn't come on her anymore.

"Why not?"

"I'm Muslim."

"You're Muslim? You could've fooled me."

"At least I'm trying to be one."

"So if you're Muslim, you can get blow jobs all day long, as long as you don't do anything for the girl?"

"I'm sorry for disrespecting you."

"Whatever, I'm fine with it. But you're fucked up."

"There's a girl I'm supposed to marry; I've been talking to her family for some time now." I couldn't remember the last time I had spoken to Maryam or her mom; it had to have been a year. Googly-Eyed Bitch walked out.

ONCE I GOT going, the move from repressed religious fanatic to college-boy-who-just-wants-head was a surprisingly easy transition. I had been at the International Islamic University and Canton Agricultural Technical College and found the same idea about women; all that differed was their application of the idea. One man wants to put a veil on a woman and cut off her clitoris, and another just hopes to jizz in her hair and shuffle off into the night; but either way, woman was as Wesley told me, "nigger of the world." Between cultures of honor-killings and cultures of date-rape drugs, a woman couldn't go anywhere in the world and be regarded as a full human being.

The kind of stuff you think about as a rape-son graduating from the distinct misogynies of two hemispheres: There had to be something terrible about being male, born with a part of your body that was made to split people open and stab them. What did that do to your brain? Had to do something.

25 manchild in the north country

The sides of the couches in the Heritage Hall lounge were hard wood and completely flat, which meant that you could turn a couch on its side and make it stand like a pillar. Then you could climb up it with reasonable confidence.

"You're not going to hurt me, right?" asked Jim, lying on his back on a pile of mattresses.

"I know what I'm doing," I assured him, nearly eight feet above the floor. The couch wobbled a little but Tom held it in place. "I went to wrestling school."

"Shit, don't land on my face."

"I won't."

"Punks have bad teeth anyway, but still—"

"Don't worry."

"Jim's done," said Rob, sitting on the other couch with his guitar. "Jim, you're fuckin' *done.*"

"Oh my god," cried one of the girls watching. "You guys are crazy."

"That's at least forty feet off the ground!" Tom exclaimed in the shrill hyperbole of wrestling announcer Jim Ross.

"I'm holding my nuts just in case," said Jim, closing his eyes.

After steadying myself, I raised my arms like Randy "Macho Man" Savage. The trick to a flying elbow drop was to have your legs and ass hit the ground first, absorbing the impact before your elbow hit the guy's chest.

"OH MY!" shrieked Tom-as-Jim-Ross. "OH MY GOD, GET SOME MEDICAL ATTENTION OUT HERE!"

"That was nothing," Jim shrugged.

It gave the guys across the hall the idea to make a wrestling movie in which we'd all play characters and wrestle on stacked mattresses in the dorm lounge. I thought that the lounge did look like an arena, especially with the surrounding balcony above. Tom and I decided to model the film after an old wrestling movie, *I Like to Hurt People*, which revolved around the villainous Sheik and a variety of good-guy wrestlers trying to take him down. I'd be the Sheik of our story, causing mayhem in the dorm wrestling circuit until my main event with our hero: Big Daddy Beans, the kid who owned the camera. For our championship we used my Egyptian Wrestling Federation belt, which had finally arrived. It was a beautiful thing, a sacred object in my hands, and to wear it felt like I really was the champion of Egypt.

We all wanted to be someone else. Rob still wanted to be Peter North, who had supposedly parlayed his porn money into a string of restaurants. Jim aspired to be Dropkick Murphys' singer Mike McColgan, who was such a working-class hero that he quit the band to join the Boston Fire Department.

I called myself "Manchild" after Mankind, who fashioned a Christ of himself every time he went to the ring; in fact he even made the point at the Kawasaki King of Death Match Tournament, coming to the ring with a giant cross wrapped in barbed wire on his back.

WITH TOM'S DRUG relationships connecting us to every faction of Canton social life, we developed a diverse roster of wrestlers—almost enough for a full-fledged league. Tom even arranged for me to wrestle at the Alpha Theta Gamma frat house against a brother named Bailey who we knew back in DeSales. Bailey threw down some mattresses outside the house and made a costume of his karate ghee, a pair of sparring gloves, and a horned Viking helmet. His wrestling moniker was a simple "Mr. Bailey," and with every fake punch or kick he made video game sounds.

The wrestling was all slapstick and harmless—even my climactic battle with Big Daddy Beans in the Heritage Hall lounge was only a comedy bit, besides my slam into the drinking fountain and a death-defying leap from the balcony onto the mattresses. It only changed with a botched spot against Kid Kato, whose character was supposed to be a boxer (North Country welterweight champion). Our match started with him slamming me onto a table, but the table legs gave way and sent me headfirst into a door hinge. I touched the top of my head and saw blood on my hand.

"Fuck, Mike!" snapped Kid Kato. "You gotta get that taken care of."

"No, I'm good. Let's go." I could feel it coming down my face.

"Mike, fuckin' serious dude, you're fuckin' spurtin'—"

"The blood is real in wrestling."

"No way, no fuckin' way."

"The blood is real in wrestling, dude. They don't use fucking ketchup."

"Fuck that, Mike," said the kid working the camera. "You're really bleeding, you need to go to—"

"THE BLOOD IS REAL IN WRESTLING!"

"All right," said Kid Kato. "Jesus Christ, let's just do this." So we rolled around on the mattresses for half an hour, just doing lame punches and clotheslines. My head left big red blotches on the mattresses. Kid Kato's clothes were ruined but I could barely see him, the blood pouring into my eyes.

I heard giggling from somewhere. After defeating Kato I realized that two girls had been watching us.

"That's so fake," one of them said. So I walked over and lowered my head, guessing that they'd be able to see my open wound. I was right. "Oh my god," she cried, running off with her friend. Kid Kato disappeared and tracked down the RA, who called an ambulance. They wheeled me out on a stretcher and drove me to Canton hospital.

The aftermath turned me into a campus legend: The cut was good for four stitches, the girl who saw me had thrown up on herself, the lounge was closed off for a week as a biohazard, and the bloody mattresses were burned. As kids came around Tom's suite to watch the tape and copies made their way through the dorms, my wrestling persona consumed my real self. "Oh shit," yelled the kids in the dining hall, "that's the fuckin' Manchild right there!" A few even treated me like an actual fighter, saying stuff like "I don't want to piss off *that* guy," like I could really do something. To live up to the character, I started wearing my bloody T-shirt and carrying a steel folding chair—a pro wrestler's weapon of choice—everywhere I went, even to class.

By the next semester our tapes had circulated throughout the campus, finding their way to another aspiring Mankind. He called himself Cracker Jack, which I guessed made reference to Mankind's earlier persona, Cactus Jack. Our matches were something like a parody vs. a parody, each of us trying to out-Foley the other with a baseball bat wrapped in barbed wire. Immortalizing ourselves with the camcorder, he gladly let me swing hard at him, cutting up his arm and back. After he took the bat and got his own shots in, I turned from the camera, pulled out a razor blade that I had hidden in my shoe and sliced my left arm deep in the same place that Mankind sported a long scar (and I knew the match in which he had earned it, the bed-of-nails match with Shoji Nakamaki in the King of Death tournament). Blood streamed down the length of my arm. Cracker Jack kept wailing on my bare skin with the barbed-wire bat, scratching me all to shit. The sight of your own blood and a rush of endorphins will have you feeling religious— with every shot I'd say "Ya Husayn" under my breath for the Prophet's slaughtered grandson, though in my head I *was* Husayn, the goat spilling blood all over the barn floor. Our choreographed violence was something special, a ritual even, at least in the fucked-up ways that I saw it. Through Husayn, I understood Mankind showing up at the King of Death matches with a cross on his back, and I was sure that no one else got it like me.

SEEING A FLIER on the dorm bulletin board for the Canton Interfaith Club, I decided to volunteer as a representative for Islam. Who else could they have? I hadn't seen any evidence of Muslims in the North Country.

The dean of students was a pasty white guy named Dan Sweeney.

"You're not what I'd expect," he said. "Islam is kind of . . . it's not really a *world* religion, right? It's limited to one part of the world, like the Arabs, am I right?"

"Only a third of Muslims are Arab," I told him. "The world's largest Muslim country is Indonesia."

"Oh, that's fascinating. Now in Islam, you're not supposed to have premarital sex, right?"

"Right," I answered.

"So what do you do? Do you masturbate?"

It turned out that the Interfaith Club already had a Muslim representative, a middle-aged Indian man who ran the school library. One Friday he drove me to prayers in Potsdam. The mosque was a trailer and I wouldn't have known that it was a mosque from the outside. That might have been the way that they wanted it, the safest way to have a mosque in the back-woods white North Country.

My encounters with Islam then were rare enough that when I made wudhu and listened to khutbahs, it was like meeting up with an old friend. Islam and I could relive the memories and miss what we'd lost, but part again and return to our current lives. Later that same Friday night, I was on the roof of the pizza place on Main Street, wrestling a thumb-tack match against a three-hundred-pound asshole who was too drunk to fully understand that we weren't really fight-ing. Every punch came stiff and he kept trying to get me into the piledriver. Just to get it over with, I whispered in his ear, "clothesline me," so he smashed his fat forearm across my chest and I fell hard, shirtless, onto the tacks. The crowd of a dozen or two wasted Canton kids cheered. My opponent then put both hands on my sternum and pressed with all of his weight for the pin. I thought that my chest would cave in before the referee finished his count.

Walking home with my roommate, who sometimes wrestled in a red jumpsuit as the Flying Gimp, I still had my shirt off and the tacks in my back and arms. I had wrestled in thumbtacks a bunch of times at parties. It wasn't nearly as bad as it looked, and only seriously hurt after the adrenaline wore off and I kept them in; and even then it was more the discomfort of feeling something under your skin and inside you that doesn't belong there. I wanted so bad to pull them out—there was a real pleasure in the relief, like scratching an itch or taking a really satisfying shit—but we hadn't videotaped the match, so I at least had to get some good post-match photos back at the dorms.

We were nearing the footbridges to campus when a car full of girls drove by and then turned around.

They stopped in front of us.

"What's up?" asked the driver.

"I just wrestled in thumbtacks," I answered, turning around to show off the sparkling brass in my skin.

"Go! Go!" whispered the girl in the passenger seat. They sped off without saying a word.

"That's their story for the night," I said.

"That's their story for the year," said the Flying Gimp.

As we crossed the Grasse River, I stopped him to look over the bridge.

"It's not too deep," I said. "Up to your knees, maybe."

"What are you thinking?"

"And it's not that much of a drop; I could jump off here and give a flying elbow onto somebody."

"That'd make some good film," he said.

"A Grasse River Death Match, we should do it." Then we

kept walking, passing Greek letters spray-painted on all the boulders and trees. I got another idea. "Ryan's still got his shotgun, right?"

"No fucking way. I mean, yeah, he's got it, but no to whatever you're thinking."

"Just think about it, though. If it was a controlled environment, and we did it in such a way that it just looked like a hunting accident . . . And Ryan knows what he's doing with a gun; he could just graze me in the leg. I'd completely trust him—"

"I'm pretty sure that Ryan wouldn't shoot you. Better forget about that one, Manchild." I knew he wouldn't do it, and I knew it was crazy, and not just crazy in the dumb-college-stunt way but a whole other darker level where you don't get to have a normal life later and laugh about your wild youth. It was just seriously fucking wrong, so wrong that it pushed you out of the sociological mainstream, and I couldn't figure out why that was so cool, but it was.

IN THE DORMS we convinced some girls to do a catfight. The plan was for the Flying Gimp to serve as special guest referee, and the Manchild, who was feuding with the Gimp, would run in and kick his ass. Then the Manchild would beat up the two girls and threaten to slam them onto thumbtacks. That would get me the heat as a villain, I figured, and show the full extent of the Manchild's sadism; but just before I did it, a third girl would attack me from behind, choking me out and then clotheslining me onto the tacks.

"Why are we doing this?" asked our third catfighter, a tiny dark-haired girl named Maureen. She had gone to high school with the Flying Gimp.

"We've done tons of thumbtack matches, but none of them are on tape," I told her.

"So if I put you in thumbtacks and it's on tape, then you never have to do it again?"

"I guess not."

"Then promise that you won't do that to yourself anymore."

"What?"

"I'll do this if it means you stop hurting yourself."

"Okay, whatever."

"You promise?"

"Yeah, I promise."

We shot the scene, and while I was lying in the thumbtacks she stood on me for good measure. Afterwards she helped pull out the tacks and wiped the blood off my shoulders and arms.

"No more," she whispered in my bed later, her head on my shoulder. "I don't like that you do that." I liked that she didn't like it.

"Well, we got it on tape now, I don't have to."

"And no more of the other stuff. No more barbed wire. No more cutting yourself with razor blades."

"Okay," I said. "I might pass out soon, so if I do, good night."

"Good night."

Then I kissed her on the forehead and waited to see how she'd react. Nothing happened, but at least she didn't get up and run away, so I repositioned myself to kiss her on the lips. She kissed me back, and we just did that for six hours without my ever going for more.

One of the weekends that the Flying Gimp went home, she stayed over and we tried but I kept going soft at the point of entry. We'd go at it with urgency; I'd work up my interest and then think I was ready but still lose it. I always had to pee first, and when it didn't work I'd have to keep getting up to pee between attempts; but then nothing came out, just a nervous dribble while I tugged to keep my penis from shrinking like a closed accordion. It reminded me of hallucinating piss in Islamabad.

"If you try too hard, it's not going to happen," she said. "It's like you're not even trying because you *want* to do it, you're just afraid of it not happening."

"I have a lot of conditioning," I told her. "Religion will do a number on you."

"You have such a big brain and you don't know how to shut it off. It's going to think you to death."

Things worked themselves out on their own. One night I got it in, found my bearings and pounded on her for an hour but never came, going soft only from fatigue. Anyway, I felt good about the *fact* of having sex, the crossing of the line that made me call Jim and Rob to announce my successful initiation. I wished that I could call Siddique too, and even Wesley.

The second time I lasted three minutes and came on her stomach. After that I was fine.

THAT YEAR SAW a great deal of news coverage devoted to "backyard wrestling," the phenomenon of kids all over the country trying to be the next Mankind, jumping off their roofs and smashing fluorescent light tubes on each other's heads. Even if I had promised Maureen that I wouldn't wrestle anymore, I was still entitled to my share of the glory, so I emailed *Inside Edition* and told them about our footage. They wanted to come up and do a story, but there was no easy way of sending a crew to the North Country; the nearest airport to Canton was Syracuse, at least two hours away. Then they found kids in Cincinnati doing the same stunts and had no need for us.

"What the shit are we gonna do?" I asked the Flying Gimp.

"It's hard to get anyone to come up to the North Country," he said. Then came the idea—there were already TV people in the North Country, news reporters in Watertown who never had any news. We'd give them some.

They showed up at our dorms early the next morning. It hadn't dawned on me that they'd bring a camera and do interviews. The cameraman took shots of all the wrestling posters on my walls and the Manchild action figure I had made (painting my Shawn Michaels figure and cutting off his long plastic hair), then rearranged our room so that I could sit in front of my full-length Stone Cold Steve Austin poster while answering questions.

The reporter didn't look too much older than us. She asked if I had any wrestling T-shirts, so I changed into my AUSTIN 3:16 shirt, and they ran the microphone wire underneath to clip onto my collar.

"For a test, can you say your name?" asked the cameraman.

"Michael Schutt."

"Okay, he's good."

"Can you hold the wrestling belt while you talk?" asked the reporter. I put the Egyptian belt on my shoulder, proud like a real wrestler with his real title. "So Mike, what's going through your mind when you do this stuff?"

"When I'm bleeding from the forehead and bleeding from the arm," I told her, "and people are looking at me, and they just have this look like . . . they're either unwilling or unable to do what I've done . . . it's just the fantasy of being their hero."

They aired it that evening, frumpy Watertown anchors Brian Ashley and Anne Richter introducing us as a scourge upon the North Country. The Flying Gimp and I watched from our dorm room. "It's called backyard wrestling," said Anne Richter, "but it's probably something you wouldn't want to see in your backyard—in fact you may not want to see it right now. We have some graphic pictures for you, be warned."

Unable to scream because we still had to hear what they said, we just looked at each other.

"Pro wrestling fans," added Brian Ashley, "are setting up makeshift rings, creating characters, and fighting for their own championship belt. It could be dangerous." As he told viewers, "This is amateur video given to us by a student at SUNY Canton," it cut to me from the Kid Kato match, stumbling breathlessly toward the camera with my face and CANTON INTRAMURALS T-shirt completely covered in blood. "It supposedly shows young men using barbed-wire bats and chairs as weapons—" Cut to clips from the match with Cracker Jack: "The young man tells us that the blood you see is real," with a shot of me on the lounge floor with my left arm sliced open. Then back to the desk, where he handed it over with "7 News reporter Theresa Fulcher has the exclusive story of one college student pushing the line between play . . . and *pain.*"

It was perfect, so cheesy and serious that we couldn't tell who it embarrassed more, us or them or the whole North Country. Then came the boom. "And what do SUNY Canton officials have to say about this backyard wrestling in their backyard?" For some reason we didn't see that coming.

"The blood concerns me; the safety concerns me," said Dean Sweeney, "and we're going to investigate it—"

The piece concluded with an interview of some goofy doctor

who compared our wrestling stunts to reckless drug use and warned that we had a strong chance of killing ourselves.

"These people get high not only on the violence," he told the anchors, "but also on the acting component as well. As one of them said, 'to be a hero,' not just for himself but probably for others as well."

"We're dead!" I told the Flying Gimp. We kept saying it over and over. *We're dead, we're dead, oh shit we're dead, we're so fucking dead, we're dead and we're dead and we're dead, and we're stupid for not even thinking they'd talk to the school, oh fuck, we're dead . . .* but we were laughing as we said it.

"Fuckin' Sweeney," said the Gimp.

"Whatever," I smirked. "That guy asked me if I jerked off."

The next morning I was awakened by a call from the reporters.

"Mike, we were wondering how you felt about getting kicked out of school."

"I'm kicked out?"

"That's what they're saying."

"It's news to me," I said. It wasn't even nine-thirty. "But whatever, I'll go to another school if I have to." Then I tried going back to sleep, only to have the RD knock on our door.

"Mike, Dean Sweeney wants to see you in his office."

First I called Mom at work.

"I think I've been kicked out of school," I said.

"I figured that much. You can't embarrass them on the news, bud."

"I know. I'm supposed to go talk to the dean of students."

"If they're going to kick you out, at least see if you can apply to other schools without this showing up on your record."

"Okay, Mom."

"You'll be okay, just no more wrestling."

"I'm retired, Mom."

Dean Sweeney asked if I had any scars. I told him that I just had the one on my head and the one on my arm.

"I'm not a believer," he said. "Can you lift up your shirt?" So I pulled up my shirt. "Why do you hurt yourself, Michael? Do you get some kind of pleasure out of it?"

"No, it's nothing like that."

He played the good cop. The bad cop was school president Joe Kennedy, who wanted me expelled, but the dean hoped that I could just move off campus for the remainder of the semester, finish out my classes, and then leave Canton forever. I did as Mom suggested and asked about my chances with other schools. Sweeney promised that my disciplinary records wouldn't be included in my academic transcripts. "Fine," I said, waiving my right to a hearing. Then he sent me to the school health center, where my scars were measured and a psychiatrist asked me the same kinds of masochism-type questions.

A few days later I saw Sweeney again.

"You know, Michael, when I asked if you got pleasure out of wrestling, I didn't mean in a sexual way."

"Okay, I didn't think you did."

"I just wanted to make sure you knew that."

Exiled from the dorms, I was allowed on campus only for a half hour before and after my classes. A guy named Rich let me crash at his off-campus apartment.

The North Country was really hurting for news; even my suspension made the top story, and then the night after that they found a real professional wrestler from the local circuit to say that we knew nothing about his great sport. Then the Fox News affiliate from New York sent up a crew. I taped their broadcast off Rich's TV and then brought it to a party down the street.

"It all went on secretly for months," said the Fox reporter, walking by the big SUNY Canton sign with a stack of our tapes in her hand. When it showed my face and said, "also known around campus as the Manchild," the drunk guys standing around the TV cheered like I was Hulk Hogan; then it showed Joe Kennedy saying, "I hope he has a good academic career *somewhere else*," and they all booed like he was Nikolai Volkoff singing the Soviet national anthem in the ring.

The Fox anchor said, "He was even given a psychiatric evaluation to determine if he was a threat" over the clip from my Kid Kato match where I scream "MASH'ALLAH!" at the camera.

Tom plastered fliers all over campus reading SCHUTT 3:16, FUCK KENNEDY! THE MANCHILD LIVES while I tried to smooth things over with the school, writing my professors a letter with the false claim that we had used fake blood and knew what we were doing. Both Kennedy and Sweeney knew that the blood was real, since a whole dorm lounge had been declared a biohazard over it, but still gave my fake-blood story to the local paper for their own damage control. Then *Inside Edition* decided that they were willing to come up to Canton after all, to feature my expulsion story in their piece on backyard wrestling.

The *Inside Edition* segment showed Kennedy saying, "We don't tolerate violence on this campus" and me arguing, "It's not violence. It's performance art." A clip of the Flying Gimp pulling thumbtacks out of the Manchild's arm was juxtaposed with thumbtack scenes from Mankind's Hell in a Cell match. "Where did he get the idea?" asked the voiceover; "From watching his favorite wrestler on TV!" Best of all, they interviewed Vince McMahon himself, who claimed, "We often say on the air, 'don't try these moves,'" which wasn't even true; I had been obsessively watching wrestling on and off for ten years and never heard them say that. But they sure say it now.

manned missiles

26

That fall I was at Buffalo State College.

"Hey Mike Knight," said a girl, "don't you go to school for free or something?"

"I get a check from the government because my dad's insane."

"Oh man, that's awesome." She and her friend laughed. "You're such a character."

At Buffalo they never called me just Mike or even Michael, it was always *Mike Knight*. Legally it was Michael Edward Muhammad Knight; Mom had paid for me to take her name and the Prophet's on the condition that I also include Edward, Gramps's name. In the course of switching schools I killed not only the Manchild, but also Michael Schutt and hopefully the decade-plus of bad feelings that I had with the name.

Socially speaking, I hit my stride in Buffalo. Canton had been an orientation exercise for the sake of learning how to be funny and talk to girls and function at parties. The person-alities of Canton were like my trainers: Tom had shown me around the college drug culture, Rob qualified me to discuss porn and express frat-boy heterosexism, and Jim endowed me with a cool factor for having knowledge of the punk underground.

Being older than most of Porter Hall's residents also pro-vided some leverage, as though I had been able to practice being their age for a few years. They couldn't get over my stories. Fresh out of high school, they just wanted to meet wild college characters like they had seen in dumb movies, and there I was: the guy who lived in a mosque in Pakistan, got kicked out of his old college for running a fight club in the dorms, engaged in written correspondence with Charles Manson, and went to school for free because his dad was insane. I kept my own life at arm's length; stories of thumb-tack wrestling, psychotic fathers, and aspirations of jihad in Chechnya could even be funny, since with my new name they seemed far away—almost like they had happened to someone else, or were just things I had watched on TV.

I WAS SITTING in an awful statistics class when a lady walked into the room and stopped the professor to tell us that a plane had just crashed into the World Trade Center. The professor said that anyone with relatives in New York was free to go call them, and then went on with his lecture. A short time later the lady came back and said that another plane crashed into the World Trade Center, and that both of the towers were gone.

That's how she said it. *Gone.* Not even *collapsed*, which could have provided an image of how it happened, but *gone* as though nothing was left behind, no rubble, no smoke, just an empty space. She added that there were other planes that might have been hijacked, more planes that could come down and hit anything.

The professor still had over an hour left to class and kept going, after which I walked back to the dorms and sat around the TV. I watched replays of the towers falling for fifteen to twenty hours every day. With my brain fried, my eyes heavy and burning, I'd look at the maps on CNN with names like Peshawar jumping out at me, and I'd remember the fantasies I had as Malik al-Kafi Khan, not having any idea what to do.

"I think I want to join the army," I told Mom on the phone.

"You're not joining the army, bud."

"Great-Gramps fought in World War I, Gramps fought in World War II, and Uncle Ed went to Korea. Mine's the first generation of Knights without a veteran."

"Michael, you're all that I have in the world. You're not joining the army."

Thank Allah for moms.

BUSH DECLARED SEPTEMBER 14th a national day of prayer, asking Americans to visit their respective houses of worship. It just so happened to be a Friday. I attended my first jum'aa in two years, but it wasn't for Bush or even Muhammad.

One thing was for sure: I had no interest in questioning whether Islam was inherently a religion of peace or one of war, whether the terrorists had misappropriated an innocent faith or the liberal Muslims were only in denial of what Islam actually taught. I'd never claim to know what "true" Islam stood for; religions were too big to make it that simple, there was too much history and too many verses, and everyone just took the parts that they wanted anyway. For a prophet's message to become what they call a *world* religion, it'd have to be big enough to accommodate all kinds of personalities. Good ones, mean ones, greedy ones, kind ones, hard ones, soft ones, and they all own Islam as much as it owns them. The water has no shape; it's shaped by the bottle. I could see that as a Muslim, contrasting Qari Saheb's sweetness with that maniac Rushdie, and I even saw it with Catholics in Geneva, between sweet Gramps and that dickhead monsignor or Fat Ed.

Arriving at the mosque early I found only one brother, a well-dressed man in sunglasses. We embraced three times in the manner of the Prophet; he said *al-hamdulilah* on the first, *subhanahu Allah* on the second, and *Allahu Akbar* on the third. To hear just that much had me missing everything and wishing I was a real Muslim again—*again?* Was I ever a real Muslim? How was it measured?

After washing and making a short prayer, I took a Qur'an from the shelf and sat in a lonely corner of the room. The walls were white with big windows that brought in the sun, the kind of mosque I liked. It reminded me of the Islamic Center of Rochester.

I had never picked up any substantial amount of Arabic. I could sound out letters and recognize certain words, mainly *Allah*. For the convert, Allah stands out in a swirl of unknowable Arabic, and we're always trying to spot it like with those Waldo books.

Flipping through the pages I found Ya Sin, sura for the dead and dying, "Heart of the Qur'an" as some hadiths said. It began with a series of sharp squiggles and two dots underneath. My ability to sound out the words had decayed over the years, so I paused on nearly every letter. The only parts

I could read with any grace were those beginning lines that I had memorized so long ago. Giving up on Ya Sin, I put the Qur'an back on the shelf and skimmed through an English translation of hadiths. Then I laid down with my head facing Mecca and closed my eyes, awakening some time later to find the mosque filling up, brothers all around me whispering their prayers, standing up, sitting down, touching their foreheads to the floor, counting Allah's Name on their fingers.

Sitting through the sermon reminded me of how bad my posture had become. It was hard not to slouch. There was also a special way that I'd position my right foot behind me while sitting in the mosque—I had seen guys doing it and figured it might have been how the Prophet sat—but my body was no longer used to it, and I had to change position a few times.

The imam knew what he had to do, focusing his sermon on the Prophet's friendship with a Jewish boy and our universal brotherhood as sons of Adam, the entire human race coming from a single womb. And he told us that suicide was not allowed in Islam, nor was the fighting in places other than the battlefield, nor the killing of noncombatants.

With the khutbah's end came the fast rising action toward prayer—the imam's supplication, the brothers standing up, someone in front repeating the call, the imam telling us to straighten out our lines and stand shoulder to shoulder, feet to feet. I looked down at my bare pale feet and the bare black feet to my right and all the shades of bare feet down the line. There we were, all brothers and sons of Adam like the imam said. To think of that reminded me of Malcolm X at Mecca, and then for the first time I wondered what Malcolm would have said about the attacks.

The imam turned his back to us, lifted his hands to his ears and said *Allahu Akbar*. We followed, most of us in silence. The imam recited short parts of the Qur'an that I still knew by heart. At the last verse of al-Fatiha I braced myself for what I saw coming, the overwhelming "AAAAAAMEEEEEEEN" of hundreds of men in unison. The rest went on as I remembered. I felt the comfort of my forehead on the soft carpet, the peace of rising and descending, the sense of completion when we greeted the angels on our shoulders. When it was done I chose not to stick around, instead weaving my way through my brothers for the door, stepping out with my left foot first and passing police officers on the way to my car.

At the time I only knew one Muslim, a bisexual Afghan girl who would dye her hair pink and put a big ring in her lip and sing in punk bands. She lived several hours away. We had met on a punk rock website and exchanged phone numbers but didn't hang out in real life.

Sometimes I wondered how she still considered herself Muslim, despite her life of running around doing coke and boys and girls.

"And you're a Muslim too."

"How's that?" I asked her.

"Look at you, you're *so* Muslim. You can't walk away from it anymore than I can."

Even if labels were stupid, I still found comfort in the word. The way she said *Muslim* made it weightless; it was now just a love word that didn't really mean anything. Or it was family, a label that both trapped and blessed us, a part of yourself that you could love and hate at the same time but ultimately had to learn to live with. I wanted for there to be more of that girl, a mass of Muslim punk rockers to form our own tribe and be confused and conflicted together.

Everyone loves a dramatic conversion story. They want to

hear how low you had fallen, what a sad and rotten scumbag you were until the Truth arrived and changed you forever. And if you lose your faith it's the same treatment: People take all of your doubts and disillusionment and compress it into one heartbreaking scene. First you *are not*, and then you *are*, or first you *are*, and then you *are not*, and there can be no overlapping between the conditions. That's not how it worked for me. I stumbled around on both sides of the trip. For a long time after I was in, I wasn't really *in*; and even if I left at some point, I don't think that I've ever been really out.

"I got into Islam for dumb reasons," I told her.

"Not any dumber than just being born into it."

AT THE END of the semester I called Mom and she wanted to know if I had heard about *that kid*.

"What kid?" I asked.

"Sunday morning I'm sitting on the living room floor cutting coupons, got CNN on, and I hear a reporter say something about 'reading Malcolm X's autobiography.' So I look up at the TV and there's this *kid*, he's got mud all over his face, they found him over *there* . . ."

They found him in Afghanistan. Reporters were calling him the "American Taliban." He had come from a middle-class home in California and was younger than me, just twelve years old when his mom took him to see the Spike Lee movie. A few years later his dad left them to live with another man. The boy didn't know what to do but change his name and hide in a new costume.

"I was a student in Pakistan, studying Islam," he told the reporters. It seemed likely that the United States would charge him with something and put him away forever.

"He didn't know what he was doing," my mother insisted, a slight tremble in her voice. She pleaded with me as though I'd be the judge in his trial. "How could he have known anything? He was just a kid; a little boy on the other side of the world."

dutch sailors

27

"Don't forget who you are and where you come from," continued his father proudly, "and you can do nothing to harm you. You are an Unger—from Hades."

—F. Scott Fitzgerald, "The Diamond as Big as the Ritz"

In my younger, more vulnerable years, my father told me that if I had sex with a white girl on a freshly covered grave, she would turn into an African American. I can't say that I've been turning that over in my mind, and I have no plans to test the theory, but I think about him when I find myself in his country.

His country is West Virginia. The year 2002 would have made it seven years since I last saw him.

Naomi told me that he had since bought a house on top of a mountain and lived there all alone. Most of my drive was a straight line on the I-81; then I'd have to follow Naomi's directions, since his house didn't really have an address. As much as it felt like a different country, West Virginia also felt like a different time in history, as though I had crossed a physical point of separation between the present and past. My cell phone lost its signal near the state line.

This past belonged to me. My great-great-great-great-great-great-grandfather Johannes George David Unger arrived in Philadelphia on the ship *Phoenix* in 1743. His son Johannes Nicholas Unger left the Pennsylvania Dutch for Morgan County in then Virginia, settling at what would become the town of Unger's Store.

There was a period when Virginia, right on the edge of the Mason-Dixon Line, could not decide if it was a Northern or Southern state. In the secession years, Virginia was home to two state governments, one loyal to the Union and the other to the Confederacy. Pro-North delegates broke away to form West Virginia, the only state born from the Civil War.

After the war, pro-Southerners in Romney erected the first monument to the fallen rebels, an open violation of federal law banning any memorial to the Confederacy. The monument was smuggled into Hampshire County under the cover of night, its inscription left incomplete in case it was discovered en route: THE DAUGHTERS OF OLD HAMPSHIRE ERECT THIS TRIBUTE OF AFFECTION TO HER HEROIC SONS WHO FELL IN DEFENCE OF—the last two words were engraved on site—SOUTHERN RIGHTS.

Wesley lived near Romney, which had been passed back and forth between the Union and Confederacy dozens of times. Naomi's directions had me losing my way on nameless dirt roads that went deep into the woods and the hills, sometimes driving a road to its fenced-off end—at which point I'd get out, hop the fence and walk a mile into the wilderness without finding anything. There was also a thick fog, the wrong food for my religious imagination. Sometimes I thought I found Wesley's house shrouded in the mist, only to get closer and discover an abandoned shack or hunters' shelter.

When it became too dark I retreated across the state line into Virginia. Winchester served as my base of operations—there were hotels, the Shenandoah University campus (for checking my email) and Apple Blossom Mall within short walks from each other. I called Naomi to go over the directions again, but she said that I had them right. I tried the next day, lost myself once more in the woods and again called Naomi. She said it was near his nephew's house, which I found, but the woman who answered the door had never heard of a Wesley Unger.

Allah didn't want me to find him, I figured. Maybe ten miles from Romney and on the road that would take me back to the I-81, back north and home and away from those sticks forever, I pulled into a gas station to fuel up.

Then I saw him by the entrance, sitting on a cement step with a cigarette.

After seven years I wasn't sure that it could really be him, so I called out his name.

"Wesley?" He turned his head. "Hi, Dad."

"Hey," he said with a smile. "This is quite a surprise." I approached him cautiously and we shook hands. He invited me to have a seat next to him. "Who are you with?" he asked.

"Nobody."

"You didn't bring anyone with you?"

"Nope."

"Where's your mother?"

"Home."

"Did she ever tell you that I'm not your father?"

Then someone who knew Wesley interrupted us on his way

into the gas station. "Hey there," said Wesley. I only saw the man's tan work boots as he passed. "I think it's okay for you to hear the truth," Wesley continued. "You see, your real father is Dan Aykroyd."

"The actor?" I looked at him. He remained fully serious.

"If not Dan Aykroyd, then someone within Dan Aykroyd's sphere of influence."

"How do you know this?"

"Your earlobes. Yours are attached, mine are not. If you were to examine Dan Aykroyd, I believe that his earlobes would be identical to your own." Hitler held attached earlobes to be the mark of Jewish ancestry, and Dan Aykroyd grew up Catholic but his maternal grandmother was a Russian Jew. Wesley had the separated earlobes of a good Aryan.

"I never knew that," I said.

"Have you seen my new house?" he asked.

"No, I've actually been trying to find it for the past two days."

"Well, come on, I'll show you."

I left my car there and climbed into his black truck. As he drove I imagined what my childhood might have been like with a father, but replaced Wesley in the fantasy with Dan Aykroyd, Dr. Ray Stantz in full Ghostbuster uniform with his proton pack strapped on, throwing me a baseball in our backyard. Back to reality: Just a mile from the gas station, Wesley took us up his hidden driveway at a sharp angle over rocks and bumps and dips. Passing it at least a dozen times that day, I never could have seen that driveway, and my car never would have made it up the hill. "You won't like my house," he warned, "and you won't like my lifestyle." At the top of the hill I saw a long row of rusted engine parts, a broken-down white truck, a shed with rain buckets lining the side and stacks of firewood. At the end of all the junk, a series of wooden planks led to the door of his house.

"You should know," he said, reaching over me to the glove compartment, "that I'm not a dangerous person." With his West Virginia dialect he pronounced "person" as *puh-sun*. From the glove compartment he pulled out a small handgun. I didn't see where he put it; in an inside pocket of his denim jacket, or tucked in his jeans in front or behind? It seemed like something I should have kept track of. We both got out. Walking past the shed, I read its door—engraved by my father's hand, Psalm 23: THE LORD IS MY SHEPHERD, I SHALL NOT WANT. HE MAKES ME TO LIE DOWN IN GREEN PASTURES; HE LEADS ME BESIDE QUIET WATERS. HE RESTORES MY SOUL; HE GUIDES ME IN THE PATHS OF RIGHTEOUSNESS FOR HIS NAME'S SAKE. EVEN THOUGH I WALK THROUGH THE VALLEY OF THE SHADOW OF DEATH, I FEAR NO EVIL; FOR THOU ART WITH ME; THY ROD AND THY STAFF, THEY COMFORT ME. THOU DOST PREPARE A TABLE BEFORE ME IN THE PRESENCE OF MY ENEMIES; THOU HAST ANOINTED MY HEAD WITH OIL; MY CUP OVERFLOWS. SURELY GOODNESS AND LOVING KINDNESS WILL FOLLOW ME ALL THE DAYS OF MY LIFE, AND I WILL DWELL IN THE HOUSE OF THE LORD FOREVER.

The inside of his house was a big room with a lumpy bed, wood-burning stove, and kitchen occupied by a table saw and piles of sawdust on the floor. Wesley poured me a glass of milk and we talked for two hours. At one point he had his back to me and I noted the pistol tucked in his jeans.

"I'm going to tell you about 9/11," he said. "I want you to understand why that happened."

"Why'd it happen?"

"During the construction of the World Trade Center, there was a Mafia hit. A Mafia hit man pushed someone down one of the Twin Towers' elevator shafts, and he stayed at the bottom through the years drawing negative energy upon the buildings."

"So 9/11 was the result of bad karma?" I asked. He looked up at me.

"What is your present relationship to Islam?" Karma was the wrong way to put it, I knew, and it put Wesley on guard. He might have thought that karma was an Islamic term.

"I don't know," I said. "I still have the emotional ties to Islam, but I don't know what I believe."

"Listen to this: There is nothing holy about the month of Ramadan."

"Muhammad's legally my middle name," I told him. "So it's like, still there, you know what I mean? But I don't know how I feel about it, how I feel about *him* . . ."

"You changed your name?"

"My full name now is Michael Edward Muhammad Knight."

For Wesley, my new names made a string of rejections: I now wore the names of my mother's father, the man who aimed a shotgun at him and had me baptized in the Catholic Church, and Muhammad, *Mahomet*, cursed thrall of the Arabian moon god. Most importantly, the change from Schutt to Knight was as much a decision to *not* call myself Unger.

"You are F. Scott Fitzgerald," he said.

"You mean, like reincarnated?"

"I don't use that word, but you are him. You could be him in some other way, because I don't use that word. But if that's the word that works for you, then you can use it and let it be valid. I want you to think about F. Scott Fitzgerald at the Hermitage; I need you to be at the Hermitage and think about him and know what you know, without everyone else needing to know it. Because the secret vanity is better, you understand? You are the only one who needs to know."

"I understand."

"There is something called the secret vanity, and it's better for you."

Naomi claimed to be firm with her brother when he got in his crazy talk but I couldn't, I never had the confidence with him. Instead I asked what it meant to be F. Scott Fitzgerald, and Wesley brought me into his own customized belief system. "When you're killed by a certain spiritual reality," he said, "the one that comes after you will belong to that same reality."

"Okay," I said, waiting for more.

"Look, you're not my son. My son was Michael Roland, but the Roman Catholic Church killed Michael Roland so that the next boy would be born into their reality."

"And that's me."

"Yes." He took a drag from his cigarette and almost seemed to be speaking to it under his breath, but I couldn't make out the words.

"Why did the Church want me to be born a Catholic?"

"Because they knew that the one who came after Michael Roland would be F. Scott Fitzgerald. You see, F. Scott Fitzgerald died outside the Church. He died in a state of self-condemnation. The Roman Catholic Church wanted to bring him back into their fold, so to speak."

"What was so important about F. Scott Fitzgerald?"

"You know who the Desert Fathers were?"

"Yes," I answered.

"The Desert Fathers were the founders of Christianity. You know about the Council of Nicea?"

"Yeah, Emperor Constantine and—"

"Okay," he said. "F. Scott Fitzgerald—and you can call this

reincarnation if that's what you need to do—F. Scott Fitzgerald was one of the early founders of what we call Christianity and the Roman Catholic Church. So when the Church lost F. Scott Fitzgerald, you see, they lost their father."

With that he stood up and offered his hand, my cue to leave. "No hard feelings," he said. We shook hands and then he drove me back to my car.

WESLEY MIGHT HAVE suffered from mental illness but he was at least well-read, so perhaps his random shit-piles weren't so random. Guessing that he had a real reason for saying Fitzgerald and not Faulkner or Sherwood Anderson or someone else, upon returning home I bought everything by or about Fitzgerald that I could find. It was the kind of spiritualized research that I hadn't tasted since high school, in which Allah was laying out a path of books for me to follow, each volume unveiling a piece of my new shape.

The first thing I learned was that F. Scott Fitzgerald and I shared a birthday: September 24, also the birthday of Ayatollah Khomeini. Like mine, his mother was an Irish Catholic from the north. She married a man from Maryland. Before Scott was born she had two children who both died in infancy, leading her to see his life as particularly precious. Before me, my mom had two miscarriages.

I read *The Great Gatsby*, which I only vaguely remembered from sophomore English at DeSales; and I read *Tender is the Night*, in which protagonist Dick Diver steals the Shah's car and inadvertently offends a character named Hosain. The first paragraph of the novel compares the beach to a "bright tan prayer rug." At the end of the novel, Dick Diver goes from his fabulous life and career on Lake Geneva in Switzerland to lose it all and end up in Geneva, New York. They didn't teach that book at DeSales, which might have been for the best; for Fitzgerald, the whole town was only a symbol of failure and disappointment.

Also in *Tender is the Night*, Dick Diver takes a train from Buffalo to Virginia for his father's funeral. Reading multiple biographies of Fitzgerald, I learned that he spent a portion of his childhood in Buffalo, within walking distance of Buffalo State College. In his later years he lived at a Los Angeles hotel called the Garden of Allah. Then I got into Fitzgerald's best-known short story, "The Diamond as Big as the Ritz," which featured a protagonist named Unger, and *Save Me the Waltz* by his wife Zelda, which starred a couple named David and Alabama Knight. That coincidence was weird enough for me to get weird along with it.

I read about how Fitzgerald was religious early on, nearly becoming a priest; Andrew Turnbull writes that "though a renegade Catholic, he was not unspiritual and part of him hated being at odds with the Church." I could handle being ex Catholic, I hadn't felt anything for the Church in nearly twenty years . . . but it still ripped me up to stand on the outside of Islam.

Like me, Fitzgerald did poorly in school because he read so much and so indiscriminately. And his father, though present, seems to have been absent to him; so Fitzgerald heroes became their own fathers, creating overblown personas that they tried to wear like coats—like Jay Gatsby, Jay Gatz's new name and life born from his own "Platonic conception of himself." I had once fashioned my own Gatsby and made him everything that a fifteen-year-old Michael William Schutt hoped to be; but before that I was an honorary Jedi Knight, the kind that a six-year-old Michael Roland Unger would imagine.

Zelda was a real Southerner from Montgomery, Alabama. Fitzgerald's father came from Maryland, and both of our ancestries included active Confederates. I read his story "Ice Palace" from *Flappers and Philosophers*, with the boy and girl walking through the Confederate cemetery and the girl saying that he'll never understand her love for the South. Fitzgerald loved the dead South with faith that its noble breeding could win over Northern money, but they called that the Lost Cause. He also admired the doomed-underdog charm of the Confederacy, which I guess is a gift of white privilege; only Caucasians can see slave owners as charming underdogs.

I started to read pro-Southern histories of the Civil War, which painted the conflict as having less to do with slavery than state rights and federal tyranny—again a prize of whiteness, to spin a slave owners' crusade as a fight *against* oppression. I read *Co. Aytch*, the memoir of a Confederate soldier, which I liked because the guy said that he had seen the most beautiful woman of his whole life right in Berkeley Springs; she could have been an Unger. Then I bought William C. Davis's *An Honorable Defeat*, which told the fall of the South like a classical tragedy. The book centered on Jefferson Davis, first and only president of the Confederate States of America, who did what he could to hold up the illusion of a functioning government while living as a fugitive, refusing to admit defeat even as his treasurer threw armfuls of Confederate money into the fireplace.

Following a Fitzgerald conception of Southern chivalry, I could revert to whiteness like a prodigal American son, no longer Elijah Muhammad's Exceptional Devil, and embrace the myths of Dixie while avoiding the facts. The tragedy of the South became fused with my sense of Shi'a tragedy, the Stars and Bars like a flag for Karbala, the cursed desert in Iraq where Muslims butchered the Prophet's grandson—because the Sixth Holy Imam, Ja'far as-Siddiq, said that every land was Karbala, right? I even drew up a Confederate battle flag with the starry blue *X* cutting the red field into four triangles; on the top triangle I wrote Muhammad's name in Arabic, Ali's in the one below him, and in the right and left triangles I wrote the names of his martyred sons, Hasan and Husayn. It reminded me of those redneck assholes wearing their T-shirt with the Confederate flag reading, YOU HAVE YOUR X, I HAVE MINE! If only in my own story, it now seemed almost funny; which was *my* X, the old world I had lost?

Scott Fitzgerald himself was a tragedy, maybe the Imam Husayn of American letters. The Hemingway Century should have been the Fitzgerald Century, but Scott was forced to write commercial short stories to pay for Zelda's psychiatric treatment while Hemingway could just live for the craft and pound out sincere novels. Scott might have had three or four other *Gatsby*s in him, who knows. Hemingway was the Yazid, then, the usurper of power and birthright and the murderer of Husayn—or maybe Zelda was Yazid, or it could have been Fitzgerald's own alcoholism. Either way, I was starting to build my own religion, one blending a cathartic embrace of Fitzgerald's suffering with the noble fatalism of the South and that of the Twelve Shi'a Imams. They all made powerful portraits of defeat as virtue; winners write the history, but losers cope with myths of consolation. And from this semiotic clusterfuck I'd reinvent myself again as a new kind of culture-mutant with my own jumbled set of symbols, sacraments, texts, metaphors, and heroes—an Appalachian Twelver, Stonewall Ali-Asghar.

The Southern apologia couldn't hold up for long, but still I made an F. Scott Fitzgerald pilgrimage that summer. First I stopped at his grave in Rockville, Maryland, and slept there for the night, right by the long stone slab bearing the final words of *The Great Gatsby:* "So we beat on, boats against the current, borne back ceaselessly into the past." The headstone gave his full name, Francis Scott Key Fitzgerald; he had been named after his second cousin three times removed, the author of the Star-Spangled Banner.

In the car I had my bottle from Mecca's holy well of Zamzam that I had bought at Faisal Mosque years ago. Sometime around sunrise I emptied it onto Scott's grave, pouring one dream into another, and then drove a little more than an hour to Wesley's house.

"Where are you going?" he asked.

"The Hermitage," I told him.

"Are you thinking about F. Scott Fitzgerald?"

"Of course."

"When F. Scott Fitzgerald is at the Hermitage, only he knows who he really is; he doesn't go around making everyone recognize him. He has the secret vanity, which is better." I let him go on that again and then he told one of his girl stories. One night in his younger years he met a girl, took her to his place, and did what he wanted. When he offered to drive her home, she answered, "I have a way." Wesley insisted but again she said only that she had a *way*, and soon he was screaming at her that it was a crazy hour of night and that she needed a ride. "I have a way," she repeated before walking out the door. "I was right behind her," said Wesley, "barely three steps behind. But when I got outside she had just disappeared— and bear in mind, you understand, this was a wide-open area. There was nowhere she could have run to that fast and nothing to hide behind. She was just gone." With that he held up his open hands as if to say *poof.*

"Wow," I said.

"They always have a way. That's what you need to remember."

From Wesley's house I drove back to Winchester and the I-81, which I'd take further south until its absorption into the I-40, heading for Nashville and the Hermitage. On the way I stopped at the home of Stonewall Jackson in Lexington and went along the tour with a small group of Civil War buffs.

The Hermitage was the mansion and cotton plantation owned by Andrew Jackson. F. Scott Fitzgerald's last novel, his unfinished *The Love of the Last Tycoon*, opens with a film studio executive, a screenwriter, and the daughter of a producer in front of the house at dawn. The executive compares himself unfavorably to Jackson, finding it hard to say both of their names in the same sentence. When the other two leave, he chooses to stay behind and shoot himself in the head.

According to Jeffrey Meyers, their failure to get into the locked Hermitage reflects the inability of Hollywood to comprehend America's real heart, its "ideals and traditions"; but for Fitzgerald, the historic sites themselves had failed. In *The Beautiful and Damned*, Anthony and Gloria pay a visit to the home of Robert E. Lee in Arlington, but the annoying tourists and fraud of historic preservation leave Gloria disappointed. She wishes that they'd just let the places properly rot and die, out of genuine respect for the past that is gone whether the house still stands or not. "Do you think they've left a breath of 1860 here?" she asks Anthony.

Like the Hollywood people, I came upon those cedar-lined driveways too early, and had to go find a parking lot to sleep in until the place opened. When I came back at noon there was a serious Andrew Jackson impersonator walking up and down the footpaths in full costume.

"Welcome to our home," he said with conviction.

I joined the tour, waiting for my turn to stand in the doorways of the parlors and bedrooms and cultivating what Wesley called my inner "secret vanity," really trying to see myself as F. Scott Fitzgerald, after which we visited the Jackson graves behind the house. The president and his wife rested in a domed tomb that he had personally designed. Off to the side was a little grave covered in leaves and dead brown grass, the tombstone reading UNCLE ALFRED. He was Old Hickory's favorite slave, who outlived his owner and begged the Ladies' Hermitage Association to be buried near him.

With the end of the tour, the group dissipated. I sat in the grass, leaning against the slave quarters and reflecting on my father's instructions. I couldn't find any reference in my reading to F. Scott Fitzgerald actually visiting the Hermitage, but I wanted to know what he would think if he was here at the "great grey hulk of the Andrew Jackson house," contrasting and comparing it to the "huge incoherent failure of a house" that was Gatsby's mansion. One was only a lesser version of the other; the promise had been corrupted and now destroyed the man who chased it.

Andrew Jackson was born in the Carolinas without a distinguished family name to get him through life, so he came out here to Tennessee—America's lawless western edge, not even yet a state—and *created himself.* The first president to come from the frontier, he was also in a sense Fitzgerald's First Tycoon, having successfully attained the American Dream that would consume and murder Gatsby. The glory of the past could not be preserved, as Gloria argues at the home of General Lee, no more than it could be duplicated, as I learned at the Hermitage. If Wesley wanted me to think and feel as Fitzgerald would here, it could have only been for Fitzgerald's sense of decline—

Or perhaps the religious hope that Fitzgerald might have felt at this house, with the secret vanity being that he considered himself a personage also capable of self-creation and renewal. Anyway, it didn't matter so much since the nobility was never really noble and the dream had never been pure. Gatsby's adolescent vision of fate reminded me of that John Gast painting *American Progress*, showing the giant ethereal blonde woman dressed like a Greek goddess floating over the plains, the rising sun and Mississippi River and cities and a trail of telegram wires behind her while the white men march forward and the Indians, bisons, and bears flee off the canvas. She has the Star of Empire on her forehead; she is Manifest Destiny, America as Idea, and certainly a religious idea, which makes it illusion. "I see America through the eyes of the victim," said Malcolm Little, who renewed himself first as Detroit Red, then Malcolm X, and finally El-Hajj Malik El-Shabazz. "I don't see any American Dream; I see an American nightmare."

The real object of my pilgrimage was not even the Hermitage but something further south on the I-65, the Scott and Zelda Fitzgerald Museum in Montgomery, Alabama—in the same part of town as the First White House of the Confederacy, which was designed by Zelda's uncle. The museum was located in a house where Scott and Zelda used to live during the time that he worked on *Tender is the Night*. When I got there it was closed. The sign in front read, THEY BELONG TO THE WORLD, and was made with bricks from Zelda's childhood home. I stole a loose brick and began the long drive north.

SEVERAL MONTHS LATER I went back to Rockville, deciding that Fitzgerald's death anniversary of December 21 would be my date for observing Ashura, and I would commemorate Imam Husayn's martyrdom at Fitzgerald's grave. In the car I packed my piles of Fitzgerald books and also whatever Islamic books I still had, along with Joseph Campbell's *The Hero with a Thousand Faces* and Carl Jung's *Synchronicity*. I stopped at Princeton and walked across the frozen dead campus, saying "labbayk Allahumma labbayk" (Here I am, O God, here I am) like pilgrims in Mecca, searching *This Side of Paradise* with cold, hurting fingers for named buildings or streets. When it came time to walk off the campus and resume the journey, I tried to imagine Fitzgerald's mixed affection and bitterness for the place and feel what he would about being there again.

From there I did the three-hour-plus drive straight to St. Mary's cemetery, finally parking my car by the neighboring Tiger Mart. In my car I called Mom.

"I made it to Rockville."

"Good, are you having fun?"

"It's not about fun, Mom. It's like the opposite of fun."

"I know, bud. How is it?"

"Cold."

"Well, be sure to bundle up. You have your gloves?"

"I don't know if I brought them."

"You can just sit in your car too, if you get cold."

"I'm in the car right now."

"Okay."

"Mom, what do you think about this?"

"F. Scott Fitzgerald? It's interesting. I was wondering

how Wesley came up with that. He used to read a lot, you know—"

"No. I mean, what I'm doing right now is kind of strange, I think."

"You're not hurting anyone, bud. You get into this, you get what you want out of it, and then it's on to the next thing. It's been like that since you were six years old."

I got off the phone and ventured out of my car to step over the little graveyard fence. St. Mary's had originally refused to bury Scott and Zelda in his family's plot because they did not die as practicing Catholics. It wasn't until 1975 that their daughter Scottie convinced the Baltimore diocese to change its ruling and permit the remains to be moved. It helped my larger story, since disrespect and disturbance of the dead fit the motif of Karbala.

What am I doing here? I asked the headstone, slapping my chest and trying hard to cry. Celebrating loss. I'm here to feel F. Scott Fitzgerald's pain because he's dead and can't feel it himself anymore, and I'm here to feel Imam Husayn's pain because he felt it for my sake, to save the Islam that I'm not good enough for anyway. And I'm feeling my own pain too, I guess.

What am I doing here in my silver shirt and gold tie? Mourning the end of romantic illusions? The dream of our Islamic brotherhood, the ummah, was broken prior to Karbala, but with Husayn's martyrdom it became shattered beyond repair. With Karbala I had lost the faith that Muslims somehow functioned in a way that was superior to other religious communities. And Fitzgerald wrote of his own failed mythology with heroes who had the gift of eternal optimism in the face of sure doom, but the doom was real and they were meant to lose big. Both historical (but mythologized) Husayn and fictional (but historicized) Gatsby occupied enough of my thought to become equally real and deserving of analysis. Whatever Husayn had that made him stand his ground at Karbala, he had it for real—when he stood his ground he stood firm, his legs were like pegs driven into the earth. I wasn't sure if Gatsby really had it or just yearned for it. I knew that I didn't really have it; there was a missing piece and I only dealt with *symbols* of what could fill the gap. Champions of Allah's straight path, champions of the World Wrestling Federation, it's all the same. They were models for how to swing your penis, but that's still valid: You need to know how to swing it to know that you have it, and sometimes you're not born with your balls, you have to go out into the world and capture them.

Why the hell am I here, cracking up? Well, my father is a schizophrenic and there's no hope for a real relationship with him; the best I have is to let him concoct a crazy path for me and at least halfway entertain it. Amory Blaine said something about life being either a search for the Holy Grail or just an amusing game—here it's both, with the game still earnest enough. I'm also trying to figure myself out as an American who has washed his hands of America, as well as a Muslim who forgot all his Arabic but still loves Allah. F. Scott Fitzgerald said that the test of a "first-rate mind" was to simultaneously hold two contradicting ideas; maybe I could pull it off.

Fitzgerald used to prank people who wrote him letters. When someone writing a paper on his work asked for suggested reading materials, he provided a list full of nonexistent books—one of them being *F. Scott Fitzgerald and the Rise of Islam.* If that book was real, it'd have my answers; perhaps to develop this new Fitzgeraldiyya sect, I'd have to actually write *F. Scott Fitzgerald and the Rise of Islam* and *make* it real, or at least meditate upon it as an unreachable cosmic Qur'an floating in the clouds above me. I already had a few notebooks filled with my new novel, an immature tribute to *The Great Gatsby* with Gatsby as a Muslim punk rocker, a Pakistani kid with tall mohawk and spiked leather jacket.

There was a possibility, though it seemed less likely each year, that someday I'd be a father and perhaps whisper the call to prayer in my own child's ear. I knew that I wanted my kids to see the insides of mosques, but what would I teach them at home? There's no god but God, and Scott Fitzgerald's the Hidden Imam? I hoped for some line of continuity between dead Ungers and unborn Muhammad Knights, or perhaps a mosaic formed in the displaced scraps of pasts that I had stitched together. In the end I faced the consequence that I had no past at all, none that came to me from the old world with any organic authenticity.

The *old* world . . . my great-great-great-great-great-great-grandfather Johannes George David Unger was born just four decades after the Battle of Vienna, the macrohistorical event that halted Islam's spread into Europe (September 11 and 12, 1683). Johannes had sprung up from the old world possessed by its Orientalist nightmares, but he left the old world to escape violence of other Christians, an Anabaptist refugee seeking religious freedom across the Atlantic. I couldn't know what he dreamed for his American future—there wasn't really such a thing as America yet—but I had to wonder whether he'd have boarded the ship *Phoenix* if he saw the trouble ahead: a half–Irish Catholic branch of his own bloodline disowning Christendom altogether to follow Mahomet, who Martin Luther had called a first-born child of Satan.

Then I considered that Irish Catholic half. When we first

met, Wesley told me that I was Frederick the Great, that Barbarossa lived in our Prussian blood. Now he called me F. Scott Fitzgerald, and I found the real truth of it: I was more my mother than my father, and if anyone has been the masculine figure in my life, the real Impossible Man, it's her.

Remembering my parents and everything that happened, including my own madness—youth itself is a "chemical madness," wrote Fitzgerald—I could only explain my life with a story from Islamic tradition, in which the Prophet Muhammad watched a mother and her small child sitting around a bonfire. Whenever the child got up and walked too close to the fire, the mother would pull him back; and as the Prophet saw this he wept, because it reminded him of Allah.

The old world? Nothing to brood over. But there was a Shi'a mosque in Manassas, and a chance that I could crash there through Christmas. I pulled myself up and looked at the stone a final time—*if I'm supposed to feel anything, it'd better be fast*—before leaving the cemetery.